Teacher's Resources

Goals for Living

Managing Your Resources

by

Nancy Wehlage
Portage, Wisconsin

and

Mary Larson-Kennedy, CFCS
Delavan, Wisconsin

Publisher
The Goodheart-Willcox Company, Inc.
Tinley Park, Illinois
www.g-w.com

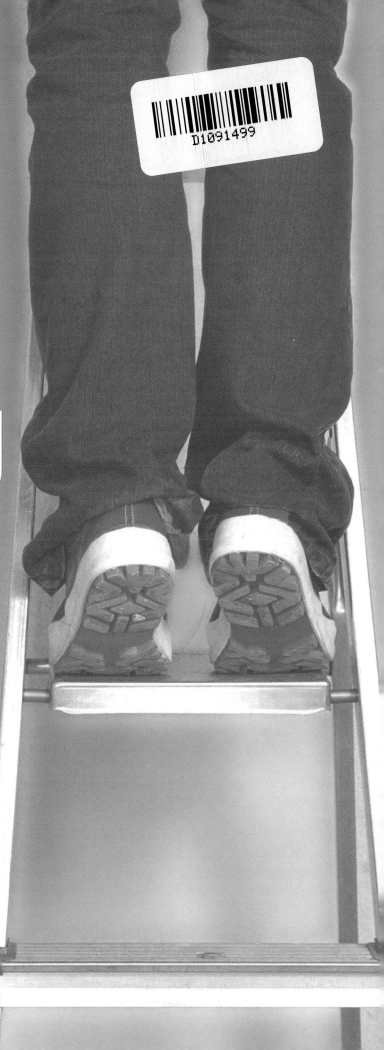

Contents

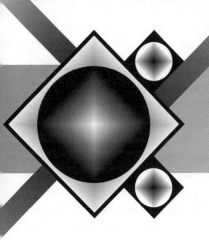

Introduction

Goals for Living: Managing Your Resources is a comprehensive text concerned with life management. The *Goals for Living* learning package includes the student text, *Student Activity Guide, Teacher's Resource Guide, Teacher's Resource Portfolio,* and *Teacher's Resource CD with* **Exam***View® Test Generator Software.* Using these products can help you develop an effective life management program tailored to your students' unique needs.

Using the Text

Goals for Living is designed to give students the knowledge they need to effectively manage their daily lives. The text begins with a basic introduction to the management process. The remaining parts of the book represent areas of life in which management decisions are made daily. Managing personal and family life, relationships with others, physical and mental health, child care and guidance, meal planning and preparation, clothing, housing, finances, and consumer and career choices are covered. *Goals for Living* emphasizes how management skills in these areas can help students control their lives.

The text includes an expanded table of contents to give students an overview of the wide variety of topics they will be studying in this book. A glossary is included to help students learn terms found in the text. A complete index is provided so students can find the information they want quickly and easily.

The "To Know" Section

Vocabulary words appear at the beginning of each chapter under the heading "To Know." This list is designed to help students identify important terms from the chapter. These terms appear in bold type in the text where they are defined so students can recognize them as they read. Discussing these words with students will help familiarize them with concepts to which they are being introduced. To be sure students are familiar with these important terms, you may want to ask them to:
1. look up, define, and explain each term
2. relate each term to the topic being studied
3. match terms with their definitions
4. find examples of how the terms are used in current newspapers and magazine articles, reference books, and other related materials

The Objectives

Each chapter opening page has a list of behavioral objectives. You may wish to go over these objectives with students before they study the chapter. The objectives will tell students the skills they will be expected to demonstrate on completion of the chapter.

Boxed Features

The boxed features in *Goals for Living* fall into three categories: "Use Your Reasoning Skills," "Brainstorming," and "Getting Involved." "Use Your Reasoning Skills" provides an activity to challenge students' thinking. "Brainstorming" offers opportunities for classroom participation and interaction. "Getting Involved" focuses on activities either in the school community or the wider neighborhood community. One of each of these boxes appears in every chapter.

The Chapter Summary

A chapter summary is located at the end of each chapter. This section reviews the major concepts covered in the entire chapter.

The "To Review" Section

The questions at the end of each chapter under the heading "To Review" cover the basic information presented in the chapter. These review questions are designed to help students recall, organize, and use the information presented in the text. The review section for each chapter consists of a variety of true/false, completion, multiple choice, and essay questions. You may wish to supplement these questions with other study and evaluation strategies. Answers to these questions appear in the *Teacher's Resources*.

The "To Challenge Your Thinking," "To Do with the Class," and "To Do with Your Community" Sections

A variety of activities are listed under these headings. The activities in the "To Challenge Your Thinking" section are designed to stimulate critical thinking skills. The "To Do with the Class" section lists activities that may be done as a class or in small groups. The "To Do with Your Community" section lists activities that students can extend what they have learned.

Many activities in the "To Do" sections give students the opportunity to reinforce concepts learned in the chapter through hands-on experiences. Some activities also encourage students to extend and enrich learning of text material. Some activities are designed for students to complete individually; others are designed to be completed in group situations. Activities also vary in degree of difficulty. Activities may be chosen or assigned according to students' interests and abilities. Additional reteaching, reinforcement, extension, and enrichment activities for each chapter are provided in the *Teacher's Resources*.

Using the *Student Activity Guide*

The *Student Activity Guide* for *Goals for Living* is divided into chapters that match the chapters in the text. Each chapter contains exercises designed to increase student interest and understanding of text material. Some of these exercises allow students to extend and enrich learning by applying and expanding on the information provided in the text. Other activities provide a means of reteaching and reinforcing learning through direct review of text material.

By reading the text first, students will have the information they need to complete all the activities. Some activities relate to only a section of a chapter. You may wish to have students read only the section that pertains to an activity before completing that activity. This will facilitate student learning of one topic before moving on to other topics.

Students should try to do the activities without looking in the book. Then they can use the text to check their answers after they have completed the activities.

Answers to learning experiences in the *Student Activity Guide* are provided in the *Teacher's Resources*. You may wish to go over answers with students. This will enable you to answer students' questions and emphasize any text material students are having difficulty understanding.

The pages of the *Student Activity Guide* are perforated for easy removal. They are also drilled for ease of placement in student notebooks.

Using the *Teacher's Resource Guide*

The *Teacher's Resource Guide* for *Goals for Living* includes a variety of materials to assist you in presenting the concepts in the text and help you make management concepts interesting and meaningful to students. The individual and group activities will allow students to apply the concepts learned to realistic situations.

Like the *Student Activity Guide*, the *Teacher's Resource Guide* is divided into chapters that match the chapters in the text. Each chapter contains the following:

- **Behavioral Objectives.** These are the objectives that students will be able to accomplish after completing the chapter activities.

- **Bulletin Board Ideas.** One or two bulletin board ideas are described in each chapter. Many of these ideas are illustrated for you.

- **Teaching Materials.** A list of all materials available to supplement each chapter in the text is conveniently located at the beginning of each chapter. The list includes the names of all activities contained in the *Student Activity Guide*. It also lists names of the reproducible masters and color transparencies.

- **Introductory Activities.** These motivational activities are designed to stimulate your students' interest in the chapter they will be studying. These activities encourage a sense of curiosity that students will want to satisfy by reading the chapter.

- **Instructional Concepts and Student Learning Experiences.** A variety of student learning experiences are described for teaching each of the major concepts discussed in the text. This allows you to meet the needs of your students by giving you options for reteaching, reinforcing, extending, and enriching learning. Each of the major concepts is listed, followed by student learning experiences for teaching each concept. The student learning experiences can help you meet the following goals:

  - *To Reteach Concepts.* Studies have shown that students respond differently to different teaching techniques. Therefore, these materials provide suggestions for several strategies that can be used to teach each concept in the text. This allows you to choose a different strategy to reteach students who showed low response to a previous strategy.

  - *To Reinforce Learning.* It is generally accepted that the more ways in which a student is exposed to a given concept, the greater his or her understanding and retention will be.

  - *To Extend Learning.* The activities are directed to students at a variety of ability levels. You may choose some of the application exercises to encourage highly motivated students to extend their learning beyond the realm of the classroom. These activities give students the opportunity to relate text information to other situations, particularly experiences in their own lives.

  - *To Enrich Learning.* Some activities, such as research activities, are designed to help students learn more about topics introduced in the text. These activities give students the opportunity to enrich their learning through more in-depth study.

Activities that are found in the accompanying *Student Activity Guide* are also described for your convenience in planning daily lessons. These are identified with the letters *SAG* following the title and the letter of the activity.

- **Answer Keys.** These sections contain the answers for the "To Review" questions at the end of each chapter in the text. Any answers needed for the learning experiences in the *Student Activity Guide* are provided. Answers needed for the reproducible masters and chapter tests are also found in this section.

- **Reproducible Masters.** At least one reproducible master is included for each chapter. The masters are designed to enhance the presentation of concepts. Some of the masters are designated for use as transparency masters with an overhead projector. These masters are often charts or drawings you can use to illustrate key concepts for students during class discussion. They can also be used as student handouts. Some of the masters are designated to be used as student activities. These masters include activities designed to encourage creative and critical thinking. The masters can be copied and given to students to complete individually. They can also be used as the basis for class discussion.

- **Test Masters.** Individual tests with clear, specific questions that deal with topics presented in each chapter are provided. True/false, multiple choice, and matching questions are used to measure student learning about facts and definitions. Essay questions are also provided in the chapter tests. Some of these require students to list information, while others allow students to express their opinions and creativity. You may wish to modify these tests to tailor the questions to your classroom needs.

Correlation of National Standards for Consumer and Family Resources

As you plan your program, you may find the *Correlation of National Standards for Consumer and Family Resources* chart on pages 19-25 useful. This chart correlates the Family and Consumer Sciences Education National Standards with the content of *Goals for Living: Managing Your Resources.* It lists the competencies for each of the content standards for Consumer and Family Resources. It also identifies the major text concepts that relate to each competency.

Scope and Sequence Chart

In planning your program, you may want to use the *Scope and Sequence Chart* found on pages 26-30. The chart identifies the major concepts presented in each chapter of the text.

Basic Skills Chart

Students enrolled in your course have the opportunity to develop and use the following basic skills: verbal, reading, writing, mathematical, scientific, and analytical. (Analytical skills involve the higher-order thinking skills of analysis, synthesis, and evaluation in problem-solving situations.)

A *Basic Skills Chart*, found on pages 31-35, has been included in the *Goals for Living Teacher's Resources* to identify those activities that encourage the development of basic skills. This chart includes activities from the *Student Activity Guide* (identified as *SAG*) and student learning experiences from the *Teacher's Resources* (identified as *TR*). Incorporating a variety of these activities into your daily lesson plans will assure your students of receiving vital practice in the development of their basic skills. Also, if you find that students in your class are weak in a specific basic skill, more activities can be selected that will develop that particular skill area. In addition, you may wish to use this chart to show others outside the field of family and consumer sciences how basic skills are taught in your classroom.

Using the *Teacher's Resource Portfolio*

The *Teacher's Resource Portfolio* for *Goals for Living* combines the *Teacher's Resource Guide* with a set of color transparencies. All of the materials are included in a convenient three-ring portfolio. Reproducible materials can be removed easily. Handy dividers included with the portfolio help you organize materials so you can quickly find the items you need.

Color transparencies for *Goals for Living* are provided to add variety to your classroom lecture as you discuss topics included in the text with your students. You will find some transparencies useful in illustrating and reinforcing information presented in the text. Others will give you an opportunity to extend learning beyond the scope of the text. Attractive colors are visually appealing and hold students' attention. Suggestions for how the transparencies can be used in the classroom are included in the *Teacher's Resources*.

Using the *Teacher's Resource CD with ExamView® Test Generator Software*

The *Teacher's Resource CD with* **Exam**View® *Test Generator Software* includes all of the contents of the *Teacher's Resource Portfolio* plus **Exam**View® *Test Generator Software* on a convenient CD. The transparencies are in both PowerPoint format as well as PDF format. Lesson planning guides are also included. The CD format allows you to view and print resource pages exactly as they appear in the *Teacher's Resource Portfolio*.

To produce overhead transparencies, print transparency master pages onto acetate film designed for your printer. If you are printing a color transparency, you will need a color printer to produce a transparency that appears as it does on your screen. However, you can print color transparencies in gray scale using a black ink printer.

The **Exam**View® *Test Generator Software* database includes all the test master questions from the *Teacher's Resources* plus an additional 25 percent new questions prepared just for this test bank. You can choose to have the computer generate a test for you with randomly selected questions. You can also opt to choose specific questions to create customized tests to meet your classroom needs. You may wish to make different versions of the same test to use during different class periods. Answer keys are generated automatically to simplify grading.

Using Additional Resources

Much student learning in your class can be reinforced by allowing students to see, analyze, and work with examples. Your providing samples of materials, pictures, demonstration samples, and articles related to a variety of family and consumer science and management topics can greatly enhance student learning. Students can use these items in many activities related to the text.

You may be able to acquire some items through local stores. Old pattern catalogs, fabric remnants, and other items can often be purchased

inexpensively. Many stores may be willing to donate items. You may be able to obtain pamphlets and project ideas by contacting consumer product manufacturers.

Magazines, catalogs, and sales brochures are excellent sources of photos. Having a large quantity of pictures available for clipping and mounting will be helpful to students. Students may analyze and discuss the pictures in a variety of activities.

Current magazines and journals are also good sources of articles on various family and consumer science and management topics. Having copies in the classroom will encourage students to use them for research and ideas as they study family and consumer sciences. The following publications may be helpful to you or your students:

Better Homes and Gardens
bhg.com

Choices
scholastic.com

Consumer Reports
consumerreports.org

Family and Consumer Sciences Research Journal
fcs.sagepub.com

Journal of Family and Consumer Sciences
aafcs.org

Newsweek
newsweek.com

Sew News
sewnews.com

Time
time.com

What's New
whats-new-mag.com

Other information may be obtained through various government offices and trade and professional organizations.* The following may be able to provide you with resources:

American Association of Family and Consumer Sciences (AAFCS)
(703) 706-4600
aafcs.org

American Council on Consumer Interests
(573) 882-3817
consumerinterests.org

American Financial Services Association
americanfinsvcs.com

American Gas Association
(202) 824-7000
aga.org

American Society of Interior Designers
(202) 546-3480
asid.org

American Textile Manufacturers Institute, Inc.
(202) 862-0518
atmi.org

Chamber of Commerce of the United States of America
(202) 659-6000
uschamber.com

Council of Better Business Bureaus, Inc.
(703) 276-0100
bbb.org

Federal Citizen Information Center
pueblo.gsa.gov

Food and Drug Administration (FDA)
(888) 463-6332
fda.gov

Home Sewing Association
(412) 372-5950
sewing.org/

Insurance Information Institute
(212) 346-5500
iii.org

National Safety Council
(630) 285-1121
nsc.org

United Fresh Fruit and Vegetable Association
(202) 303-3400
uffva.org

USDA Food and Nutrition Services
(703) 305-2281
fns.usda.gov/fns/

*Note: These phone numbers and Web sites may have changed since the publication of these *Teacher's Resources*.

Current information, catalog, and/or instructional materials may be obtained from the following product and service companies:

Coats & Clark
(800) 648-1479
coatsandclark.com

Georgia-Pacific Corp.
(800) 284-5347
gp.com

Gerber Products Company
(800) 443-7237
gerber.com

Haan Crafts Corporation
(800) 422-6548
haan.com

S.C. Johnson
(800) 494-4855
scjbrands.com

Kirsch
(800) 817-6344
kirsch.com

McCall Pattern Company
(800) 782-0323
mccall.com

Nasco
(800) 558-9595
enasco.com

Owens-Corning Fiberglas Corp.
(800) 438-0465
owenscorning.com

Pineapple Appeal Kits
(800) 321-3041
pineappleappeal.com

Proctor & Gamble Co.
(513) 945-8787
pg.com

Simplicity Pattern Company, Inc.
(888) 588-2700
simplicity.com

Singer Sewing Co.
(800) 474-6437
singerco.com

To-Sew, Inc.
(818) 700-9374

Strategies for Successful Teaching

You can make the *Goals for Living* subject matter exciting and relevant for your students by using a variety of teaching strategies. Many suggestions for planning classroom activities are given in the various teaching supplements that accompany this text. As you plan your lessons, you might also want to keep the following points in mind.

Helping Your Students Develop Critical Thinking Skills

As today's students leave their classrooms behind, they will face a world of complexity and change. They are likely to work in several career areas and hold many different jobs. Besides providing young people with a knowledge base of facts, principles, and procedures, you must help prepare them to solve complex problems, make difficult decisions, and assess ethical implications. In other words, you must help students learn how to use critical thinking skills. These skills are often referred to as the higher-order thinking skills. Benjamin Bloom listed these as

- analysis—breaking down material into its component parts so its organizational structure may be understood;

- synthesis—putting parts together to form a new whole; and

- evaluation—judging the value of material for a given purpose.

In a broader perspective, students must be able to use reflective thinking in order to decide what to believe and do. According to Robert Ennis, students should be able to

- define and clarify problems, issues, conclusions, reasons, and assumptions;

- judge the credibility, relevance, and consistency of information; and

- infer or solve problems and draw reasonable conclusions.

Students have the right to learn critical thinking skills. These skills cannot be an optional part of the curriculum. To think critically, students must have knowledge. However, critical thinking goes beyond memorizing or recalling information. Critical thinking cannot occur in a vacuum; it requires individuals to apply what they know about the subject matter. It requires students to use their common sense and experience. It may also involve controversy.

Critical thinking requires creative thinking to construct all the reasonable alternatives, consequences, influencing factors, and supporting arguments. To help students develop this type of thinking, you need to encourage learners to value unusual ideas and seek perspectives outside the obvious.

Teaching critical thinking does not require exotic and highly unusual classroom approaches. You can incorporate complex thought processes in the most ordinary and basic activities. With careful planning and skillful execution, you can even incorporate complex thought into reading, writing, and listening exercises.

Help your students develop their analytical skills and go beyond what they see on the surface. Rather than allowing students to blindly accept what they read or hear, encourage them to examine ideas in ways that show respect for others' opinions and different perspectives. Encourage learners to think about points raised by others. Ask students to evaluate how new ideas relate to their attitudes about various subjects.

Debate is an excellent way to explore opposite sides of an issue. You may want to divide the class into two groups, each to take an opposing side of the issue. You can also ask students to work in smaller groups and explore opposing sides of different issues. Each group can select students from the group to present the points for their side.

Problem-Solving and Decision-Making Skills

An important aspect in the development of critical thinking skills is learning how to solve problems and make decisions. Some very important decisions lie ahead for your students, particularly those related to their future education and career choices. The steps in the decision-making process are outlined in Chapter 1, "Decision Making in Your Daily Life." You can encourage students to apply the decision-making process to all their important decisions.

Simulation games and role plays are activities that allow students to practice solving problems and making decisions in nonthreatening circumstances. Role playing allows students to examine others' feelings as well as their own. It can help students learn effective ways to react or cope when confronted with similar situations in real life.

Using Cooperative Learning

The use of cooperative learning groups in your classroom will give students a chance to practice teamwork skills, which are critical in today's workplace. During cooperative learning, students learn interpersonal and small-group skills that will allow them to function as part of a team. These skills include leadership, decision making, trust building, communication, and conflict management.

When planning for cooperative learning, you will have a particular goal or task in mind. You will first specify the objectives for the lesson. You will match small groups of learners to complete the task or goal. You or the group will assign each group member a role.

Interdependence is a basic component of any cooperative learning group. Success is not measured only in terms of outcome. It is also measured in terms of the successful performance of each group member in his or her role. Students understand that one person cannot succeed unless everyone succeeds. The value of each group member is affirmed as learners work toward their goal.

The success of the group depends on individual performance. Mix groups in terms of abilities and talents to create more opportunities for students to learn from one another. As groups work together over time, rotate the roles so everyone has an opportunity to practice and develop different skills.

You will need to monitor the effectiveness of cooperative groups. Intervene as necessary to provide task assistance or to help with interpersonal and group skills. Finally, evaluate students' achievement and help them discuss how well they worked together.

Helping Students Recognize and Value Diversity

Your students will be entering a rapidly changing workplace—not only in the area of technology, but also in the diverse nature of the workforce. Years ago, the workforce was dominated by white males, but 85 percent of the new entrants into the workforce at the start of this century were women, minorities, and immigrants. The workforce is also aging. Over half of the workforce will be people between the ages of 35 and 54. Because of these changes, young workers will need to be able to interact effectively with those who are different from themselves.

The appreciation and understanding of diversity is an ongoing process. The earlier and more frequently young people are exposed to diversity, the better able they will be to bridge cultural differences. If your students are exposed to different cultures within your classroom, they can begin the process of understanding cultural differences. This is the best preparation for success in a diverse society. In addition, teachers have found the following strategies to be helpful:

- Actively promote a spirit of openness, consideration, respect, and tolerance in your classroom.

- Use a variety of teaching styles and assessment strategies.

- Use cooperative learning activities whenever possible. Make sure group roles are rotated so everyone has leadership opportunities.

- When grouping students, make sure the composition of each group is as diverse as possible with regard to gender, race, and nationality. If the groups present information to the class, make sure all members have a speaking part. (Sometimes females and minorities are under-represented in speaking roles.)

- Make sure one group's opinions are not over-represented during class discussions. Seek opinions of under-represented persons/groups if necessary.

- If a student makes a sexist, racist, or other offensive comment, ask the student to rephrase the comment in a manner that will not offend other members of the class.

Remind students that offensive statements and behavior are inappropriate in the workplace as well as the classroom.

- If a difficult classroom situation arises based on a diversity issue, ask for a time-out and have everyone write down his or her thoughts and opinions about the incident. This allows everyone to cool down and allows you to plan a response.

- Arrange for guest speakers who represent diversity in gender, race, and ethnicity even though the topic does not relate to diversity.

- Have students change seats from time to time throughout the course, having them sit next to people they do not know and introducing themselves.

- Several times during the course, have students do anonymous evaluations of the class, asking them if there are any problems with which you are unaware.

Assessment Techniques

Various forms of assessment need to be used with students to evaluate their achievement. Written tests have traditionally been used to evaluate performance. This method of evaluation is good to use when assessing knowledge and comprehension. Other methods of assessment are preferable for measuring the achievement of the higher-level skills of application, analysis, synthesis, and evaluation.

Included in the *Goals for Living Teacher's Resources* are two means of assessing learning. For each chapter in the text there is a reproducible objective test. The end-of-chapter Review in the text can be used to evaluate students' recall of key concepts. The boxed features ("Getting Involved," "Use Your Reasoning Skills," and "Brainstorming") and activities suggested at the end of each chapter ("To Challenge Your Thinking," "To Do with the Class," and "To Do with Your Community") will provide opportunities for you to assess your students' abilities to use critical thinking, problem solving, and application.

Performance Assessment

When you assign students some of the projects described in the text, a different form of assessing mastery or achievement is required.

One method teachers have successfully used is a rubric. A **rubric** consists of a set of criteria including specific descriptors or standards that can be used to arrive at performance scores for students. A point value is given for each set of descriptors, leading to a range of possible points to be assigned, usually from 1 to 5. The criteria can also be weighted. This method of assessment reduces the guesswork involved in grading, leading to fair and consistent scoring. The standards clearly indicate to students the various levels of mastery of a task. Students are even able to assess their own achievement based on the criteria.

When using rubrics, students should see the criteria at the beginning of the assignment. Then they can focus their effort on what needs to be done to reach a certain level of performance or quality of project. They have a clear understanding of your expectations of achievement.

Though you will want to design many of your own rubrics, several generic ones are included in the front section of the *Goals for Living Teacher's Resources*. These are designed to assess the following:

- *Individual Participation*
- *Individual Reports*
- *Group Participation*

These rubrics allow you to assess a student's performance and arrive at a performance score. Students can see what levels they have surpassed and what levels they can still strive to reach.

Portfolios

Another type of performance assessment that is frequently used by teachers today is the portfolio. A **portfolio** consists of a selection of materials students choose to document their performance over time. Students select their best work samples to highlight their achievements. These items might provide evidence of employability skills as well as academic skills. Some of the items students might include in portfolios are

- work samples (including photographs, videotapes, assessments, etc.) that show mastery of specific skills
- writing samples that show communication skills

- a resume
- letters of recommendation that document specific career-related skills
- certificates of completion
- awards and recognition

The portfolio is assembled at the end of a course to provide evidence of learning. A self-assessment summary report should be included. This report explains what the student has accomplished, what he or she has learned, what strengths he or she has gained, and any areas that need improvement. Students may present their portfolios to the class. Students can also discuss with you how items in their portfolios demonstrate their achievement of educational goals and outcomes. At the end of the course, portfolios should remain the property of students. Students may use the portfolios for interviews with potential employers.

Portfolio assessment is only one of several evaluation methods you can use, but it is a powerful tool for both you and your students. It encourages self-reflection and self-assessment of a more global nature. Traditional evaluation methods of tests, quizzes, and papers have their place in measuring the achievement of some course objectives. However, using a variety of assessment tools can allow you to fairly assess the achievement of all desired outcomes.

Goodheart-Willcox Welcomes Your Comments

We welcome your comments and suggestions regarding *Goals for Living: Managing Your Resources* and its ancillaries as we are continually striving to publish better educational materials. Please send any comments you may have to:

Editorial Department
Goodheart-Willcox Publisher
18604 West Creek Drive
Tinley Park, IL 60477-6243

Or to send a memo to the editor, visit our Web site at:
www.g-w.com

Evaluation of Individual Participation

Name _____ **Date** _____ **Period** _____

The rating scale below shows an evaluation of your class participation. It indicates what levels you have passed and what levels you can continue to try to reach.

Criteria:

1. Attentiveness

1	2	3	4	5
Completely inattentive.	Seldom attentive.	Somewhat attentive.	Usually attentive.	Extremely attentive.

2. Contribution to Discussion

1	2	3	4	5
Never contributes to class discussion.	Rarely contributes to class discussion.	Occasionally contributes to class discussion.	Regularly contributes to class discussion.	Frequently contributes to class discussion.

3. Interaction with Peers

1	2	3	4	5
Often distracts others.	Shows little interaction with others.	Follows leadership of other students.	Sometimes assumes leadership role.	Respected by peers for ability.

4. Response to Teacher

1	2	3	4	5
Unable to respond when called on.	Often unable to support or justify answers when called on.	Supports answers based on class information, but seldom offers new ideas.	Able to offer new ideas with prompting.	Often offers new ideas without prompting.

Total Points: _____ **out of 20**

Comments:

_____

_____

_____

Evaluation of Individual Report

Name _____ Date _____ Period _____

The rating scale below shows an evaluation of your oral or written report. It indicates what levels you have passed and what levels you can try to reach on future reports.

Report title _____ Oral _____ Written _____

Criteria:

1. Choice of Topic

1	2	3	4	5
Slow to choose topic.	Chooses topic with indifference.	Chooses topic as assigned, seeks suggestions.	Chooses relevant topic without assistance.	Chooses creative topic.

2. Use of Resources

1	2	3	4	5
Unable to find resources.	Needs direction to find resources.	Uses fewer than assigned number of resources.	Uses assigned number of resources from typical sources.	Uses additional resources from a variety of sources.

3. Oral Presentation

1	2	3	4	5
Uses no notes or reads completely. Poor subject coverage.	Has few good notes. Limited subject coverage.	Uses notes somewhat effectively. Adequate subject coverage.	Uses notes effectively. Good subject coverage.	Uses notes very effectively. Complete coverage.

4. Written Presentation

1	2	3	4	5
Many grammar and spelling mistakes. No organization.	Several grammar and spelling mistakes. Poor organization.	Some grammar and spelling mistakes. Fair organization.	A few grammar and spelling mistakes. Good organization.	No grammar or spelling mistakes. Excellent organization.

Total Points: _____ out of 15

Evaluation of Group Participation

Group _____

Members _____   _____

_____   _____

_____   _____

The rating scale below shows an evaluation of the efforts of your group. It indicates what levels you have passed and what levels you can try to reach on future group projects.

Criteria:

1. Teamwork

1	2	3	4	5
Passive membership. Failed to identify what tasks needed to be completed.	Argumentative membership. Unable to designate who should complete each task.	Independent membership. All tasks completed individually.	Helpful membership. Completed individual tasks and then assisted others.	Cooperative membership. Worked together to complete all tasks.

2. Leadership

1	2	3	4	5
No attempt at leadership.	No effective leadership.	Sought leadership from outside group.	One member assumed primary leadership role for the group.	Leadership responsibilities shared by several group members.

3. Goal Achievement

1	2	3	4	5
Did not attempt to achieve goal.	Were unable to achieve goal.	Achieved goal with outside assistance.	Achieved assigned goal.	Achieved goal using added materials to enhance total effort.

Total Points: _____ **out of 15**

Members cited for excellent contributions to group's effort are:

_____   _____

Members failing to contribute to group's effort are:

_____   _____

Correlation of National Standards

for

Consumer and Family Resources

with

Goals for Living: Managing Your Resources

In planning your program, you may want to use the correlation chart. This chart correlates the Family and Consumer Sciences Education National Standards with the content of *Goals for Living: Managing Your Resources.* It lists the competencies for each of the content standards for Consumer and Family Resources. It also identifies the major text concepts that relate to each competency. Bold numbers indicate chapters in which concepts are found.

After studying the content of this text, students will be able to achieve the following comprehensive standard:

2.0 Evaluate management practices related to the human, economic, and environmental resources.

Content Standard 2.1 Demonstrate management of individual and family resources, including food, clothing, shelter, health care, recreation, and transportation.	
Competencies	**Text Concepts**
2.1.1 Apply management and planning skills and processes to organize tasks and responsibilities.	**1:** Daily decision making; Factors affecting decisions; Values, goals and resources influencing decisions; Using the decision-making process. **2:** Understanding values; Understanding goals; Standards as measures. **3:** Types of resources; Scarcity of resources; Changing resources; Using resources; Managing resources; Using the management process; Management skills. **4:** Technology as a resource in daily living; The workplace at home; Benefits of technology; Concerns in the use of technology. **14:** Factors affecting family management; Family decision making; Sharing family management responsibilities. **15:** Trends—family and work; The impact of family and work; Successfully combining family and work. **18:** Understanding stress; Managing stress; Personal skills for effective coping. **22:** Savings and investment alternatives; Insurance; Retirement plans and estate planning. **23:** Consumer responsibilities.

Competencies	Text Concepts
2.1.1 (Continued)	**24:** Factors affecting decision making; The decision-making process in consumer choices. **25:** Guidelines in meal planning; Time management in meal planning; Shopping skills; Avoiding waste. **26:** Efficient meal preparation. **31:** Career planning; Career options; Management-related careers.
2.1.2 Examine how individuals and families make choices to satisfy needs and wants.	**1:** Daily decision making; Factors affecting decisions; Values, goals, and resources influencing decisions; Using the decision-making process. **2:** Understanding values; Understanding goals; Standards as measures. **3:** Types of resources; Scarcity of resources; Changing resources; Using resources; Managing resources; Using the management process; Management skills. **4:** Technology as a resource in daily living. **11:** The importance of families; Families in crisis; Resources for families. **12:** Factors influencing marital success; Mutual adjustments in marriage. **14:** Factors affecting family management; Family decision making; Sharing family management responsibilities. **15:** Trends—family and work; The impact of family and work; Employers, governments, and communities—responding to family needs; Successfully combining family and work. **17:** Basic concepts of nutrition; Food guides and eating patterns; Selecting nutritious foods; Factors that influence food choices. **20:** Financial management throughout life; Understanding a paycheck; Basic banking; Record keeping; Developing a budget—a spending plan. **21:** Credit use; Managing credit use throughout life; Laws and regulations governing credit. **22:** Savings and investment alternatives; Insurance; Retirement plans and estate planning. **24:** Factors affecting decision making; The decision-making process in consumer choices. **25:** Guidelines in meal planning; Time management in meal planning; Shopping skills; Avoiding waste. **27:** The significance of clothing; A wardrobe plan; The elements of design; Knowledge and skill in clothing selection. **29:** The home—meeting human needs; Factors affecting satisfaction with housing; Housing alternatives. **31:** Career planning; Career options; Management-related careers.
2.1.3 Implement decisions about providing safe and nutritious food for individuals and families.	**16:** Factors that contribute to good health; Factors affecting good health; Dietary Guidelines for Americans. **17:** Basic concepts of nutrition; Food guides and eating patterns; Selecting nutritious foods; Factors that influence food choices. **25:** Guidelines in meal planning; Time management in meal planning; Shopping skills; Avoiding waste.

Competencies	Text Concepts
2.1.3 (Continued)	**26:** Efficient meal preparation; Nutrition and meal preparation; The significance of heat in cooking; Food preparation techniques; Serving the meal.
2.1.4 Implement decisions about purchasing, creating, and maintaining clothing.	**27:** The significance of clothing; A wardrobe plan; The elements of design; Knowledge and skill in clothing selection. **28:** Techniques of clothing care; Laundry and cleaning techniques.
2.1.5 Implement decisions about housing and furnishings.	**29:** The home—meeting human needs; Factors affecting satisfaction with housing; Housing alternatives. **30:** Design in home furnishings; The selection of home furnishings; Maintaining a clean home; Preventive maintenance.
2.1.6 Examine information about procuring and maintaining health care to meet the needs of individuals and family members.	**16:** Factors that contribute to good health; Factors affecting good health. **17:** Basic concepts of nutrition; Food guides and eating patterns; Selecting nutritious foods; Factors that influence food choices. **18:** Understanding stress; Managing stress; Personal skills for effective coping. **19:** Hazardous environmental conditions; Prevention techniques.
2.1.7 Implement decisions about recreational needs.	**4:** Technology as a resource in daily living; Benefits of technology. **16:** Factors that contribute to good health.
2.1.8 Apply consumer skills to acquire and maintain transportation that meets the needs of individuals and family members.	**22:** Automobile insurance. **24:** Factors affecting decision making; The decision-making process in consumer choices.

Content Standard 2.2 Apply the relationship of the environment to family and consumer resources.

Competencies	Text Concepts
2.2.1 Determine individual and family responsibility in relation to the environmental trends and issues.	**3:** Types of resources; Scarcity of resources; Changing resources; Using resources; Managing resources. **4:** Technology as a resource in daily living; Benefits of technology; Concerns in the use of technology. **19:** Hazardous environmental conditions; Prevention techniques. **25:** Avoiding waste.

Competencies	Text Concepts
2.2.2 Examine how environmental trends and issues affect families and future generations.	**3:** Types of resources; Scarcity of resources; Changing resources; Using resources; Managing resources; Using the management process; Management skills. **4:** Technology as a resource in daily living; Benefits of technology; Concerns in the use of technology. **5:** The role of heredity and environment; Patterns in growth and development; Character; Self-concept. **19:** Hazardous environmental conditions; Prevention techniques.
2.2.3 Examine behaviors that conserve, reuse, and recycle resources to maintain the environment.	**3:** Types of resources; Scarcity of resources; Changing resources; Using resources; Managing resources; Using the management process; Management skills. **19:** Hazardous environmental conditions; Prevention techniques. **25:** Avoiding waste.
2.2.4 Investigate government regulations for conserving natural resources.	**19:** Hazardous environmental conditions; Prevention techniques.

Content Standard 2.3 Analyze policies that support consumer rights and responsibilities.

Competencies	Text Concepts
2.3.1 Examine state and federal policies and laws providing consumer protection.	**21:** Credit use; Managing credit use throughout life; Laws and regulations governing credit. **23:** Consumer rights; Consumer responsibilities.
2.3.2 Investigate how policies become laws related to consumer rights.	**21:** Credit use; Managing credit use throughout life; Laws and regulations governing credit. **23:** Consumer rights; Consumer responsibilities.
2.3.3 Examine skills used in seeking information related to consumer rights.	**21:** Credit use; Managing credit use throughout life; Laws and regulations governing credit. **23:** Consumer rights; Consumer responsibilities. **24:** Factors affecting decision making; The decision-making process in consumer choices.

Content Standard 2.4 Analyze policies that support consumer rights and responsibilities.	
Competencies	**Text Concepts**
2.4.1 Review types of technology that impact family and consumer decision making.	**4:** Technology as a resource in daily living; Benefits of technology; Concerns in the use of technology. **24:** Factors affecting decision making; The decision-making process in consumer choices.
2.4.2 Examine how media and technological advances impact family and consumer decisions.	**4:** Technology as a resource in daily living; Benefits of technology; Concerns in the use of technology. **10:** Types of communication; Levels of communication; The importance of active listening; Skill in conflict resolution. **24:** Factors affecting decision making; The decision-making process in consumer choices.
2.4.3 Assess the use of technology and its impact on quality of life.	**4:** Technology as a resource in daily living; The workplace at home; Benefits of technology; Concerns in the use of technology.

Content Standard 2.5 Analyze interrelationships between the economic system and consumer actions.	
Competencies	**Text Concepts**
2.5.1 Examine the use of resources in making choices that satisfy the needs and wants of individuals and families.	**1:** Daily decision making; Factors affecting decisions; Values, goals, and resources influencing decisions; Using the decision-making process. **3:** Types of resources; Scarcity of resources; Changing resources; Using resources; Managing resources; Using the management process; Management skills. **4:** Technology as a resource in daily living; The workplace at home; Benefits of technology; Concerns in the use of technology.
2.5.2 Examine individual and family roles in the economic system.	**20:** Financial management throughout life; Understanding a paycheck; Basic banking; Record keeping; Developing a budget—a spending plan. **21:** Credit use; Managing credit use throughout life; Laws and regulations governing credit. **22:** Savings and investment alternatives; Insurance; Retirement plans and estate planning. **23:** Consumer rights; Consumer responsibilities. **24:** Factors affecting decision making; The decision-making process in consumer choices.

Competencies	Text Concepts
2.5.3 Examine economic impacts of laws and regulations that pertain to consumers and providers of services.	**21:** Credit use; Laws and regulations governing credit. **22:** Savings and investment alternatives; Insurance; Retirement plans and estate planning. **23:** Consumer rights; Consumer responsibilities.
2.5.4 Determine practices that allow families to maintain economic self-sufficiency.	**20:** Financial management throughout life; Understanding a paycheck; Basic banking; Record keeping; Developing a budget—a spending plan. **21:** Credit use; Managing credit use throughout life; Laws and regulations governing credit. **22:** Savings and investment alternatives; Insurance; Retirement plans and estate planning. **23:** Consumer rights; Consumer responsibilities. **24:** Factors affecting decision making; The decision-making process in consumer choices.

Content Standard 2.6 Demonstrate management of financial resources to meet the goals of individuals and families across the life span.

Competencies	Text Concepts
2.6.1 Examine the need for personal and family financial planning.	**1:** Daily decision making; Factors affecting decisions; Values, goals, and resources influencing decisions; Using the decision-making process. **2:** Understanding values; Understanding goals; Standards as measures. **3:** Types of resources; Scarcity of resources; Changing resources; Using resources; Managing resources; Using the management process; Management skills. **20:** Financial management throughout life; Understanding a paycheck; Basic banking; Record keeping; Developing a budget—a spending plan. **21:** Credit use; Managing credit use throughout life; Laws and regulations governing credit. **22:** Savings and investment alternatives; Insurance; Retirement plans and estate planning. **23:** Consumer rights; Consumer responsibilities.
2.6.2 Apply management principles to individual and family practices.	**1:** Daily decision making; Factors affecting decisions; Values, goals, and resources influencing decisions; Using the decision-making process. **2:** Understanding values; Understanding goals; Standards as measures. **3:** Types of resources; Scarcity of resources; Changing resources; Using resources; Managing resources; Using the management process; Management skills.

Competencies	Text Concepts
2.6.2 (Continued)	**4:** Technology as a resource in daily living; The workplace at home; Benefits of technology; Concerns in the use of technology. **10:** Types of communication; Levels of communication; The importance of active listening; Skill in conflict resolution. **14:** Factors affecting family management; Family decision making; Sharing family management responsibilities. **16:** Factors that contribute to good health; Factors affecting good health. **17:** Basic concepts of nutrition; Food guides and eating patterns; Selecting nutritious foods; Factors that influence food choices. **18:** Understanding stress; Managing stress; Personal skills for effective coping. **20:** Financial management throughout life; Understanding a paycheck; Basic banking; Record keeping; Developing a budget—a spending plan. **25:** Guidelines in meal planning; Time management in meal planning; Shopping skills; Avoiding waste. **27:** The significance of clothing; A wardrobe plan; The elements of design; Knowledge and skill in clothing selection. **29:** The home—meeting human needs; Factors affecting satisfaction with housing; Housing alternatives. **31:** Career planning; Career options; Management-related careers.
2.6.3 Apply management principles to decisions about individual and family insurance.	**22:** Savings and investment alternatives; Insurance; Retirement plans and estate planning.
2.6.4 Obtain personal and legal documents related to individual and family finances.	**20:** Financial management throughout life; Understanding a paycheck; Basic banking; Record keeping; Developing a budget—a spending plan. **21:** Credit use; Managing credit use throughout life; Laws and regulations governing credit. **22:** Savings and investment alternatives; Insurance; Retirement plans and estate planning. **32:** Sources of job leads; Job-seeking skills; Traits leading to job success; Employer responsibilities.

Scope and Sequence Chart

In planning your program, you may want to use the Scope and Sequence Chart. This chart identifies the major concepts presented in each chapter of the text. Refer to the chart to select for study those topics that meet your curriculum needs. Bold numbers indicate chapters in which concepts are found.

Part One: Learning to Manage

Skills for Managing Resources

1: Decisions: related to stage in life, role in daily living; Using the decision-making process
2: Identifying and clarifying needs, wants, and values; Standards in management; Flexible standards
3: Scarcity of resources; Changing resources throughout life; Resource use: exchanging, developing, and sharing; Identify resources and planning resource use; Management skills; Time and energy management; Work simplification; Using the management process
4: Recognizing benefits and concerns of technology

Personal and Family Resources

1: Values, goals, and resources
2: Categories of values; needs and value conflict, values sources, and changing needs and values; Goals: short-term, long-term, and changing goals
3: Human and nonhuman resources; Changing resources throughout life
4: Technology at home; Benefits of technology

Financial and Economic Resources

4: Knowledge of technology uses

Consumer Resources

4: Computers in the home

Career Planning Resources

4: Technology brings the workplace home

Part Two: Development Across the Life Span

Personal and Family Resources

5: Understanding self-concept: formation of self-concept and healthy self-concept; Character; Hereditary and environmental influences on development; Patterns of human development
7: Developmental tasks of infants and toddlers, preschool children, and school-age children
8: Developmental tasks of adolescence, young adulthood, middle age, and late adulthood

Parenting Resources

6: Patterns of children's development: physical, social, emotional, intellectual; Infants and toddlers, preschool children, school-age children; Development of self-concept
7: Developmental tasks of infants and toddlers, preschool children, and school-age children

Part Three: Understanding Relationships

Skills for Managing Resources

10: Communicating with yourself; Communicating with others: open communication, full communication, two-way communication; Conflict resolution; Problem ownership

Personal and Family Resources

9: Respect, trust, responsibility, and openness in relationships; Relationships throughout life
10: Communicating with yourself; Communicating with others: open communication, full communication, two-way communication; Conflict resolution; Problem ownership

Parenting Resources

9: Relationships of children within the family and outside the family

Part Four: Family Living

Skills for Managing Resources

14: Family decision making; Family management tasks; Sharing family responsibilities
15: Impact of work on home management; Skills helpful in combining family and work; Recognizing resources; Decision-making skills

Personal and Family Resources

11: Family forms; Families meeting needs; Characteristics of a caring family; Skill in dealing with family crises; Resources for families
12: Factors influencing marital success; Marital adjustments
14: Family management throughout the family life cycle
15: Trends related to family and work; How family and work impact each other; Child care services offered by employers; Government policies to help working parents; Child care options

Parenting Resources

13: Parental responsibilities to children: meeting physical and psychological needs; Changes in children's dependency on parents
15: How family and work impact each other; Child care services offered by employers; Government policies to help working parents; Child care options

Financial and Economic Resources

15: Why people work

Consumer Resources

15: Choosing child care

Career Planning Resources

15: Why people work; Work patterns; Impact of family on the workplace; Employers' response to working parents; Flexible personnel policies

Part Five: Managing Health and Wellness

Skills for Managing Resources

16: Recognizing nutritious foods: labeling, dating; Selecting nutritious foods at home and when eating out

18: Managing stress; Skills for coping

Personal and Family Resources

18: Understanding stress; Stressful reactions; Causes of stress

Health and Safety Resources

16: Good eating habits; Physical activity; Sufficient sleep; Good mental health; Defense mechanisms; Dietary Guidelines for Americans; Lifestyle diseases; Sexually transmitted diseases

19: Knowledge of hazardous conditions; Recycling; Medical exams; Medical records; Vaccinations; Signs of illness; Emergency care of the sick and injured

Food and Nutrition Resources

16: Dietary Guidelines for Americans

17: Nutrients; Functions of food; Food Guide Pyramid; Special nutritional needs; Eating patterns; Influences on food choices and eating habits

Part Six: Managing Finances

Skills for Managing Resources

20: Understanding a paycheck; Managing a checking account; Developing a budget

Financial and Economic Resources

20: Recordkeeping

22: Savings and investment alternatives; Life insurance; Health insurance; Government health insurance; Property insurance; Automobile insurance; Retirement plans and estate planning

Consumer Resources

21: Credit: advantages and disadvantages, types, sources; Obtaining credit; Credit laws and regulations

Part Seven: Managing as a Consumer

Skills for Managing Resources

24: Making consumer decisions

Personal and Family Resources

24: Family's influence on consumer decisions

Financial and Economic Resources

24: The economy and consumer decisions

Consumer Resources

23: Consumer rights; Consumer responsibilities; Misleading advertising; Consumer complaints

Part Eight: Managing Food

Skills for Managing Resources

25: Food shopping skills; Time management in meal preparation
26: Organization in the kitchen; Work centers, equipment, and storage space; Serving meals

Food and Nutrition Resources

25: Planning meals; Avoiding food waste
26: Retaining nutrients; Understanding heat in cooking; Specific food preparation techniques: milk, cheese, eggs, meat, grain products, fats and oils, fruits, vegetables

Part Nine: Managing Clothing

Skills for Managing Resources

27: Decision-making skills for clothing selection; Sewing skills; Shopping guidelines; Judging performance of clothing

Textiles and Clothing Resources

27: Clothing and basic needs; Style and fashion; Wardrobe plan; Elements of design; Fiber, fabric, finish
28: Clothing care and storage; Laundering and cleaning, stain removal techniques; Care labels; Laundry products and procedures

Part Ten: Managing Housing

Skills for Managing Resources

30: Maintaining a clean home

Personal and Family Resources

29: Physical and psychological needs met by the home

Housing and Home Furnishings Resources

29: Space needs in a home; Storage needs in a home; Influences on satisfaction with housing; Renting and buying housing; Types of housing; Financing a home purchase; Legal aspects of buying housing
30: Elements and principles of design; Walls and wall treatments; Ceilings; Floors and floor coverings; Windows and window treatments; Furniture; Lighting; Accessories; Preventive maintenance; Maintenance for energy efficiency

Part Eleven: Preparing for Your Career

Skills for Managing Resources

31: Management skills for careers

Personal and Family Resources

31: Self-study for career planning: interests, abilities, personal characteristics
32: Traits leading to job success

Career Planning Resources

31: Career planning; Sources of career information; Career and technical student organizations; Management-related careers; Management level and training required; Occupational trends
32: Sources of job leads; Job seeking skills; Cover letter; Resume; Job application; Interview; Employment tests; Employer responsibilities

Basic Skills Chart

This chart has been designed to identify those activities in the *Goals for Living Student Activity Guide* and *Teacher's Resource Binder* that specifically encourage the development of basic skills. The following abbreviations are used in the chart:

SAG...Activities in the *Student Activity Guide* (designated by letter)

TR...Strategies described in the *Teacher's Resource Binder* (referred to by number)

Activities listed as "Verbal" include the following types: role-playing, conducting interviews, oral reports, and debates.

Activities listed as "Reading" may involve actual reading in and out of the classroom. However, many of these activities are designed to improve reading comprehension of the concepts presented in each chapter. Some are designed to improve understanding of vocabulary terms.

Activities that involve writing are listed under "Writing." The list includes activities that allow students to practice composition skills, such as letter writing, informative writing, and creative writing.

The "Math/Science/Technology" list includes activities that require students to use computation skills in solving typical problems they may come across in their everyday living. Any activities related to the sciences and computers are also listed.

The final category, "Analytical," lists those activities that involve the higher order thinking skills of analysis, synthesis, and evaluation. Activities that involve decision making, problem solving, and critical thinking are included in this section.

Additional activities that promote the development of basic skills are included in the text at the end of each chapter. "To Challenge Your Thinking" activities are designed to encourage critical thinking. "To Do with the Class" and "To Do with Your Community" activities provide a variety of learning experiences for students and involve a variety of basic skills outlined in the chart.

	Verbal	**Reading**	**Writing**	**Math/Science**	**Analytical**
Chapter 1	TR: 2, 6, 8, 9, 13, 15, 17	TR: 12, 15	TR: 10	TR: 11	SAG: A, B, C, D TR: 1, 12, 13, 17
Chapter 2	TR: 1, 2, 6, 7, 9, 10, 11, 15, 16, 20, 23, 24, 25	TR: 10, 17			SAG: A, B, C, D TR: 5, 6, 18, 19, 20
Chapter 3	TR: 2, 3, 10, 12, 13, 14, 15 21, 23, 27, 33, 43, 44, 45	TR: 1, 6, 13	SAG: A, B TR: 1, 6, 13, 22, 46	SAG: C TR: 6, 20	SAG: A, B, C, D TR: 5, 7, 8, 11, 19, 26, 30, 34, 35, 36
Chapter 4	TR: 1, 2, 5, 13, 16, 18, 23, 25, 26, 28, 29, 31, 32	SAG: C TR: 1, 6, 8, 12, 14, 16, 19	SAG: A, C TR: 1, 27, 33	SAG: A, B,C TR: 6, 7, 8, 9, 14, 18, 19, 24, 26, 29, 32	SAG: B TR: 8, 15, 20, 23

	Verbal	Reading	Writing	Math/Science	Analytical
Chapter 5	SAG: A TR: 1, 6, 7, 11, 12, 13, 15, 21, 22, 25, 28, 30, 31, 32, 37, 38, 39, 40, 41, 43, 47	SAG: C TR: 4, 13, 14	SAG: A, B TR: 4, 18, 24, 27, 29, 33, 44	SAG: A TR: 4, 5, 6, 7, 8	SAG: A, D TR: 2, 9, 10, 14, 16, 23, 26, 33, 36, 42, 47
Chapter 6	TR: 1, 2, 6, 8, 10, 12, 14, 15, 17, 23, 24, 26, 28, 29, 35, 39, 40, 41, 42, 43	SAG: A TR:13, 19, 20, 33	TR: 1, 13, 14, 19, 22	SAG: A, B, C TR: 7	SAG: A, B, C, D TR: 33, 34, 37
Chapter 7	TR: 1, 2, 3, 5, 6, 7, 8, 11, 13, 16, 19, 21, 22, 24, 25, 26, 27, 29, 30, 33, 34, 35, 36, 37, 38, 40	TR: 20, 23	TR: 20, 32	SAG: A, B, C	SAG: A, B, C TR: 18, 31
Chapter 8	TR: 2, 4, 5, 7, 9, 14, 17, 18, 20, 22, 23	TR: 1, 17, 20, 25	TR: 1	SAG: A, B, C, D	SAG: A, B, C, D TR: 6, 10, 12
Chapter 9	SAG: D TR: 1, 3, 5, 7, 10, 11, 12, 14, 21, 22, 23, 25, 29	TR: 1, 18, 24, 26	SAG: C TR: 1, 6, 17, 18, 19, 28		SAG: A, B, D TR: 2, 4, 8, 26, 32
Chapter 10	TR: 1, 2, 3, 4, 6, 7, 12, 15, 18, 19, 22, 23	TR: 5, 25	TR: 3, 13		SAG: A, B, C, D TR: 4, 10, 17, 24
Chapter 11	TR: 2, 3, 7, 11, 15, 16, 19, 22, 25, 26, 29	SAG: D TR: 2, 10, 31	SAG: D TR: 1, 6, 14, 20		SAG: A, B, C TR: 4,9

	Verbal	**Reading**	**Writing**	**Math/Science**	**Analytical**
Chapter 12	SAG: A, B TR: 2, 3, 7, 8, 14, 15, 16, 17, 18, 19, 24, 27, 28, 29	TR: 4, 25	TR: 9, 13, 20, 25		SAG: A, B, C, D TR: 6, 23
Chapter 13	TR: 1, 2, 4, 5, 7, 9, 10, 12, 15, 20, 21, 28, 29	TR: 1, 23	TR: 4, 12, 14, 22, 25, 27		SAG: A, B, C, D TR: 13, 17, 19
Chapter 14	TR: 1, 3, 6, 7, 12, 13, 14, 16, 19, 20, 21, 22, 23, 24, 25, 32, 36	SAG: A TR: 20	SAG: D TR: 8, 17, 29		SAG: A, B, C, D TR: 8, 11, 15, 31
Chapter 15	TR: 1, 4, 5, 8, 11, 13, 19, 25, 29, 33, 40, 43	TR: 3, 14, 16, 27, 36, 38	TR: 2, 13, 14, 26	TR: 12	SAG: A, B, C, D TR: 7, 12, 22, 25, 39, 44, 45
Chapter 16	TR: 1, 5, 15, 20, 23, 25, 33, 34	SAG: C TR: 1, 12, 19, 29, 32, 34	SAG: C TR: 11, 15, 17, 19, 25, 29, 32, 35	SAG: A, B	SAG: A, B TR: 5, 7, 8, 16, 26, 29, 30
Chapter 17	TR: 14, 23, 25, 28, 34, 38, 40	TR: 2, 14, 41	TR: 14, 30, 33	SAG: A, B TR: 5, 6, 9, 20	SAG: A, B, C, D TR: 4, 10, 14, 16, 18, 27, 34, 35, 37, 41
Chapter 18	TR: 4, 5, 14, 16, 24, 25, 27, 29, 31, 32, 33, 35, 36, 37, 38	TR: 4	TR: 23, 28, 30, 37		SAG: A, B, C, D TR: 8, 9, 17, 18, 19, 20, 34
Chapter 19	TR: 2, 4, 5, 8, 10, 14, 16, 18, 24, 26, 28, 35, 37, 40, 41	SAG: B TR: 3, 7, 18, 37, 38	SAG: B TR: 7, 25, 38, 41	SAG: A, B, C TR: 6, 8, 10, 12, 16, 18, 19, 20, 23, 24	SAG: A, C TR: 9, 29

	Verbal	**Reading**	**Writing**	**Math/Science**	**Analytical**
Chapter 20	TR: 1, 15, 19, 22, 23, 24, 27, 29	TR: 3	SAG: A TR: 3, 26	SAG: B, C TR: 9, 16	SAG: A, B, C TR: 7, 21, 25, 28, 31
Chapter 21	TR: 1, 2, 3, 5, 13, 18, 22, 23, 25	TR: 6, 8, 11, 13, 19, 20, 22	TR: 11, 22, 24		SAG: A, B, C, D TR: 10, 12, 16, 18
Chapter 22	SAG: E TR: 1, 2, 5, 6, 13, 14, 15, 19, 29	SAG: B, D TR: 9, 10, 15, 19, 23, 29, 31	TR: 9, 14, 21, 23, 30, 31	SAG: C TR: 10, 12, 18, 24	SAG: A, C, D TR: 4, 10, 12, 24, 30
Chapter 23	TR: 2, 3, 4, 5, 6, 9, 15, 16, 19, 22, 23, 26, 27, 30, 31, 32, 33	SAG: A, B, C TR: 1, 6, 9, 10, 11	SAG: A, B, C TR:7, 11, 29		SAG: B, C TR: 7, 8, 11
Chapter 24	SAG: A TR:1, 4, 6, 7, 8, 10, 11, 13, 21, 24, 30, 34	SAG: A TR: 9, 11, 14, 16	SAG: A TR: 9, 14, 18, 36		SAG: B, C, D TR: 2, 3, 8, 30, 35
Chapter 25	TR: 3, 6, 10, 16, 20, 21, 25, 27, 31, 35, 41, 44, 47, 48	SAG: A TR: 4, 9, 25	TR: 7, 46, 48	SAG: A, B, D TR: 14, 42	SAG: A, B, C, D, E, F TR: 11, 13, 14, 22, 23, 30, 32, 38, 40
Chapter 26	TR: 4, 9, 12, 17, 20, 24, 25, 27, 36, 45	TR: 19, 32	TR: 16, 19	SAG: B, E, F TR: 13, 17, 19, 27, 33, 34, 38, 39, 40, 42, 43	SAG: A, B, C, D, E, F TR: 2, 5, 6, 11, 13, 15, 16, 20, 21, 27, 33, 34, 38, 39, 40, 41, 42
Chapter 27	TR: 2, 3, 6, 8, 9, 10, 14, 17, 18, 21, 23, 24, 27, 28	TR: 8, 37, 40	TR: 15, 29, 38, 40	TR: 32	SAG: A, B, C, D TR: 17, 29, 33, 34, 39, 42

	Verbal	Reading	Writing	Math/Science	Analytical
Chapter 28	TR: 3, 9, 12, 18, 20	TR: 19		SAG: D TR: 14, 15, 16, 20, 21	SAG: A, B, C, D TR: 6, 7, 13, 16, 21, 22
Chapter 29	SAG: B TR: 2, 3, 5, 7, 8, 9, 19, 22, 23, 24, 25, 26, 27, 29	TR: 5	SAG: B TR: 3, 11	TR: 34	SAG: A, C, D, E TR: 10, 12, 14, 15, 27, 28
Chapter 30	SAG: C TR: 1, 2, 3, 6, 9, 11, 14, 16, 30, 34, 36	SAG: C TR: 10, 36	SAG: C TR: 15	TR: 23	SAG: A, B, D TR: 18, 21, 23, 26, 32, 35
Chapter 31	SAG: C TR: 1, 5, 6, 8, 14, 15, 21, 24	SAG: C TR: 19, 24, 30	SAG: C TR: 1, 11, 20		SAG: A, B, D TR: 26
Chapter 32	TR: 2, 3, 5, 6, 11, 18, 20, 21, 24, 25, 26, 28, 31, 33, 34	SAG: A TR: 27	SAG: A, B TR: 13, 14, 23, 27, 34		SAG: C, D TR: 15

Decision Making in Your Daily Life

Objectives

When students have completed this chapter, they will be able to
- recognize how the decisions they make affect their lives.
- describe how the changing world affects their decision making.
- explain how values, goals, and resources influence management decisions.
- apply the decision-making process to their daily lives.

Bulletin Board

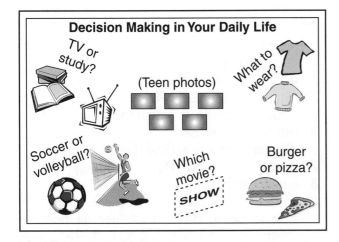

Decision Making in Your Daily Life

TV or study?

(Teen photos)

What to wear?

Soccer or volleyball?

Which movie?

SHOW

Burger or pizza?

Title: *Decision Making in Your Daily Life*

Cut out pictures from magazines and use them to create a bulletin board illustrating decisions teenagers make in their daily lives. Examples include choices regarding food, clothing, friends, activities, job, family, etc. The meaning will be more complete if a written question is placed next to each picture. For instance, next to a picture of some books might be the question, "Should I study now or watch TV?"

Teaching Materials

Text, pages 11-26
To Review
To Challenge Your Thinking
To Do with the Class
To Do with Your Community
Student Activity Guide
A. *Daily Decision Making*
B. *Decisions, Decisions, Decisions!*
C. *Recognizing Your Resources*
D. *Skills in Solving Problems*
Teacher's Resources
The Patterning Technique, reproducible master 1-1
Roles and Decisions, transparency master 1-2
Chapter 1 Test
Decision Making, color transparency CT-1

Introductory Activities

1. *The Patterning Technique,* reproducible master 1-1, and *Roles and Decisions,* transparency master 1-2, TR. Patterning is a technique that can help people to organize their thoughts and capture information and ideas as they are generated. Use the masters to explain to students the technique of patterning. Then have students try out the technique for themselves to illustrate the variety of roles and decisions in their lives.
2. Ask students to list simple, routine decisions that teenagers are likely to make. Then ask them to list more complex decisions that may also have to be made by teenagers. Discuss students' ideas.

Instructional Concepts and Student Learning Experiences

Decisions You Make Daily

3. Ask students to identify life stages and to brainstorm examples of decisions typical of each particular stage.
4. *Daily Decision Making,* Activity A, SAG. Students are asked to give examples of decisions related to various areas in life and to list values, goals, and resources related to each decision.
5. *Decisions, Decisions, Decisions!* Activity B, SAG. Students are asked to give examples of decisions typically made in various stages in life and roles in life.
6. Ask students to interview people who are at different life stages about decisions they make that are related to their stage in life.
7. Ask students to list the various roles that people may assume during their life.
8. Ask students to brainstorm a list of decisions that teenagers make about family, relationships with others, health, food and clothing, and buying consumer goods.
9. As a class, have students develop a list of 10 different attitudes or emotions. Then have students discuss how each item listed might influence a decision.

Factors Affecting Decisions

10. Have students write a fictional story describing a situation in which peer pressure would affect a person's decision. Read a few stories aloud and have the class discuss them.
11. Have students identify social and technological changes that have occurred in their lifetime. Discuss how these changes might affect decision making.
12. Ask students to analyze the front section of a newspaper. Have them discuss stories they find that involve situations or problems associated with social and technological change.

Values, Goals, and Resources Influence Decisions

13. *Decision Making,* color transparency CT-1, TR. Use this transparency as a basis of discussion on how values, goals, and resources influence decisions. Ask students to identify decisions they or other family members have made based on values, goals, and resources.
14. *Recognizing Your Resources,* Activity C, SAG. Students are asked to list three resources that could be used to reach each goal listed.

Using the Decision-Making Process

15. Ask each student to interview five people in different roles about decisions they make that are unique to their role. Have students discuss what they have learned.
16. *Skills in Solving Problems,* Activity D, SAG. Students are to think of a problem they would like to solve, then follow the steps of the decision-making process to solve the problem.
17. Have students work in small groups to solve a given problem using the decision-making process. Students should share their results with the other groups.
18. Invite a panel of several people to speak to your class on the challenge in decision making today for individuals and families. People such as doctors, teachers, social workers, and bankers might make good panel members.

Answer Key

Text

To Review

1. decisions, goals
2. (Student response. List two.)
3. (Student response. List four.)
4. (Student response. Name four.)
5. (Student response.)
6. (Student response. Give three examples.)
7. (Student response. Describe three.)
8. goals, values
9. 1. Identify the problem to be solved or decision to be made. 2. Consider all possible alternatives to reach that goal. 3. Recognize the consequences of each alternative. 4. Choose the best alternative. 5. Evaluate the decision and the process.
10. goal

Teacher's Resources

Chapter 1 Test

1. C
2. H
3. D
4. I
5. A
6. J
7. E
8. B
9. F
10. G
11. F
12. T
13. F
14. T
15. T
16. T
17. F
18. T
19. T
20. T
21. B
22. D
23. B
24. C
25. A
26. D
27. (Student response.)
28. (Student response.)
29. (Student response.)
30. (List five: Student response.)

Reproducible Master 1-1

The Patterning Technique

Name _____ **Date** _____ **Period** _____

Patterning is a way to recognize your thoughts. It is an easy technique that allows you to capture information and ideas as they come to mind. With this technique, you need not organize ideas first as done when making an outline.

The patterning technique can be helpful whenever you want to examine information or gather your thoughts quickly. You could use this technique as a tool for organizing your life. For instance, you could organize your roles and decisions in life using patterning.

Patterning begins with a blank sheet of paper. The first step is to write the main topic in the middle of the page and draw a circle around it. In this case, you are the main topic, so you write your name in the center of the page. Next, begin listing your various roles in life on branches extending out from the circle. Turn the paper around as you need to. You will be able to read the pattern more easily if you print. Include just enough words so that you understand what you mean. When you have listed all your roles, begin writing related decisions on branches that extend out from those roles. You may have several decisions related to certain roles.

Soon the pattern will begin to bristle with branches. Patterns are as unique as fingerprints. No one will have one just like yours. Now try out the patterning technique for yourself.

Transparency Master 1-2

Roles and Decisions

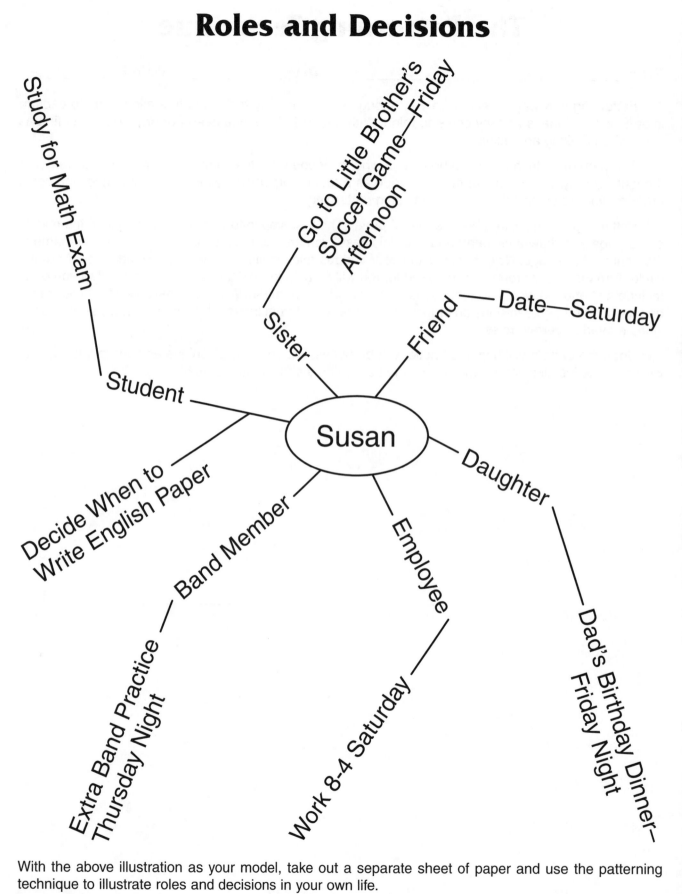

With the above illustration as your model, take out a separate sheet of paper and use the patterning technique to illustrate roles and decisions in your own life.

Decision Making in Your Daily Life

Name _____

Date _____ Period_____ Score _____

Chapter 1 Test

Matching: Match the following terms and identifying phrases.

_____ 1. The ends of purposes toward which managers work that provide them with direction.

_____ 2. Used to help reach your goals.

_____ 3. A certain function you assume in life.

_____ 4. Various options available from which to choose.

_____ 5. Affect the types of decisions made because of one's position in the lifespan.

_____ 6. Things that are important to you and provide motivation in your life.

_____ 7. End results that can have advantages and disadvantages.

_____ 8. Judging the decision-making process and the end result to learn from your mistakes and accomplishments.

_____ 9. People who make choices or decisions that move them toward specific goals.

_____ 10. A resource to help you solve problems and reach personal goals.

A. stages in life

B. evaluation

C. goals

D. role

E. consequences

F. managers

G. decision-making process

H. resources

I. alternatives

J. values

True/False: Circle *T* if the answer is true or *F* if the answer is false.

T F 11. Although managing your life involves many decisions, you do not make decisions each day.

T F 12. In your community member role, you make decisions related to volunteer work.

T F 13. Making decisions is less challenging today than in the past due to technological advances and social changes.

T F 14. The more skilled you become in managing daily living, the greater control you have over your life.

T F 15. Your choices are based mainly on your resources and guided by your goals.

T F 16. Many resources go unused because people do not recognize their resources or their possible uses.

T F 17. When making decisions, you need not consider more than two or three alternatives.

T F 18. An evaluation of a decision is successful if you use what you learn to prevent future mistakes.

T F 19. If people fail to consider all possible alternatives, they may miss an important step for making successful decisions.

T F 20. Standards help you decide if you have reached your goals.

(Continued)

Name _____

Multiple Choice: Choose the best answer and write the corresponding letter in the blank.

_____ 21. Decisions made are often related to life stages. Which of the following is NOT a stage in life?
   A. Teenager.
   B. Parent.
   C. Senior citizen.
   D. Young adult.

_____ 22. Decisions are made in various roles you assume. Which of the following is an example of a role in life?
   A. Family member.
   B. Parent.
   C. Employee.
   D. All of the above.

_____ 23. Which of the following decisions is related more to a stage in life than to a role in life?
   A. Where to go on a family vacation.
   B. What to do after high school graduation.
   C. Whether or not to change jobs.
   D. Whom to vote for as governor.

_____ 24. Which of the following statements about the challenge of decision making is NOT true?
   A. Changing technology has brought new challenges into our lives.
   B. Consumer decisions are more challenging because of the variety of products from which to choose.
   C. A person can learn to control the external forces in life.
   D. Changing social customs create new situations related to decision making.

_____ 25. Which of the following is NOT true about the first step of the decision-making process?
   A. It is always easy to identify the true problem.
   B. Sometimes the real problem remains hidden among events that are happening.
   C. Sometimes people have a difficult time admitting that a problem exists.
   D. When identifying the problem, it is helpful to state it in terms of a goal.

_____ 26. Which of the following is true of the evaluation step of the decision-making process?
   A. If you stated the problem in terms of a goal, you will have standards by which to judge whether or not goals have been accomplished.
   B. Both the decision and the entire decision-making process should be evaluated.
   C. In evaluating the process, check to see whether you thought through the outcomes of each alternative.
   D. All of the above are true.

Essay Questions: Provide the answers you feel best show your understanding of the subject matter.

27. List four decisions related to the role of a community member.

28. Describe five social or technological changes that have made decision making more difficult.

29. Describe a situation that includes each of the following: (A) a person making a decision, (B) a decision based on certain values, (C) a decision guided by a goal or goals. Be sure to identify each of these items in your description.

30. Name the steps of the decision-making process and describe each step briefly.

Your Values, Goals, and Standards

Objectives

When students have completed this chapter, they will be able to
- identify values.
- explain how needs and values influence their behavior.
- distinguish between higher values and instrumental values.
- describe how values form and change.
- analyze the relationship between values, goals, and standards.
- describe the importance of flexible standards.
- use values, goals, and standards to become better managers.

Bulletin Boards

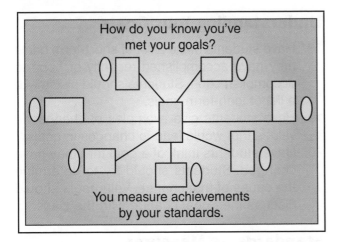

How do you know you've met your goals?

You measure achievements by your standards.

Title: *How Do You Know You've Met Your Goals?*

Find small pictures of seven people who vary in age and sex and place them on the board as indicated by the small ovals. Beside each picture, place a picture depicting the kind of vacation that the person might consider to be wonderful. For instance, next to a young boy might be a picture of an amusement park. In the center area, place the following explanation: "The types of vacations that each of these people prefer are quite different. However, they are all considered wonderful vacations because they fit each person's standards for a wonderful vacation."

Title: *What You Do Reflects Your Values*

Place several pictures of people doing different activities on the board. Place a blank sheet of paper under each picture and allow students to write down the values that they think are being reflected in the pictures. Have students discuss the values chosen as a class.

Teaching Materials

Text, pages 27-38
  To Review
  To Challenge Your Thinking
  To Do with the Class
  To Do with Your Community
Student Activity Guide
  A. *Value Identification*
  B. *Values and Behavior*
  C. *Values and Value Sources*
  D. *Goals and Standards*
Teacher's Resources
  Human Need Values, reproducible master 2-1
  Chapter 2 Test
  What Higher Values Do You Reflect? color
    transparency CT-2

Introductory Activities

1. Choose a group of students and give each student in the group a list of five values. Each student's list may contain some similar items, but the total lists should all be different. Instruct the group to role-play coming to a group decision on such an action as a vacation, what to do for a weekend activity, or how to spend a gift of $1000. Each student in the group should provide input based on the values they have been given. Have the rest of the class discuss what values are being shown and how they affect the decision being made.
2. Have students make a list of five activities they saw someone doing recently. Have the class discuss each activity and determine what values might be indicated by the activity.

Instructional Concepts and Student Learning Experiences

Understanding Your Values

3. *Value Identification,* Activity A, SAG. Have students list and describe the three main categories of higher values, giving examples of each. Then have students indicate which category of higher values relates to each of the items listed.

4. *Values and Behavior,* Activity B, SAG. Have students use the form provided to analyze how values and behavior are related. Have students save their responses and evaluate them again when they finish studying Chapter 2.

5. Have students think of some decisions that did not turn out very well for them. Students should analyze whether these decisions were based on the values most important to them.

6. Have students make a list of five instrumental values. Students should analyze each value and determine to which higher value each instrumental value would lead. Then students should categorize each higher value as a moral value, a human need value, or an aesthetic value. Students should discuss their lists as a class.

7. *What Higher Values Do You Reflect?* color transparency CT-2, TR. Under each of the higher values listed in the mirror, write examples of each type of value. Ask students to share personal stories or personal examples to show how their actions reflected their values. Discuss how other people may reflect their values in daily life.

8. Guest speaker. Invite a representative of a mental health clinic to discuss healthy ways of dealing with conflicts in values.

9. *Human Need Values,* reproducible master 2-1, TR. Use the master to present Maslow's arrangement of human need values. Students should discuss their reactions to this arrangement.

10. Have each student write a short paragraph describing a fictitious situation in which values conflict. The conflict may be between two people or within one person. Put the paragraphs into a container. Have each student draw a paragraph, read it, and identify the conflicting values.

11. Have students discuss value conflicts that are typical at their stage of life.

12. Have students list some possible sources of values and the specific values that may result from those sources.

13. *Values and Value Sources,* Activity C, SAG. Have students determine instrumental values that lead to various higher level values. Students should then list actions of adults and teens that would influence a child's values.

14. Have students list 10 of their own values and try to determine the sources of those values. Students should not be required to share these responses with the class.

15. Have students interview an adult to find out how their values have changed in the last 10 years. Students should share their findings with the class.

16. Have students discuss the phrase "Absence makes the heart grow fonder" in terms of changing values.

17. Have each student write an anonymous example of changing values that he or she has experienced. Choose some examples and read them to the class.

Understanding Your Goals

18. Have students make a list of short-term goals they have accomplished recently or hope to accomplish soon. Students should also make a list of long-term goals.

19. Have students give examples of changes in values that would lead to changes in goals.

20. Have students think of a goal that they have changed. Students should try to determine the cause of that change. Volunteers should discuss their goal change with the class.

Standards as Measures

21. *Goals and Standards,* Activity D, SAG. Have students complete the given charts with information related to short-term and long-term goals. Students should list several goals, the value or values on which each goal is based, and the standards that could be used to judge whether the goal has been reached.

22. Have students explain how subjective and objective standards differ. Students should give several examples of each.

23. Have students discuss some conventional standards in current society, such as grades, common table manners, or dress codes. Students should discuss how these standards influence their own standards and how they feel if their standards differ from conventional standards.
24. Have students work in groups to develop and perform skits illustrating people using flexible standards.
25. Have students discuss reasons why families who have flexible standards are likely to be more relaxed and have less strained relations than families with rigid standards.
26. Panel discussion. Invite an officer in the armed services, a coach, a child care supervisor, and other professionals who are involved in shaping the skills of others to discuss how goals and standards are used to guide people in their charge.

Answer Key

Text

To Review
1. (Student response. List four.)
2. A. higher value
   B. instrumental value
   C. instrumental value
   D. higher value
   E. instrumental value
   F. higher value
3. Physical, Psychological
4. (Student response. Describe five.)
5. (Student response.)
6. between, within
7. (Student response. List five.)
8. (Student response. List three of each.)
9. Standards are measures or clues that show your progress. They help measure performance and tell you when a goal has been reached to your satisfaction. They help you identify what is acceptable and what is not acceptable to you.
10. A. subjective standards
    B. objective standards
    C. subjective standards
    D. subjective standards
    E. objective standards
    F. objective standards

Student Activity Guide

Value Identification, Activity A
1. Moral values have to do with conduct and what you feel is right and proper. Examples of moral values include freedom, equality, and honesty.
2. Human need values relate to your physical and psychological needs. Examples of human need values include food, water, air, rest, and self-acceptance.
3. Aesthetic values are related to the sense of feeling, smelling, tasting, seeing, and hearing. Examples of aesthetic values include how things look and function.
   1. aesthetic
   2. moral
   3. human need
   4. aesthetic
   5. moral
   6. human need
   7. human need
   8. moral
   9. aesthetic
   10. moral
   11. human need
   12. aesthetic

Teacher's Resources

Chapter 2 Test

1. D	14. T
2. C	15. T
3. A	16. T
4. D	17. F
5. E	18. T
6. A	19. T
7. E	20. F
8. B	21. C
9. C	22. A
10. A	23. C
11. F	24. C
12. T	25. D
13. F	

26. If you are unsure of your values, you may have trouble making decisions that support those values. Clearly understanding your values will make it easier for you to make choices that will help you reach your goals.
27. (Student response.)
28. (Student response.)
29. (Student response.)
30. physical/survival needs, safety needs, love needs/social needs, ego and esteem needs, self-fulfillment needs

Reproducible Master 2-1

Human Need Values

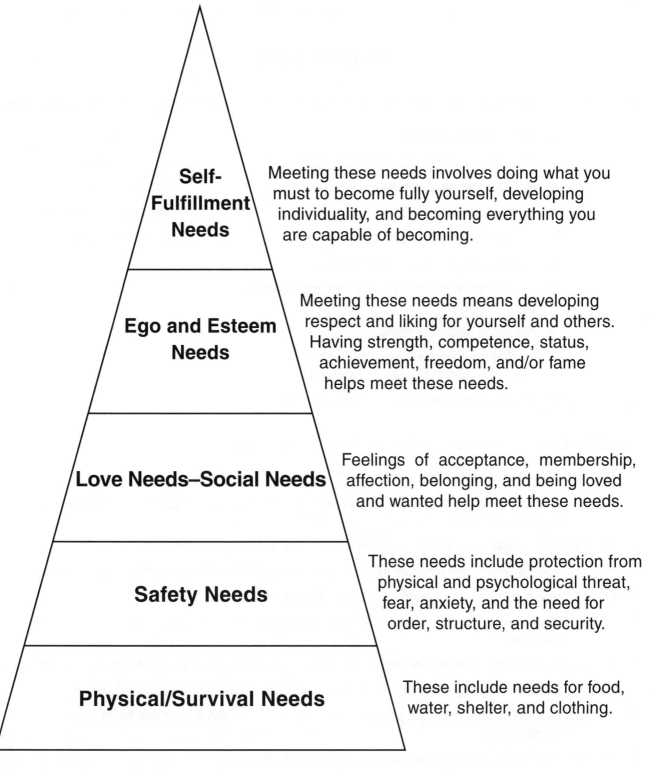

Self-Fulfillment Needs	Meeting these needs involves doing what you must to become fully yourself, developing individuality, and becoming everything you are capable of becoming.
Ego and Esteem Needs	Meeting these needs means developing respect and liking for yourself and others. Having strength, competence, status, achievement, freedom, and/or fame helps meet these needs.
Love Needs–Social Needs	Feelings of acceptance, membership, affection, belonging, and being loved and wanted help meet these needs.
Safety Needs	These needs include protection from physical and psychological threat, fear, anxiety, and the need for order, structure, and security.
Physical/Survival Needs	These include needs for food, water, shelter, and clothing.

Abraham Maslow developed a simple tool to explain why people do things. He and other researchers found that people were motivated to do things as a result of their basic human needs. He put these needs into the shape of a triangle with the basic human needs at the bottom and the higher human needs at the top.

Your Values, Goals, and Standards

Name _____

Date _____ Period _____ Score _____

Chapter 2 Test

Matching: Match the following types of values with their descriptions. (Letters may be used more than once.)

_____ 1. Often are material items.

_____ 2. Relate to physical and psychological needs.

_____ 3. Relate to the five senses.

_____ 4. Lead to higher values.

_____ 5. Involve honesty and fairness.

_____ 6. May involve an appreciation of a skill.

_____ 7. Indicate what is right, what is just, and what is good.

_____ 8. Are more abstract values.

_____ 9. Involve your desire for growth—physically, socially, emotionally, and intellectually.

_____ 10. Involve an appreciation of how things function.

A. aesthetic values

B. higher values

C. human need values

D. instrumental values

E. moral values

True/False: Circle *T* if the answer is true or *F* if the answer is false.

T   F   11. Ideally, you make decisions on the basis of your resources.

T   F   12. People who are unsure of their values may not be living life based on what is really important to them.

T   F   13. Most values can either be described as higher values or personal values.

T   F   14. People often have different instrumental values that lead to the same higher values.

T   F   15. Value conflicts force people to make choices and set priorities.

T   F   16. Experiences you have throughout life may cause you to develop new values or modify old ones.

T   F   17. Short-term goals are usually more general and more abstract than long-term goals.

T   F   18. When new experiences result in value changes, goals change accordingly.

T   F   19. Standards help measure performance and tell you when a goal has been reached satisfactorily.

T   F   20. Subjective standards are specific and easy to measure.

(Continued)

Name _____

Multiple Choice: Choose the best answer and write the corresponding letter in the blank.

_____ 21. Which of the following statements about values is NOT true?
   A. Values influence the way you act.
   B. A value is something important to you.
   C. A value may be an idea or something you only talk about.
   D. Values are revealed through your statements and actions.

_____ 22. Which of the following statements indicates a value?
   A. That flower is so beautiful.
   B. The plane is very large.
   C. Their home is painted green.
   D. All of the above.

_____ 23. Which of the following indicates the relationship between values and goals?
   A. Values and goals mean the same.
   B. Values and goals are not related.
   C. Values influence personal goals.
   D. Values are based on goals.

_____ 24. Which of the following is NOT true about changing goals?
   A. Goal setting is a continuous process throughout life.
   B. Weighing values is a step in adjusting goals.
   C. Goal changes are a result of changes in objective standards.
   D. Many goals change because they are unreasonable.

_____ 25. Flexible standards _____.
   A. are not helpful in today's society
   B. are very specific
   C. are a base to measure performance
   D. allow for adjustments to situations

Essay Questions: Provide the answers you feel best show your understanding of the subject matter.

26. Why is identifying and clarifying your values important in becoming an effective manager?

27. Name four instrumental values and the higher values to which they might lead.

28. Describe a value conflict situation that might occur in a family because of differing standards.

29. List four sources of values and describe how each influences value development.

30. Name the human needs identified by Maslow.

Managing Your Resources

Objectives

When students have completed this chapter, they will be able to
- identify a variety of human and nonhuman resources.
- explain how resources change throughout a person's life.
- describe ways to use their resources.
- apply responsible use of resources to daily life.
- identify existing resources and resources that can be developed.
- describe how the management process will help them achieve their goals.

Bulletin Boards

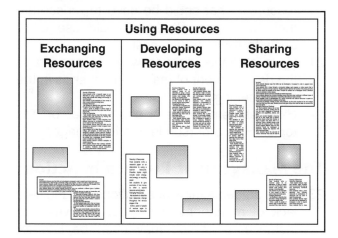

Title: *Using Resources*

Divide the board into three sections and label them with the following headings: *Exchanging Resources*, *Developing Resources*, and *Sharing Resources*. Place pictures and current articles that apply to the headings in each section.

Title: *Develop and Expand Your Resources*

Have students bring in pictures that they think show teens developing and expanding their resources. Place some of the pictures on the board and label them with the resource being developed or expanded.

Teaching Materials

Text, pages 39-55
  To Review
  To Challenge Your Thinking
  To Do with the Class
  To Do with Your Community
Student Activity Guide
  A. *Identifying Resources*
  B. *Resources to Manage*
  C. *Using the Management Process*
  D. *Managing Time and Energy*
Teacher's Resources
  *Human and Nonhuman Resources…
    A Patterning Technique*, reproducible
    master 3-1
  Management Process, transparency
    master 3-2
  Evaluation as a Resource, reproducible
    master 3-3
  Chapter 3 Test
  What Resources Do You Have? color
    transparency CT-3

Introductory Activities

1. Have students write their own definitions of human and nonhuman resources. Read and discuss some of the definitions in class. Then compare them to the definitions in the text.
2. Choose any object in the classroom and have students brainstorm to determine all of the resources involved in bringing that object to the classroom.

Instructional Concepts and Student Learning Experiences

Types of Resources

3. *What Resources Do You Have?* color transparency CT-3, TR. Have students brainstorm about various types of resources. To help students distinguish between human and nonhuman resources, write their responses on the lines provided.

4. *Identifying Resources,* Activity A, SAG. Have students complete the outline on types of resources by placing the given terms where they belong. Describe how organizational skills can improve their daily lives.

5. *Human and Nonhuman Resources...A Patterning Technique,* reproducible master 3-1, TR. Have students use the patterning technique to chart human and nonhuman resources. (Refer to Chapter 1 of the *Teacher's Resources* for an explanation of the patterning technique.)

Scarcity of Resources

6. Have students write a research paper on an alternative to using a scarce resource. Possible topics might include solar energy, wind energy, or recycling paper.

7. Ask students to give examples of how money is often a scarce resource among teens.

Changing Resources

8. Ask students to describe how resources change throughout the various stages of life.

9. Invite a panel of people of various ages to describe what resources they value most at their stage of life.

Using Your Resources

10. Have students discuss ways that families might increase their total resources by sharing and exchanging individual resources.

11. Have students make a chart depicting how different resources or combinations of resources can be used to reach the same goal.

12. Have students discuss ways that skills can be developed or increased in order to expand one's human resources.

13. Have students find a class through a community college, park program, or other source that is designed to expand a human resource. Students should interview the teacher of the class and write an article about the benefits of the class. Compile the articles into a newspaper format. Distribute copies to students in other classes.

14. Have students discuss common examples of wasted resources.

15. Have students discuss how common activities around the home may contribute to different types of pollution. Students should brainstorm nonpolluting alternatives to these activities.

16. Guest speaker. Invite a representative of a group concerned with natural resources to speak on conservation and prevention of pollution to the class.

17. *Resources to Manage,* Activity B, SAG. Have students use the chart provided to list and analyze resources that they have used. Students should also give actions that could be taken to conserve the resources listed.

Managing Resources Effectively

18. Have students make a list on their own human resources, dividing the list into the major categories of personal qualities and capabilities, talents, and skills.

19. Have each student identify a resource that he or she would like to expand. Students should write their choices on slips of paper and place them in a container. Have a student choose a slip and read the resource given. The class should suggest different ways that this resource could be developed or expanded. Repeat the exercise with other resources listed.

20. Have students figure the use-cost of various resources that could be used to redecorate their bedrooms. Students could use other goals to evaluate use-cost.

21. Have students discuss ways to encourage the development of management skills in the family setting.

22. Have students write a short paper on the topic, "How a person learns to manage."

The Management Process in Action

23. Have students think of situations that indicate lack of management in people's lives. For instance, a person may often be late for appointments. Discuss management skills that seem to be lacking in each of the situations mentioned.

24. Ask students to explain how values can be a motivating force in their lives.

25. Ask students to describe a situation that illustrates how goals provide direction in decision making.

26. Ask each student to write one of his or her goals on a slip of paper. Collect all the slips of paper and have each student draw one out of a box. Ask students to determine what resources might be needed to reach the goal they have chosen. Discuss.

27. *Management Process,* transparency master 3-2, TR. Use the chart for a discussion of each step of the management process.
28. Ask students to give examples of situations when it would be helpful to use the management process.
29. *Using the Management Process,* Activity C, SAG. Students are asked to develop a plan for managing the situation described and indicate how they would implement and control the plan.
30. Ask students to consider one of their short-term goals. Have them identify the activities involved in reaching their goals.
31. Have students explain what is meant by establishing a sequence of activities and what is meant by coordinating activities.
32. Ask students to explain why controlling the management process is important.
33. Discuss situations that would require a change of plans during the controlling step of the management process.
34. *Evaluation as a Resource*, reproducible master 3-3, TR. Students are asked to choose a problem to solve or a decision to make and go through the steps of the decision-making process. They are then asked to evaluate the process by answering the questions provided.
35. Ask students to give three reasons why evaluation in the management process can be helpful.
36. Have students think of situations where the evaluating step of the management process would allow a person to learn from his or her mistakes.

Management Skills

37. Panel discussion. Invite a group of people who have proven themselves to be good managers to come to your class and discuss the managerial skills they use and how they gained these skills.
38. Guest speaker. Invite a software salesperson to demonstrate ways that computers can be used to assist in personal management.
39. *Managing Time and Energy,* Activity D, SAG. Have students choose an activity that they do repeatedly during the week and that they feel could be done more efficiently. Students should use the form provided to develop a new procedure to improve the use of time and energy in completing the activity.

40. Panel discussion. Invite representatives of the business and private sectors to discuss techniques they use to save time and energy.
41. Panel discussion. Invite representatives of local cleaning and errand services to discuss how contracting services can help families save time.
42. Have students define *attitude*. Students should discuss how a person's attitude might affect his or her ability to manage effectively.
43. Have students plan and perform skits showing how a negative attitude can interfere with management. After class discussion, students should perform the skits again replacing negative attitudes with positive attitudes.
44. Have students discuss typical aversions to certain tasks. Students should suggest management skills that could be used to change those negative situations.
45. Have students describe situations in which the satisfaction of the outcome of a task overshadows the unpleasantness experienced while doing the task.
46. Have students work as a class to develop an informational booklet that lists services that families can contract to help with household tasks. Arrange to have the booklets distributed in other classes.

Answer Key

Text

To Review
1. (Student response. List 10.)
2. (Student response. List 10.)
3. stage
4. A. developing resources
   B. developing resources
   C. developing resources
   D. exchanging resources
   E. sharing resources
   F. developing resources
   G. sharing resources
   H. exchanging resources
5. A. false
   B. true
   C. false
6. manage, resources
7. Use-cost is the use of a resource that reduces the amount that is available for future use. A resource that is important, but is

limited, has a high use-cost. A resource that is readily available has a low use-cost.
8. The management process involves three steps: (1) planning, (2) implementing and controlling, and (3) evaluating.
9. (Student response.)
10. Work simplification is the breaking down of an activity into a detailed listing of what needs to be done.

Student Activity Guide

Identifying Resources, Activity A
I. Human resources
  A. Time
  B. Personal qualities
    1. Pleasant personality
    2. Good physical health
    3. Good mental health
  C. Capabilities, talents, and skills
    1. A beautiful singing voice
    2. Skill in writing
    3. Athletic ability
  D. Other persons
    1. Family
    2. Friends
    3. Parents
II. Nonhuman resources
  A. Material possessions
    1. Car
    2. Clothing
    3. House
  B. Money and purchasing power
    1. Allowance
    2. Credit
    3. Wages
  C. Community resources
    1. Schools
    2. Police protection
    3. Natural resources
    4. Stores

Teacher's Resources

Chapter 3 Test
1. E
2. E
3. B
4. A
5. D
6. B
7. D
8. A
9. C
10. C
11. F
12. F
13. F
14. T
15. T
16. T
17. F
18. F
19. T
20. F
21. T
22. T
23. C
24. B
25. A
26. D
27. Exchanging resources means trading one resource for another. Developing resources means increasing or expanding resources. Sharing resources means more than one person is using the resources.
28. (Student response.)
29. (Student response. List four.)
30. Planning: This step involves identifying the activities necessary to carry out the plan, arranging activities in a logical sequence, and grouping activities and coordinating different parts of the plan. Implementing and controlling: Implementing means moving ahead with activities planned. Controlling means checking the progress of the plan and making any necessary adjustments. Evaluating: This step involves judging the entire process and the end result. It helps you learn from your mistakes and accomplishments.

Reproducible Master 3-1

Human and Nonhuman Resources...
A Patterning Technique

Name _____ **Date** _____ **Period** _____

The patterning technique has been begun below to chart human and nonhuman resources. Continue adding to the diagram and share your completed pattern with others in the class.

—— Parents ——
—— Sister ——
Family
—— Other People —— Human

Resources

Nonhuman —— Material Possessions ——
Car

Transparency Master 3-2

Management Process

Management Process
→ What is my goal?

Planning
→ What steps are necessary to reach my goal?

→ What is the logical sequence of these steps?

→ Can some steps be combined or coordinated?

Implementing and Controlling
→ Is each step progressing as planned?

→ Does the plan need any adjustment?

Evaluating
→ Did I reach my goal?

→ How could I have improved my plans?

→ What have I learned from this process?

Reproducible Master 3-3

Evaluation as a Resource

Name _____ **Date** _____ **Period** _____

Choose a problem to solve or a decision to make and go through the steps of the decision-making process. Evaluate the process by answering the questions below.

Problem to solve or decision to make: _____

_____

_____

Evaluation in Planning

1. What are the goals? _____

_____

2. What obstacles stand in the way? _____

_____

3. What resources are needed? _____

_____

4. Are these resources available? _____

5. Are the goals worth the use-cost? _____

Evaluating the Action

1. Is the plan working? _____

2. Is there steady progress toward the goals? _____

3. Is there need for improvement in the plans? _____

4. What changes are needed? _____

_____

5. What must be done to implement these changes? _____

_____

Evaluating the Results

1. Were the goals achieved? _____

2. Are the results satisfactory? _____

3. What weaknesses were in the plan and action? _____

_____

4. What were the strengths of the plan and action? _____

_____

5. How can I use this information to improve future decisions? _____

_____

Managing Your Resources

Name _____

Date _____ Period _____ Score _____

Chapter 3 Test

Matching: In each of the following sentences, a very specific type of resource is underlined. Write the letter of the correct type of resource beside each description: (Letters may be used more than once.)

_____ 1. Jim's friendliness helps make him a good employee at the ice cream shop.

_____ 2. All of the girls envy Sherri's natural curly hair.

_____ 3. Students attending East High School have an excellent opportunity for a good education.

_____ 4. Scott learned to fly a plane when he was 20 years old.

_____ 5. Julie took some money from her savings account.

_____ 6. Blood from the Red Cross blood bank saved Milton's life.

_____ 7. Jeanne used her credit card to pay for the new coat.

_____ 8. Mr. Pinckney plays the violin in the civic orchestra.

_____ 9. Terry's quiet room is a good place to study.

_____ 10. Mike caught nine fish with his new spinning rod.

A. capabilities, talents, and skills

B. community resources

C. material possessions

D. money and purchasing power

E. personal qualities

True/False: Circle *T* if the statement is true or *F* if the statement is false.

T F 11. Most people take full advantage of all available resources.

T F 12. The possibilities for developing resources are actually quite limited.

T F 13. People with more resources are always more successful in reaching their goals.

T F 14. In most cases, using a resource reduces the amount that is available for future use.

T F 15. Energy might be one of the resources used to help reach the goal of cleaning the house.

T F 16. Planning provides the guidance you need to reach your goal.

T F 17. All decisions require careful planning.

T F 18. Implementing the plan means checking to see if things are going according to the time schedule.

T F 19. Time management is a method of organizing your life so you accomplish what needs to be done.

(Continued)

Name _____

T   F   20. Energy is a unique resource because everyone has the same amount of it.

T   F   21. Fatigue can be caused by environmental factors as well as by physical activity.

T   F   22. Work simplification is a way to manage your time more wisely.

Multiple Choice: Choose the best answer and write the corresponding letter in the blank.

_____ 23. Which of the following is an example of exchanging resources?
  A. Jim and his neighbor both use one lawn mower.
  B. Mary reads a book from the library to learn how to build a bookshelf.
  C. Phil bought a new bike, which was on sale.
  D. Julie washes the dishes after dinner.

_____ 24. Which of the following statements about time and energy is NOT true?
  A. Both time and energy are limited.
  B. People have equal amounts of time and energy.
  C. Use of both time and energy can be planned for more satisfying results.
  D. When a person uses energy, he or she also uses time.

_____ 25. Which of the following is NOT true about resources?
  A. Purchasing power is a human resource.
  B. No one has unlimited resources.
  C. Natural resources are considered community resources.
  D. Personal resources are often shared.

_____ 26. Which of the following would help you increase and improve your management skills?
  A. Becoming more aware of your values.
  B. Learning to recognize your resources.
  C. Using the management process.
  D. All of the above.

Essay Questions: Provide the answers you feel best show your understanding of the subject matter.

27. Describe what is meant by each of the following: exchanging resources, developing resources, and sharing resources.

28. Describe a situation in which two resources could be used to help reach the same goal. Indicate what you feel would be the use-cost of each resource.

29. List four examples of responsible use of resources.

30. Name and briefly describe the steps in the management process.

4

Technology as a Resource

Objectives

When students have completed this chapter, they will be able to
◆ identify some of the technological advances used in the world today.
◆ determine forms of technology that will help you manage your resources.
◆ explain how technology can benefit individuals, families, and society.
◆ summarize some of the concerns related to technology.

Bulletin Boards

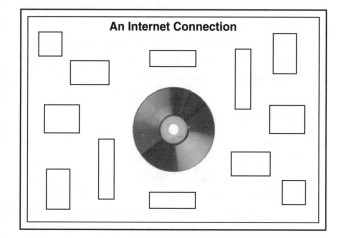

An Internet Connection

Title: *An Internet Connection*

Draw a large CD for the background of this bulletin board. Obtain brochures and information on the various ways to access the Internet and place these around the CD. Include information on such services as America Online, Yahoo, CompuServe, etc.

Title: *Technology Today*

Have each student bring in a picture or brochure describing a form of new technology for the home. Try to include examples representing all aspects of home living including food preparation, money management, clothing, home furnishings, and child care. Attach these pictures to the bulletin board making a large collage with the illustrations.

Teaching Materials

Text, pages 56-71
To Review
To Challenge Your Thinking
To Do with the Class
To Do with Your Community
Student Activity Guide
A. *Technology Today*
B. *Benefits and Concerns of Technology*
C. *Technology and the Future*
Teacher's Resources
What's New in Computer Software?
reproducible master 4-1
Weighing the Benefits and Concerns of Technology, transparency master 4-2
Chapter 4 Test
Ways Technology Shapes Your World,
color transparency CT-4

Introductory Activities

1. Ask each student to write a definition of *technology*. Then read the first sentence in this chapter, which defines technology. Compare the definitions.
2. *Ways Technology Shapes Your World,* color transparency CT-4, TR. Use this transparency as a basis of discussion about how technology influences students. Have students brainstorm about how technology shapes their world. Write their responses on the blanks provided.
3. Ask students if they carry with them any examples of technology, such as an ATM card, a beeper, or a cellular phone. What new products do they now have in their homes that were not available a few years ago? Also ask students to think about their grandparents and give examples of new technology that might have become available for the first time when they were teenagers.

Instructional Concepts and Student Learning Experiences

Technology as a Resource in Daily Living

4. Have students distinguish between computer hardware and software.
5. Discuss the concept of the "Information Superhighway" and terms associated with it.
6. In groups, have students research the various online services. Compare costs and services. As a class, summarize the findings.
7. As a class, consider important questions raised by use of the Internet. Who will control it? Will its benefits go only to those Americans who can afford to go online?
8. *What's New in Computer Software?* reproducible master 4-1, TR. Students are to use this form to identify new computer software available for home use. They are to answer the questions from information contained on the software packages. If they can actually use the software, they are asked to evaluate the product. Use these completed sheets to form a classroom file of new software available for home use. Make the file available for anyone to use.
9. Discuss the concept of biotechnology and how it is part of the technological revolution.
10. *Technology Today,* Activity A, SAG. Students are to list examples of technology in the home or workplace and then explain how each example is helpful to daily living.
11. Have students visit a large supermarket or retail store. List examples of electronic technology that they see in use in these stores. Share findings with others in the class.
12. Have students put together an exhibit of information and pictures from magazines, newspapers, brochures, and catalogs featuring electronic entertainment equipment.
13. As a class, discuss the value of play with technological equipment and games and how it affects physical, emotional, social, and intellectual development.
14. Have a student research food packaging and report on technological advances that reduce waste. Also research new products that prolong shelf life of food products.
15. Assemble a display of a variety of technological toys, games, activities, and entertainment devices. Have students categorize each according to purpose, age, safety, and value.
16. Have students research new technology used in household appliances and report their findings to the class.
17. Guest speaker. Invite someone from the medical field to discuss some of the new technology and procedures available to improve diagnosis and treatment of health problems.
18. Have students react to the following statement: "It may be possible for parents in the future to select their baby's characteristics." Discuss legal and moral concerns regarding genetic engineering.
19. Have students research the inherited diseases that are the result of defective genes. Report on the latest developments.

The Workplace at Home

20. Have students imagine they are going to be working from their home. Ask them to brainstorm a list of technological devices they will need to do the job properly.
21. Guest speaker. Invite a telecommuter to speak to the class about the pros and cons of working from home.

Benefits of Technology

22. *Benefits and Concerns of Technology,* Activity B, SAG. Have the students list various benefits and concerns related to the specific technological innovations listed.
23. Divide the class into two groups. Persons in one group will call out an existing technological innovation and someone in the other group will give a benefit or benefits of that innovation. Then the second group will call out an innovation and the other group will give the benefits.
24. Ask students to name some of the new jobs that have been created within the last ten years as a result of technology.
25. Ask students to interview parents whose young children use a computer. Ask them what their children can do and how they have benefited from using the computer. What software programs do their children use and what do they learn from these programs?

Concerns in the Use of Technology

26. *Weighing the Benefits and Concerns of Technology,* transparency master 4-2, TR. Use this transparency as you discuss with the class the various benefits and concerns of technology.
27. Have students write brief statements to identify one or more reasons why low-income persons should have access to the Internet. (Example: Information about jobs and job training would benefit poor people who need work and work skills.)
28. Discuss the problems involved with children going online and being exposed to inappropriate material. Also report on incidents where young people have been lured by adults to meet them for illicit purposes. Discuss what is being done to prevent these incidents from occurring.
29. Discuss the issue of life support systems that keep people alive when they are brain-dead. Explain the use of a Living Will in resolving such issues for family members.
30. *Technology and the Future,* Activity C, SAG. Have each student look through current magazines and newspapers to find an article about a technological innovation planned for the future. Describe this innovation and comment on how it might benefit society. Also discuss any concerns it might present.
31. Have students react to the following statement: The teacher of 2020 will be primarily a coach and intermediary between students and the (computer) world of information, helping students draw on resources around the globe.
32. Have students interview persons in the areas of communications, medicine, biotechnology, and genetics to find out what they expect to be available in the future. Report back to the class.
33. Have each student write a fictional story about life at home 50 years from now. Ask volunteers to share their stories with the class.

Answer Key

Text

To Review
1. Technology
2. Internet
3. (Student response. List three.)
4. (Student response. List two.)
5. electronic funds transfer
6. Genetics
7. (Student response. List two.)
8. (Student response. Describe three.)
9. privacy
10. (Student response. Describe three.)

Teacher's Resources

Chapter 4 Test
1. A
2. E
3. F
4. I
5. B
6. J
7. D
8. G
9. H
10. C
11. F
12. F
13. F
14. T
15. T
16. F
17. T
18. F
19. T
20. F
21. B
22. D
23. A
24. D
25. D
26. (Student response.)
27. (Student response.)
28. (Student response.)

Reproducible Master 4-1

What's New In Computer Software?

Name _____ **Date** _____ **Period** _____

New computer software is appearing on the market every day. There is a software program to meet almost any need. Visit a store that sells computer software and select two products that are designed for home use. Answer the following questions concerning the products from the information given on the software packages. If you are able to use the software, evaluate the quality of the products.

Name of product: _____

Manufacturer: _____

Purpose of software: _____

_____

Functions: _____

_____

Cost: _____

Recommended age range (if for children): _____

Do you think this is a good use of computer software? Explain your answer.

_____

_____

If you are able to use this software, how would you rate its overall quality?

_____

_____

Name of product: _____

Manufacturer: _____

Purpose of software: _____

_____

Functions: _____

_____

Cost: _____

Recommended age range (if for children): _____

Do you think this is a good use of computer software? Explain your answer.

_____

_____

If you are able to use this software, how would you rate its overall quality?

_____

Transparency Master 4-2

Weighing the Benefits and Concerns of Technology

Technology

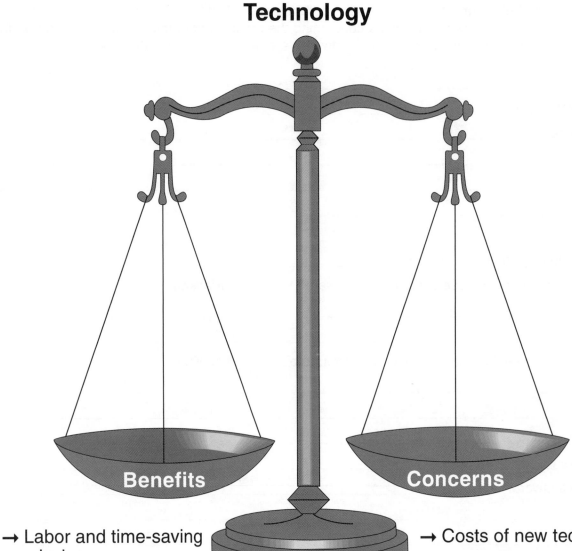

Benefits

→ Labor and time-saving devices
→ Increased productivity
→ Improved safety
→ Higher standard of living
→ Health and medical advances
→ Improved communication
→ New jobs created
→ New forms of entertainment

Concerns

→ Costs of new technology
→ Loss of jobs
→ Depletion of natural resources
→ Access by poor is limited
→ Environmental pollution
→ Privacy threatened
→ Ethical questions
→ Family life altered

Technology as a Resource

Name _____

Date _____ **Period** _____ **Score** _____

Chapter 4 Test

Matching: Match the following terms and identifying phrases.

_____ 1. The use of the computer to combine sound, graphics, animation, and information into one presentation.

_____ 2. A system that handles financial transactions without the use of cash or checks.

_____ 3. A general term that refers to the global network of computers.

_____ 4. An employee who works from his or her home.

_____ 5. The study of inherited traits in living things.

_____ 6. The field of applied biological science.

_____ 7. An electronic oraganizer about the same size as a calculator.

_____ 8. A constantly changing body of scientific knowledge that is used to solve practical problems.

_____ 9. The use of communication technology to send deliberate, repeated, hostile messages with the intent to harm another.

_____ 10. A group of computers linked together to share data.

A. multimedia

B. genetics

C. network

D. personal digital assistant

E. electronic funds transfer

F. Internet

G. technology

H. cyber bullying

I. telecommuter

J. biotechnology

True/False: Circle *T* if the statement is true or *F* if the statement is false.

T F 11. Multimedia refers to the international network of computers.

T F 12. Computers are more expensive today than they were 10 years ago.

T F 13. Digital cameras require an expensive special film.

T F 14. Technology has had a profound effect on our society.

T F 15. An increasing number of people are working out of home offices.

T F 16. Biotechnology is the study of inherited traits in living things.

T F 17. A special drive is needed to save data to a rewritable CD.

T F 18. One negative aspect of MP3 players is the additional bulky packaging that comes with the files purchased.

T F 19. Technology has reduced the amount of labor needed to produce goods and services.

T F 20. Studies show that children who use computers tend to watch more television.

(Continued)

Name _____

Multiple Choice: Choose the best answer and write the corresponding letter in the blank.

_____ 21. The closest thing to an Information Superhighway today is _____.
A. a CD-ROM
B. the Internet
C. multimedia
D. technology

_____ 22. Biotechnology _____.
A. has made it possible to create new drugs that polong life
B. is applied biological science
C. includes research on the manipulation of human genes
D. All of the above.

_____ 23. Which of the following statements about computers is NOT true?
A. Personal computers have become more difficult to use.
B. Computer-based bank-at-home systems can be used for financial transactions.
C. Computers are now in 75 percent of all homes.
D. A home computer can help a family with paying bills, setting up a budget, and compiling an inventory of household goods.

_____ 24. In banking and bill paying, which of the following statements is true?
A. ATM is a system of carrying out financial transactions by computer, such as automatic bill paying.
B. Record keeping is easy because the transactions are immediate.
C. It is necessary to have a computer to handle all bank-at-home transactions.
D. Electronic banking brings us closer to a cashless society.

_____ 25. Which of the following statements is NOT true about telecommuting?
A. The great majority of persons working out of home offices are telecommuters.
B. The increased flexibility of working at home often boosts worker productivity.
C. The computer is the main tool of the telecommuter.
D. Usually the office equipment in telecommuting is paid for by the telecommuter's employer.

Essay Questions: Provide the answers you feel best show your understanding of the subject matter.

26. Explain how technology has impacted families. Give three specific examples.

27. Explain three ways that technology has benefited society as a whole.

28. Describe three concerns related to technology.

Part Two Development Across the Life Span

5

Understanding Development

Objectives

When students have completed this chapter, they will be able to
- explain how heredity and the environment influence human development.
- describe the patterns of human development.
- explain the significance of character formation in human development.
- identify the forces that shape their self-concepts.
- describe the components of a healthy self-concept.

Bulletin Boards

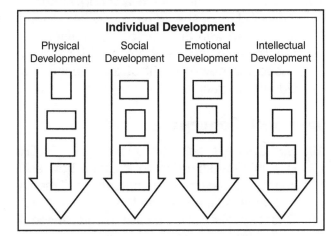

Title: *Individual Development*

Along the arrows indicating each type of development, display a series of at least four pictures which show progression in that type of development. For instance, for social development, you might show an infant with parents, a young child with a few friends in the park, a teen with team members, and an adult getting married.

Title: *Self-Concept*

Use pictures under each of the four categories that indicate self-concept as related to that category. For instance, personal self pictures could include someone's face and hair, someone exercising, someone using a skill, etc. Social self pictures could include a person in a family setting, with friends, all alone, in a large group, etc. For ideal self, pictures of an actor or actress, an athlete, a model, or any other famous person could be used. For the extended self, pictures of groups such as good friends, a band, and family members would be suitable.

Teaching Materials

Text, pages 73-89
   To Review
   To Challenge Your Thinking
   To Do with the Class
   To Do with Your Community
Student Activity Guide
   A. *Hereditary and Environmental Influences*
   B. *Patterns of Development*
   C. *Self-Concept*
   D. *Formation of the Self-Concept*
Teacher's Resources
   My Self-Concept…A Patterning Technique,
     reproducible master 5-1
   Realistic Self-Concept, reproducible
     master 5-2
   Chapter 5 Test
   Self-Concept, color transparency CT-5

Introductory Activities

1. As a class, have students brainstorm a list of words that people might use to describe themselves.

2. Have students jot down words to describe themselves in terms of physical appearance, personality, talents and skills, and how they get along with others. Students should have someone close to them, such as a family member, make a similar list describing them. Students should compare the lists before starting the chapter. Have students save the lists and analyze them again after studying the chapter.

Instructional Concepts and Student Learning Experiences

The Role of Heredity and Environment

3. *Hereditary and Environmental Influences,* Activity A, SAG. Have students analyze five statements about their characteristics to determine whether the characteristics are mainly influenced by heredity or environment.
4. Have students read an article about inherited traits, an inherited disease, or genetic counseling. Students should write a short report on the article.
5. Have students examine family pictures to determine what traits may have been passed on through heredity.
6. Have students discuss why environment can be an important factor in development even before birth.
7. Have students brainstorm lists of factors in the environment that may have negative effects on development and factors that may have positive effects on development.
8. Use models to identify the parts of the brain, targeting areas responsible for speech, movement and coordination, vision, and hearing.
9. Discuss the societal and economic implications of early brain development. If children receive excellent care during their first three years of life, what might that mean when they are grown and entering the workforce?
10. Have students consider what they can do as babysitters to promote early brain development.

Patterns in Growth and Development

11. Have students role-play family situations in which parents help children develop toward social maturity.

12. Have students prepare and perform a skit showing lack of emotional control and another skit showing control of emotions. Have the class discuss the skits.
13. Have students discuss how the ability to communicate is related to intellectual development. You may have students do reading on communication skills before this discussion.
14. Have students make a list of what a family might do to encourage intellectual development in a young child. Students should place a star by items that would cost nothing or very little. Students should discuss ways that starred items could be used to help children who are disadvantaged to develop intellectually.

Your Character

15. Have students brainstorm terms that might describe a person's character. Decide which traits are associated with strong character and weak character.
16. Have students make a list of traits that might describe the character of another person in the class, which can be shared anonymously.
17. Invite a panel including a teacher, parent, student, and religious leader to discuss their perspectives on influences on the development of character.
18. Have each student write a report about an individual he or she admires and list the traits associated with that person's character. The report could include what may have influenced the development of the chosen individual's character.

Your Self-Concept

19. *Self-Concept,* color transparency CT-5, TR. Use this transparency to illustrate how self-concept is based on the personal self, social self, ideal self, and extended self.
20. Guest speaker. Invite a psychologist to speak on the formation of self-concept.
21. Have students discuss how having specific psychological needs met or not having those needs met could affect self-concept formation. Needs to discuss could include love and acceptance, self-worth, respect, and recognition from others.
22. Have students brainstorm ideas that illustrate how parents might positively influence their child's self-concept.

23. Have students observe a young child in a group situation outside the home. Have them describe situations observed that may affect the child's self-concept.

24. For a three-day period, have each student keep a diary of experiences that he or she thinks affect his or her self-concept.

25. Have a panel of students from your class discuss peer group influence on self-concept.

26. Have students make a list of characteristics about themselves that make up their self-concept core.

27. Have students write a description of a situation involving themselves or others that may have resulted in a change in self-concept. Ask volunteers to discuss their descriptions in class.

28. Have students discuss why self-esteem is sometimes called the evaluative factor of self-concept.

29. Have students write an example of a comment or action that indicates high self-esteem and one that indicates low self-esteem. Ask students to share their examples with others.

30. Have students discuss whether it is possible to have an ideal self-concept and still have a realistic self-concept.

31. Have students discuss reasons a young child would not be expected to have a complete self-concept.

32. Have students discuss why a person who has high self-esteem and a rather complete self-concept still may not have a healthy self-concept.

33. Have students write an evaluation of their own levels of self-esteem, realistic self-concept, and complete self-concept. For each aspect of a healthy self-concept, students should write specific action plans to improve their self-concept.

34. Panel discussion. Invite a group of qualified individuals, such as a counselor, a doctor, and a social worker, to discuss the relationship between self-concept and problem behavior.

35. *Patterns of Development,* Activity B, SAG. Have students think of two teenagers they know who are the same in age but differ in terms of physical, social, emotional, and intellectual development. Students should write adjectives that describe each person.

36. Have students write down characteristics of their personal selves about which they feel good. Students should also list characteristics of their personal selves that they would like to change.

37. Have students think of people they know who are poised and seem to get along well with other people. Have students discuss words they would use to describe such a person's social self.

38. Have students list people they admire that have influenced their ideal selves. Students should discuss what qualities they admired in these people and how these people influenced their ideal selves.

39. Have students discuss instances in real life, in movies, or on television that illustrate a child developing an ideal self.

40. Have students write down people, groups, or objects that they consider part of their extended selves. Students should share their ideas with others in the class.

41. Have students plan and perform a skit illustrating a person's extended self. For instance, the plot might be based on a person's brother or sister being insulted and the person's extended self reacting as if he or she had been insulted.

42. *My Self-Concept...A Patterning Technique,* reproducible master 5-1, TR. Have students use the patterning technique to illustrate their self-concept in terms of their personal self, social self, ideal self, and extended self. (Refer to Chapter 1 of the *Teacher's Resources* for an explanation of the patterning technique.)

43. Introduce the saying, "Success breeds success," to students. Have students discuss how this saying is related to self-concept and behavior.

44. Have students research books or periodicals related to child development and write a report on how others influence the growing self-concept of preschool children.

45. *Self-Concept*, Activity C, SAG. Students are asked to indicate which aspect of self-concept is being illustrated in examples given in the activity.

46. *Formation of the Self-Concept*, Activity D, SAG. Students are asked to briefly explain how various situations might affect a person's self-concept.

47. *Realistic Self-Concept,* reproducible master 5-2, TR. Have students work in pairs to evaluate whether or not they have a realistic self-concept. In each pair, one student should circle the 10 terms that are most descriptive of him or her. The second student should circle the

10 terms he or she thinks are most descriptive of the first student. Each pair should compare their responses. Then students should reverse roles and repeat the activity. (You may also have students complete the activity with a close friend or family member outside the classroom.)

48. Guest speaker. Invite a person who works with the older adults to describe the significance of changing self-concept as a person grows older.

Answer Key

Text

To Review

1. Heredity, environment
2. people who need to understand birth defects and their causes, especially people who have given birth to a child with a disability
3. dependent; independent
4. false
5. Self-concept
6. A. extended self
   B. social self
   C. personal self
   D. ideal self
   E. personal self
   F. ideal self
   G. extended self
   H. social self
7. A. positive self-concept
   B. positive self-concept
   C. negative self-concept
   D. positive self-concept
   E. negative self-concept
   F. positive self-concept
   G. negative self-concept
   H. positive self-concept
8. A. false
   B. true
   C. true
9. A realistic self-concept means that what you know about yourself is accurate. A complete self-concept relates to how much you know about yourself. The more you know about yourself, the more complete your self-concept is.
10. Peer pressure is influence, both positive and negative, that is communicated through a person's peers.

Student Activity Guide

Self-Concept, Activity C

1.	A	14.	B
2.	B	15.	A
3.	C	16.	A
4.	A	17.	B
5.	D	18.	A
6.	B	19.	C
7.	A	20.	A
8.	C	21.	D
9.	A	22.	A
10.	A	23.	D
11.	A	24.	A
12.	D	25.	B
13.	A		

Teacher's Resources

Chapter 5 Test

1.	B	18.	F
2.	D	19.	T
3.	F	20.	F
4.	G	21.	T
5.	J	22.	T
6.	K	23.	T
7.	C	24.	F
8.	M	25.	T
9.	H	26.	T
10.	L	27.	A
11.	A	28.	A
12.	E	29.	D
13.	T	30.	D
14.	T	31.	C
15.	T	32.	B
16.	F	33.	C
17.	T	34.	D

35. (Student response.)
36. (Student response.)
37. (Student response.)
38. People with healthy self-concepts feel good about their strengths. They have bad points that they may not like, but that they accept.

Reproducible Master 5-1

My Self-Concept...A Patterning Technique

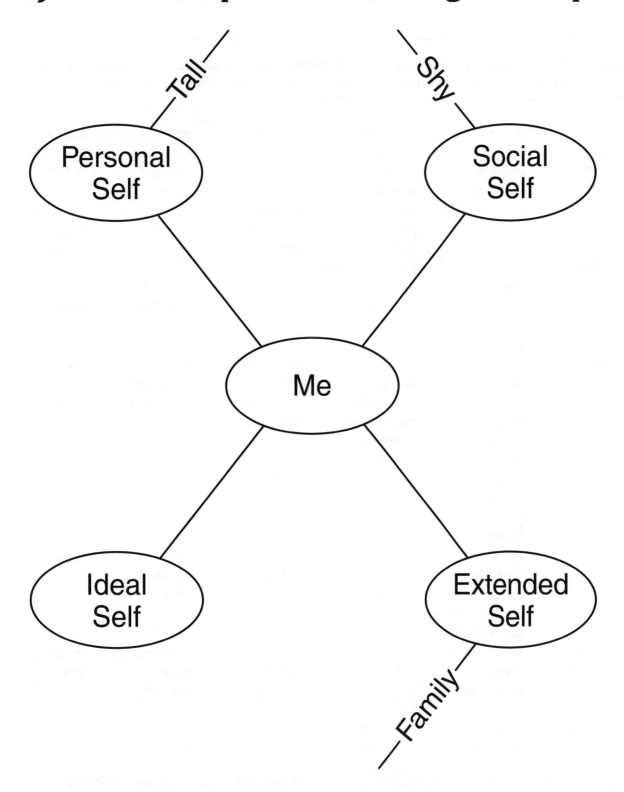

With the above illustration as your model, take out a separate sheet of paper and use the patterning technique to illustrate aspects of your self-concept.

Reproducible Master 5-2

Realistic Self-Concept

Name _____ Date _____ Period _____

Working with a classmate, circle the ten terms from the list below that you think best describe you. Then have your partner circle the ten terms he or she thinks best describe you. (Your partner should use a different color pen.) Then answer the question that follows.

able	dreamy	introverted	overprotecting	remote	tactful
accepting	dutiful	irresponsible	passive	resentful	temperamental
adaptable	efficient	irritable	patient	reserved	tender
aggressive	energetic	jealous	perceptive	respectful	tense
ambitious	extroverted	jovial	perfectionist	responsible	thoughtful
annoying	fair	juvenile	persuasive	responsive	tough
anxious	fearful	kind	petty	rigid	trusting
authoritative	foolish	knowledgeable	playful	sarcastic	trustworthy
bitter	frank	lazy	pleasant	satisfied	unassuming
bold	free	learned	pompous	scientific	unaware
brave	friendly	liberal	powerful	searching	uncertain
calm	gentle	lively	precise	self-accepting	unconcerned
carefree	giving	logical	pretending	self-assertive	uncontrolled
careless	greedy	loving	principled	self-aware	understanding
caring	gruff	manipulative	progressive	self-conscious	unpredictable
certain	guilty	materialistic	protective	selfish	unreasonable
cheerful	gullible	mature	proud	self-righteous	unstructured
clever	happy	merry	quarrelsome	sensible	useful
cold	helpful	modest	questioning	sensitive	vain
complex	helpless	mystical	quiet	sentimental	vulnerable
confident	honorable	naive	radical	serious	warm
conforming	hostile	negative	rational	shy	willful
controlled	idealistic	nervous	rationalizing	silly	wise
courageous	imaginative	noisy	realistic	simple	wishful
cranky	immature	normal	reasonable	skillful	withdrawn
critical	impressionable	objective	reassuring	sly	witty
demanding	inconsiderate	observant	rebellious	sociable	worried
dependable	independent	obsessive	reflective	spontaneous	youthful
dependent	ingenious	organized	regretful	stable	zestful
determined	innovative	original	rejecting	strained	
dignified	insensitive	overburdened	relaxed	strong	
disciplined	insincere	overconfident	reliable	stubborn	
domineering	intelligent	overemotional	religious	sympathetic	

Judging from you and your partner's choices on this activity, how realistic do you think your

self-concept is? _____

_____

Understanding Development

Name _____

Date _____ **Period** _____ **Score** _____

Chapter 5 Test

Matching: Match the following terms and identifying phrases.

_____ 1. Family, friends, life experiences, and other factors that affect growth and development.

_____ 2. Substances contained in chromosomes that carry potential for specific human traits.

_____ 3. Process of passing on biological characteristics from one generation to the next.

_____ 4. The science that studies the transmission of people's inherited traits.

_____ 5. A sequence of growth similar in most individuals.

_____ 6. Having certain ideas or impressions about oneself.

_____ 7. Ideas or images outside the individual self.

_____ 8. How a person views his or her relations with other people.

_____ 9. A feeling of oneness with a person, a group of people, or an object.

_____ 10. How worthwhile or unimportant a person feels.

_____ 11. Learning and knowing a great deal about one's abilities, relationships, and other aspects of oneself.

_____ 12. Being able to realistically judge one's strengths and weaknesses.

A. complete self-concept

B. environmental influences

C. extended self

D. genes

E. healthy self-concept

F. heredity

G. human genetics

H. identification

I. maturation

J. patterns of development

K. self-concept

L. self-esteem

M. social self

True/False: Circle *T* if the statement is true or *F* if the statement is false.

T   F   13. Genetic counseling is a service that helps people understand birth defects so that they can make informed decisions about having children.

T   F   14. Each person has his or her own unique growth pattern and rate of development.

T   F   15. Social maturity involves becoming aware of the appropriate actions in a person's environment.

T   F   16. Social development and emotional growth are mainly influenced by heredity.

T   F   17. The nervous system, the sense organs, and body control are all important in intellectual growth and development.

(Continued)

Name _____

T F 18. Getting along with others is an aspect of the personal self.

T F 19. Part of the ideal self may be the desire to become a pro basketball player one day.

T F 20. People who have developed positive self-concepts have difficulty accepting themselves and making social adjustments.

T F 21. A person's concept of self has a strong influence on that person's behavior.

T F 22. Children who receive care, love, and guidance from parents are likely to develop a positive self-concept.

T F 23. Much information about yourself is based on the reactions of other people who are important to you.

T F 24. The core of the self-concept is easily changed.

T F 25. You have a realistic self-concept when what you know about yourself is accurate.

T F 26. You do have some control over shaping your self-concept.

Multiple Choice: Choose the best answer and write the corresponding letter in the blank.

_____ 27. Which of the following statements most appropriately explains the influence of heredity on human development?
A. Heredity determines the potential in a person that can be developed.
B. Heredity causes people in the same family to develop in exactly the same way.
C. Heredity affects only the physical aspects of a person.
D. Heredity has a stronger effect on intelligence than environment.

_____ 28. Which of the following is a sign of emotional maturity?
A. Being very disappointed about losing a contest, but congratulating the winner.
B. Liking someone of the opposite sex so much that you follow the person everywhere.
C. Being so angry at a family member that you hit your CD player and break it.
D. Being so nervous about a speech that you forget every word.

_____ 29. Which is true about intellectual growth and development?
A. A person's intellect is influenced by both hereditary and environmental factors.
B. People who are the same age vary in levels of intellectual ability.
C. Language is extremely important to mental growth.
D. All of the above.

_____ 30. Formation of self-concept occurs when _____.
A. you achieve something you want
B. you are rejected and criticized
C. you receive love and attention from your parents
D. All of the above.

_____ 31. A positive self-concept is most likely to occur from _____.
A. overprotection from parents
B. being the oldest child in a family
C. receiving a compliment from a favorite teacher
D. All of the above.

(Continued)

Name _____

_____ 32. Which is NOT true about high self-esteem?
    A. People with high self-esteem feel they are worthwhile.
    B. High self-esteem is always a positive characteristic.
    C. High self-esteem gives people confidence to deal with challenges.
    D. People with high self-esteem do not need to follow the crowd to feel good about themselves.

_____ 33. People can have a more realistic self-concept if they _____.
    A. do not admit their weaknesses
    B. set goals for themselves that are too difficult to reach
    C. carefully judge the facts about themselves
    D. focus on their negative features

_____ 34. With a healthy self-concept, you _____.
    A. have high self-esteem
    B. feel good about your good points
    C. accept your weaknesses
    D. All of the above.

Essay Questions: Provide the answers you feel best show your understanding of the subject matter.

35. Choose one of the four types of self—personal self, social self, ideal self, or extended self. Describe a person who has a positive self-concept and a person who has a negative self-concept in relationship to the type of self chosen.

36. Give three examples of how experiences outside the family can affect self-concept.

37. Write a short paragraph describing a person who seems to lack a realistic self-concept.

38. Explain the meaning of this statement: People with healthy self-concepts like and dislike themselves.

Development During the Early Years

Objectives

When students have completed this chapter, they will be able to
- describe the patterns of physical, social, emotional, and intellectual development during the early years.
- predict what development to expect at various ages.
- describe influences on the development of a child's self-concept.
- explain the importance of the skill of self-observation.

Bulletin Boards

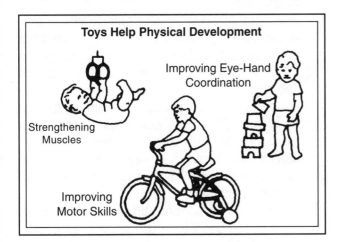

Toys Help Physical Development

Improving Eye-Hand Coordination

Strengthening Muscles

Improving Motor Skills

Title: *Toys Help Physical Development*

Draw or find pictures of children of various ages playing with different toys as shown. Label the pictures with the following phrases: *Strengthening Muscles*, *Improving Motor Skills*, and *Improving Eye-Hand Coordination*.

Title: *The Developing Child*

Divide the board into four areas. Place the following labels in the areas: *Physical Development*, *Social Development*, *Emotional Development*, and *Intellectual Development*. Have students place words or pictures depicting each type of development in the appropriate area.

Teaching Materials

Text, pages 90-109
> *To Review*
> *To Challenge Your Thinking*
> *To Do with the Class*
> *To Do with Your Community*

Student Activity Guide
> A. *Sequence of Development*
> B. *Development of Children*
> C. *Play and Intellectual Development*
> D. *The Developing Self-Concept*

Teacher's Resources
> *Emotional Needs of Children,* reproducible master 6-1
> *Children Learn What They Live,* transparency master 6-2
> Chapter 6 Test
> *Play, a Child's Work,* color transparency CT-6

Introductory Activities

1. Have students write descriptions of infants, toddlers, preschoolers, and school-age children. For each description, students should write one sentence on each of the following areas: physical appearance, social interaction, expression of emotions, and intellectual abilities. Have students discuss their descriptions.
2. Have students discuss various experiences that they have had with children. Students should try to determine what these experiences indicate about the development of children.

Instructional Concepts and Student Learning Experiences

Patterns of Development During the Early Years

3. *Sequence of Development,* Activity A, SAG. Have students select and place pictures to show the sequence of development in one of the four areas of development. Students are asked to write explanations of how each picture applies to development.

4. *Development of Children,* Activity B, SAG. Have students determine whether the descriptive phrases given describe infants and toddlers, preschool children, or school-age children. Descriptions are given for each of the four areas of development.

5. Guest speaker. Invite a child care consultant to discuss the importance of showing care and love to infants in terms of social and emotional development.

6. Have students observe an infant using his or her senses. Students should record any observations such as the infant watching a mobile, feeling a stuffed animal, looking at a person, etc. Students should share their observations in class.

7. Have students discuss how the change in proportions during the first two years of life relates to a child's ability to perform certain skills such as walking.

8. Have students interview a parent of a toddler about his or her child's first steps. Students should ask about the child's actions that led to those first steps. If possible, the student should borrow any pictures of the child's first steps to share with the class.

9. Have students observe preschoolers playing. Students should note the physical abilities of these children. Students should also note differences in ability among children. Have students discuss their findings in class.

10. *Play, a Child's Work,* color transparency CT-6, TR. Use this transparency as a basis of discussion about how play is "work" for a child. Discuss which types of toys are appropriate for various stages of development and which toys aid in the various stages of physical, social, emotional, and intellectual development.

11. Have students arrange a display of toys that would encourage physical development of preschool children.

12. Have students discuss how physical skills are related to peer approval among school-age children.

13. Have students find articles or chapters from child care books about encouraging social development in infants. Students should write short summaries of their findings and share their findings in class.

14. Have students write a short story from the perspective of a toddler that is experiencing stranger anxiety. The story should focus on why the toddler might be fearful of strangers. Have students share and discuss their stories in class.

15. Choose a group of students to try an experiment. Give one student rules for a game to be played with three to five other people. Have the student try to get the others to play the game without using any words to explain the rules. Then have the class discuss why language ability is an important part of cooperative play.

16. Field trip. Arrange for students to visit a program for preschoolers and observe preschoolers at play. Students should record observations on how these children interact socially.

17. Have students interview children in grades one through five about their friendships. Students should ask why they consider someone a friend and what they like to do with their friends. Have students share their findings in class.

18. Have students observe an infant and record actions that show the expression of emotions.

19. Have students write a research paper on the causes of temper tantrums in toddlers and ways that parents can help prevent and deal with tantrums.

20. Have students read literature on handling sibling rivalry in preschoolers. Students should share their findings in class.

21. Have students discuss what is meant by the statement, "School-age children begin to hide their feelings."

22. Have students visit a toy store and choose one toy to examine. Students should write a description of the toy and explain how the toy would help a child's intellectual development.

23. Have students discuss examples of symbolic play that they have observed or perhaps experienced as children.
24. Have students discuss types of pretend play that are common in childhood. Discuss how a child might develop intellectually through each type of pretend play.
25. *Play and Intellectual Development,* Activity C, SAG. Have students give examples of how children can learn from each of the play experiences listed.
26. Make a recording or have a group of students make a recording of the speech of infants and toddlers. The tape should progress in two-month intervals from a one-month-old infant to a 24-month-old toddler. Have students discuss the differences in language abilities among the different ages.
27. Panel discussion. Invite elementary school teachers, principals, school board members, child psychologists, and/or other qualified individuals to discuss the role of school in a child's social development.
28. Have students discuss the following statement: "Although constant questions may seem like a nuisance, they are important to the intellectual development of the preschooler and should be taken seriously."
29. Have students discuss how people's actions affect the moral development of preschoolers. Students should suggest guidelines for modeling actions that will have a positive effect on preschoolers' moral development.
30. Guest speaker. Invite a child care consultant or child psychologist to speak on how to handle questions from children on death.
31. Guest speaker. Invite an elementary school teacher to share examples of how school-age children deal with their emotions. Ask the teacher to give both positive and negative examples.
32. Field trip. Arrange for students to visit a park and observe children at play. Students should record actions and note learnings that may have resulted from the actions.
33. Collect copies of essays from children in grades one through five. You may be able to obtain copies from elementary school teachers. Have students analyze the essays and give examples of improvements in intellectual skills from year to year.

34. Field trip. Arrange to have students visit a child care center or other facility in which they can observe a number of children in the same age group. Have students chart characteristics they see in these children in each of the four development areas: physical, social, emotional, and intellectual.

Self-Concept During the Early Years

35. Have students discuss their reactions to the following statement: "Praising children will only spoil them and make them conceited."
36. *The Developing Self-Concept,* Activity D, SAG. Have students read each of the given situations and explain how the experience might affect a child's developing self-concept. Students are to indicate why they think the experience would have that effect.
37. As a class, have students develop a list of traits of a child who has high self-esteem. For each trait, ask students to suggest ways that the trait might be developed in the child.
38. *Emotional Needs of Children,* reproducible master 6-1, TR. For each of the needs listed, students are to write suggestions for specific ways that adults could meet those needs.
39. Have students role-play situations between an adult and a child in which the child is seeking attention from the adult, but the adult is busy with something else. Students portraying the adult should try to handle the situation in a way that will reinforce a positive self-concept.
40. *Children Learn What They Live,* transparency master 6-2, TR. Have students discuss their reactions to the ideas presented in the master.
41. Have students give examples of situations in which peers affect a child's self-concept negatively. Students should discuss possible ways that adults can help counteract the effects of situations.
42. Have students discuss the effect on self-concept of failing at a task that is beyond a person's abilities. Students should discuss what this means in terms of choosing toys and assigning responsibilities for children.
43. Have students role-play situations in which an adult helps a child recognize his or her good characteristics.
44. Guest speaker. Invite a preschool teacher to discuss ways to build positive self-concepts in children.

Answer Key

Text

To Review

1. physical development, social development, emotional development, intellectual development
2. muscular, nervous, senses
3. eye-hand
4. A. false
   B. false
5. helps a child learn to meet others; helps a child learn to cooperate with a group; provides the child with a feeling of identity
6. parallel
7. A. preschooler
   B. school-age child
   C. infant and toddler
   D. preschooler
   E. school-age child
   F. preschooler
8. (Describe three:) They acquire much knowledge through play. They learn about themselves and the world. They learn how things work. They develop communication skills by playing with other children. Symbolic play may be helpful when learning to read. Play experiences may help children develop concepts related to mathematical ideas. Pretend play develops symbolic thought and flexibility in thinking. Play gives children opportunities for decision making and problem solving. Play helps children develop thinking skills.
9. crying, babbling, single words, connection of meaningful words
10. (List two:) Children who have high self-esteem have greater self-confidence and can confront challenges more easily than children with low self-esteem.

Student Activity Guide

Development of Children, Activity B

1. A
2. C
3. C
4. B
5. A
6. A
7. C
8. B
9. A
10. A
11. B
12. C
13. B
14. B
15. A
16. C
17. C
18. A
19. B
20. B
21. C
22. A
23. C
24. A
25. B
26. A
27. C
28. B
29. B
30. A
31. B
32. C
33. C
34. C
35. B
36. A
37. A
38. C
39. A
40. B
41. C
42. C
43. A
44. A
45. C

Teacher's Resources

Chapter 6 Test

1. G
2. A
3. J
4. D
5. E
6. C
7. H
8. I
9. F
10. B
11. T
12. T
13. T
14. F
15. F
16. T
17. T
18. T
19. F
20. F
21. D
22. C
23. B
24. D
25. A
26. (Student response.)
27. (Student response.)
28. Infants first cry as a reflex, and then they begin to cry to communicate that they are hungry. They progress to babbling and try to copy the language of their parents. From babbling, the child begins to form single words. Toddlers make new sounds, connect meaningful words, and associate new words with particular objects. Further language development occurs as children have new experiences and develop intellectual skills. The child is able to form simple sentences. Preschoolers progress until they are able to form complex sentences by age four or five.
29. (Student response.)

Reproducible Master 6-1

Emotional Needs of Children

Name _____ **Date** _____ **Period** _____

To grow strong and healthy, children need food, sleep, and shelter. Children also have emotional needs. Meeting these emotional needs helps children develop healthy self-concepts. Several needs are explained below. For each one, give one specific way that an adult could help meet the need in a child.

Love: Children need to know that they matter very much to someone and that there are people nearby who care what happens to them.

_____

_____

Acceptance: Children need to know that the people who care for them always like and accept them, even if these people do not approve of some of the children's actions.

_____

_____

Security: Children need to know that they belong to a loving family and that family members will be there when children need help.

_____

_____

Protection: Children need to feel that family members will keep them safe and help them when they must face frightening situations.

_____

_____

Independence: Children need to be encouraged to try new things and to know that others have confidence in their ability to do things.

_____

_____

Guidance: Children need role models to help them learn how to behave toward other people and objects.

_____

_____

Moral guidance: Children need role models to help instill positive character traits such as kindness, courage, honesty, and generosity in them.

_____

_____

Discipline: Children need to understand there are limits to allowed behaviors and that family members enforce these limits. Children also need to understand that it is all right to feel such emotions as jealousy or anger, but that they are not allowed to hurt themselves or others because of those feelings.

_____

_____

Transparency Master 6-2

Children Learn What They Live

If a child lives with criticism, he learns to condemn.

If a child lives with hostility, he learns to fight.

If a child lives with fear, he learns to be apprehensive.

If a child lives with pity, he learns to be sorry for himself.

If a child lives with jealousy, he learns to feel guilty.

If a child lives with praise, he learns to be appreciative.

If a child lives with encouragement, he learns to be confident.

If a child lives with acceptance, he learns to love.

If a child lives with recognition, he learns what justice is.

If a child lives with security, he learns to have faith in himself.

If a child lives with friendliness, he learns that the world is a nice
place in which to live.

Author Unknown

Development During the Early Years

Name _____

Date _____ **Period** _____ **Score** _____

Chapter 6 Test

Matching: Match the following terms and identifying phrases.

_____ 1. Automatic, unlearned behaviors.

_____ 2. A sense of personal worth.

_____ 3. Type of play that indicates a child can hold mental images from the past; an example is a child using a cardboard box for a car.

_____ 4. When a child will play next to another child, but not with the child in a cooperative way.

_____ 5. The process that reads messages sent by the senses.

_____ 6. Voluntary, directed movements.

_____ 7. Competition between children in a family.

_____ 8. When infants between the ages of five and seven months feel anxious or afraid around unfamiliar people.

_____ 9. Exists when what you know about yourself is accurate.

_____ 10. A sense of right and wrong.

A. high self-esteem

B. moral development

C. motor skills

D. parallel play

E. perception

F. realistic self-concept

G. reflexes

H. sibling rivalry

I. stranger anxiety

J. symbolic play

True/False: Circle *T* if the statement is true or *F* if the statement is false.

T   F   11. One part of physical development includes changes in the internal organs, such as the brain and the sense organs.

T   F   12. Changing body proportions are quite noticeable in preschoolers.

T   F   13. Basic needs related to love, affection, belonging, and worth as a person motivate a child to develop socially.

T   F   14. Going to school has only a slight effect on a child's social development.

T   F   15. Most toddlers are not willing to openly express their emotions.

T   F   16. Play is an excellent opportunity for learning.

T   F   17. Babbling is a stage of language development when infants try to copy the language of their parents.

T   F   18. Children who have high self-esteem also have greater self-confidence.

T   F   19. A child's physical development is not related to the development of the self-concept.

T   F   20. Praising a child always helps his or her self-concept.

(Continued)

Name _____

Multiple Choice: Choose the best answer and write the corresponding letter in the blank.

_____ 21. Patterns of development _____.
  A. are an orderly and predictable sequence of characteristics children display as they develop
  B. include physical, social, emotional, and intellectual development
  C. can help parents predict what development to expect
  D. All of the above.

_____ 22. Which of the following is NOT true about the emotions of infants?
  A. Infants are born with certain fears.
  B. Anger is usually expressed through crying.
  C. Infants use smiling as their main method of communication.
  D. Infants are able to express a range of emotions.

_____ 23. Play _____.
  A. is not necessary for development
  B. is a major way children acquire knowledge
  C. is enjoyable for children, but does not help them learn
  D. tends to confuse children about basic mathematical concepts

_____ 24. Thinking skills include _____.
  A. being able to classify objects into certain categories
  B. ability to reason
  C. ability to understand cause-and-effect relationships
  D. All of the above.

_____ 25. Developing a positive self-concept _____.
  A. is closely related to the satisfaction of basic needs
  B. may cause children to see themselves unrealistically
  C. occurs during the infant and toddler years
  D. All of the above.

Essay Questions: Provide the answers you feel best show your understanding of the subject matter.

26. Briefly describe the sequence of a child's social development from the infant and toddler years, through the preschool years, and through the school-age years.

27. List three emotions that can be a problem for a child and explain why.

28. Describe the pattern of language development in children.

29. Describe a situation that illustrates how physical development can be related to self-concept.

7

Developmental Tasks of Childhood

Objectives

When students have completed this chapter, they will be able to

◆ describe the developmental tasks of infants, toddlers, preschoolers, and school-age children.

◆ suggest ways children can be encouraged to achieve these developmental tasks.

Bulletin Boards

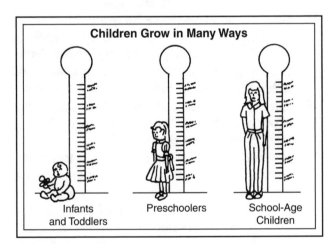

Children Grow in Many Ways

Infants and Toddlers   Preschoolers   School-Age Children

Title: *Children Grow in Many Ways*

Place three growth charts on the board and place drawings of children beside each one as shown. Place the labels *Infants and Toddlers*, *Preschoolers*, and *School-Age Children* under the drawings as shown. Write the developmental tasks of each age group on the appropriate growth chart. (See charts 7-1, 7-8, and 7-14 for tasks.)

Title: *People Who Influence a Child's Development*

Place a drawing of a child in the center of the board. Around the child, place pictures representing people who have a strong influence on a child's development. Place appropriate labels such as *mother*, *father*, *brother*, *sister*, *extended family*, *friends*, *teachers*, etc., under the pictures.

Teaching Materials

Text, pages 110-133
To Review
To Challenge Your Thinking
To Do with the Class
To Do with Your Community

Student Activity Guide
A. *Developmental Tasks of Infants and Toddlers*
B. *Developmental Tasks of Preschool Children*
C. *Developmental Tasks of School-Age Children*

Teacher's Resources
Developmental Tasks of Childhood, reproducible master 7-1
Baby Bill of Rights, reproducible master 7-2
Chapter 7 Test
Developmental Tasks of Childhood, color transparency CT-7

Introductory Activities

1. *Developmental Tasks of Childhood,* reproducible master 7-1, TR. Have students interview parents to find out how they help their children achieve the developmental tasks for their age. Students should share their findings in class.

2. Have students brainstorm a list of all the things that children need to learn to function in everyday living. Students should list items for infants, toddlers, preschoolers, and school-age children. Then divide the class into four groups. Assign each a type of development (physical, social, emotional, and intellectual). Then have each group determine which of the items listed during brainstorming apply to their type of development.

3. *Developmental Tasks of Childhood,* color transparency CT-7, TR. Use this transparency as you introduce the concept of developmental tasks. Define the tasks as goals of growth toward maturity. Discuss the various developmental tasks children go through from infancy through school-age.

Instructional Concepts and Student Learning Experiences

Developmental Tasks of Infants and Toddlers

4. Have students develop a display of objects or pictures of objects designed to make infant feedings and toddler feedings easier.
5. Have students discuss why children develop the following skills in the given sequence: holding head up, rolling over, sitting with support, sitting alone, standing with help, crawling, pulling up to stand, standing alone, and walking alone. Students should discuss what might result if a child tried to skip one or more of these tasks.
6. Have students discuss the possible emotional effects of trying to toilet train a child before he or she is physically able to control elimination.
7. *Baby Bill of Rights,* reproducible master 7-2, TR. Have students discuss how the verses apply to communicating with infants. Students should make suggestions for carrying out each of the ideas listed.
8. Have students discuss how the number and types of objects around a child and experiences a child has affect the child's vocabulary.
9. Have students react to the following statement, "I show my infant child love by working hard so that she can have the nicest toys and clothes."
10. Guest speaker. Invite a pediatrician to discuss infant and toddler feeding.
11. Have students role-play situations in which an adult must react to a toddler's temper tantrum or expression of fear.
12. Panel discussion. Invite parents to discuss their experiences in toilet training their children. Students should use the information gained from the discussion to write some guidelines for toilet training.
13. Have students discuss reasons why adults cannot expect toddlers to be responsible for their own safety. Students should suggest methods of keeping toddlers safe while allowing them to explore and learn.
14. Have students observe toddlers and record actions that indicate expression of self or awareness of self. Students should share their observations in class.

15. *Developmental Tasks of Infants and Toddlers,* Activity A, SAG. Have students list the six developmental tasks for infants and toddlers discussed in the text. For each task, students should give two suggestions for encouraging the child to accomplish the task.

Developmental Tasks of the Preschool Child

16. Have students discuss characteristics that indicate that a child is getting enough sleep. Students should also discuss characteristics that indicate that a child is not getting enough sleep.
17. Guest speaker. Invite a dietitian to speak on the importance of an adequate diet during the preschool and school-age years. The speaker should give guidelines for providing nutritious meals that appeal to preschoolers and school-age children.
18. Have students develop a list of toys and games enjoyed by preschool children. Students should indicate which of the items listed encourage small muscle development and which encourage large muscle development.
19. Have students discuss ways that adults can allow preschool children to learn while protecting them from danger.
20. Have students develop a story tape to accompany a children's book. Students should give the book and tape to a preschooler and ask the child's parent to report to them on the preschooler's experiences with the book and tape. Students should share the results with the class.
21. Have students discuss how encouraging children to explore new experiences and ask many questions can encourage characteristics in children that will be valuable in adult life.
22. Have students practice making statements that help children become aware of their feelings. Students should also practice making statements that make children aware of other people's feelings.
23. Have students find and read literature on helping preschoolers control their expressions of anger. Students should share their findings in class.

24. Have students role-play various family decision-making situations in which they include a preschooler in the process. Have the class discuss the role-plays.
25. Have students interview parents of preschool children to find out how their preschool children help with tasks at home. Students should ask parents how these tasks seem to affect their child's self-esteem and level of responsibility. Students should share their findings in class.
26. Select students to have a panel discussion on the effects of overprotective and over-restrictive parenting versus the effects of more permissive and relaxed parenting. Students should be prepared to support their discussion with research. Class members who are not panelists should prepare questions for the discussion.
27. Have students discuss the following statement: "A parent who has low self-esteem is likely to have a child with low self-esteem."
28. *Developmental Tasks of Preschool Children,* Activity B, SAG. Have students match the descriptions of actions of preschool children with the appropriate developmental tasks.

Developmental Tasks of the School-Age Child

29. Have students discuss how height and weight changes in physical development can affect children's social and emotional development.
30. Have students discuss how the phrase "practice makes perfect" relates to the development of physical skills in school-age children.
31. Have students brainstorm ways to encourage children to develop some of their weaker physical skills. For instance, some children cannot run as fast as others, so they tend to avoid play activities that involve running. How can adults encourage these children to be physically active even though they cannot match the athletic skills of other children?
32. Have students develop a pamphlet containing healthful snack ideas and recipes for school-age children. Arrange to have the pamphlets distributed to parents of elementary school children.
33. Have students discuss the relationship between family encouragement and teacher encouragement in helping children learn.

34. Have students discuss possible positive and negative effects of watching television on school-age children.
35. Have students discuss possible positive and negative results of children identifying with heroes and heroines.
36. Have students discuss how friendships can affect intellectual development.
37. Have students role-play situations in which a school-age child fails at handling a responsibility. The adult should react in ways that help the child cope with the failure.
38. Have students debate the following topics:
    - School-age children should receive an allowance.
    - School-age children should be allowed to spend their own money as they wish.
39. Have students make a list of ways that parents could help their school-age children grow in self-confidence, self-respect, and self-control.
40. Have students discuss how a school-age child's physical development might influence his or her self-concept. Students should consider how a physical disability or lack of skill might affect self-concept. Students should make suggestions for how parents can guide such children to develop good self-concepts.
41. *Developmental Tasks of School-Age Children,* Activity C, SAG. Have students list the developmental tasks of school-age children that were given in the text. Students should then list two examples of behavior that show a child has achieved each task.
42. Guest speaker. Invite a school counselor or psychologist to discuss the relationship between a child's self-esteem and his or her ability to succeed in school.

Answer Key

Text

To Review
1. By knowing the developmental tasks, these people will better understand how they can help guide the child's steps toward maturity.
2. (List three. Student response.)
3. head, foot, trunk, extremities
4. A. false
   B. true
5. (Student response.)

6. (Name three:) toys, blankets, pacifiers (Students may justify other responses.)
7. (List four:) Set a definite bedtime hour to help avoid arguments. Give the child a bath. Look at picture books. Read stories. Listen to music. Younger children may want a security object. (Students may justify other responses.)
8. (List five. Student response.)
9. The peer group begins to pull the child away from dependence on the family toward the independence necessary for maturity.
10. modeling

Student Activity Guide

Developmental Tasks of Preschool Children, Activity B

1. E
2. B
3. D
4. C
5. B
6. A
7. A
8. F
9. D
10. A
11. E
12. B
13. C
14. F
15. E
16. C
17. D
18. F

Teacher's Resources

Chapter 7 Test

1. B
2. A
3. B
4. B
5. A
6. C
7. C
8. A
9. C
10. B
11. F
12. T
13. F
14. F
15. T
16. T
17. F
18. T
19. T
20. F
21. D
22. C
23. B
24. C
25. B
26. The child's "inner clock" determines feeding, so feeding schedules may differ slightly from day-to-day. The babies are fed when they indicate hunger by waking up, crying, or being restless. The parent can still exercise some control over the feeding times.
27. Preschoolers tend to be very busy. Without routines, stopping their many activities for daily chores can be difficult. (Student response for three routines.)
28. Self-esteem may affect a child's chances for success in school even more than intelligence. Children of high intelligence and low self-esteem often do poorly in school. On the other hand, children of average intelligence and high self-esteem can usually be successful. Children with low self-esteem tend to get little satisfaction from school and lose interest easily. This lack of interest usually results in poor performance. The poor performance reinforces the low self-esteem. The child who experiences more success than failure usually maintains a confident attitude. Family members can greatly influence the child's success.
29. In order to become responsible, children need to assume responsibilities. Assuming tasks within the family gives children the opportunity to learn skills, contribute to the family, and become more independent. Children gain self-confidence as they accomplish tasks. They also develop a respect for order and organization.
30. Modeling is the most effective way for parents and other family members to influence values of children. They show their children their own values by demonstrating those values in their daily living. (Student response for two examples.)

Reproducible Master 7-1

Developmental Tasks of Childhood

Name _____ **Date** _____ **Period** _____

The developmental tasks of infants and toddlers, preschool children, and school-age children are listed below. Interview the parents of a child in one of these age groups to find out how they help their child achieve the developmental tasks for his or her age group. Record your findings in the space provided and discuss these findings in class.

	Infants and Toddlers	**Preschoolers**	**School-Age Children**
Task one:	Developing good eating and sleeping habits.	Developing healthy daily routines.	Developing and improving physical skills.
Task two:	Becoming aware of what the body can do.	Developing physical skills.	Maintaining healthful habits.
Task three:	Learning about elimination.	Learning through expanded experiences and more effective communication.	Continuing to develop basic learning skills.
Task four:	Learning to relate to others.	Learning to express feelings and control actions.	Increasing ability to relate to others.
Task five:	Learning to experience and express feelings.	Being an active member of the family.	Participating in family life as a responsible member.
Task six:	Developing self-awareness.	Strengthening self-concept while becoming more independent.	Continuing to move toward a more complete self.

Age group of child: _____

What parents do to help their child achieve his or her developmental tasks: _____

_____

_____

_____

_____

_____

_____

_____

_____

_____

_____

_____

Reproducible Master 7-2

Baby Bill of Rights

Talk to Me

Sing, hum, babble, or even read the funnies to me! I don't know exactly what you're saying, but I need to hear you. And I do know what you mean, even if I may not know words. Like your voice tones mean, "I love you." Or when you yell, I hear, "You're a pest!" Unless you communicate with me, how can I learn? I learn from you.

Hold Me

Everything is so big and new to me. I don't understand where I am. Or who I am. And I get scared. But when you hold me, I feel better. Your warmth warms me. Your breath and heartbeat make me feel I belong. Belong here. Belong to you.

Answer My Cry

I don't cry to get you upset. Or to get you mad. I cry because I can't tell you how I feel any other way. Maybe I'm cold...or wet...or hungry...or scared and lonely. Answer my cries. You'll soon know what each means. You won't spoil me. You'll help me to be a better baby—and to make you happier, too.

Love Me

Like me. Love me just as I am. Don't expect me to do what I can't do. Like being toilet-trained. My muscles aren't ready yet. I know I'm messy. But I'm growing. Overlook my baby weaknesses. You're the most important person in my world. I can't make it without you. So get to know me. Have fun with me. And love me—just as I am.

Source: "Inside Your Body, Inside Your Head," National Foundation—March of Dimes, 1978.

Developmental Tasks of Childhood

Name _____

Date _____ Period _____ Score _____

Chapter 7 Test

Matching: Match the following descriptions of children with the appropriate age group. (Letters will be used more than once.)

_____ 1. During this stage, children are quite open and frank about letting others know how they feel.

_____ 2. During these years, children form the basis for their ability to love and to be loved.

_____ 3. During this period, children consciously or unconsciously develop perceptions related to being male or female.

_____ 4. During this busy, active period, children find it hard to accept bedtime.

_____ 5. During this period, children have their first opportunity to show independence in eating.

_____ 6. These children are often interested in activities involving small muscles, such as model building or craft activities.

_____ 7. Children get their permanent teeth during this stage.

_____ 8. Physical challenges to these children include stacking blocks, buttoning clothes, and holding a glass.

_____ 9. This group of children identifies with heroes or heroines, such as baseball stars or performers on television.

_____ 10. By helping with simple tasks, children of this age group feel good about their contribution to the family.

A. infants and toddlers

B. preschool children

C. school-age children

True/False: Circle *T* if the statement is true or *F* if the statement is false.

T   F   11. A fat, cuddly baby is almost always a healthy baby.

T   F   12. Parents can influence a child's physical development by the type of play opportunities given to the child.

T   F   13. Toilet training usually begins in the child's first year.

T   F   14. When a toddler is afraid, the best way to deal with the problem is to explain why he or she shouldn't be afraid.

T   F   15. By five years of age, children use fewer aggressive actions like hitting or pushing.

T   F   16. Family rituals are a way of developing family spirit.

T   F   17. Preschoolers are too young to assume responsibilities in the family.

(Continued)

Name _____

T   F   18. Individual differences among school-age children become more obvious than differences among preschool children.

T   F   19. During early school years, most children are mature enough to learn responsibilities with money.

T   F   20. School-age children are too young to understand their own strengths and weaknesses.

Multiple Choice: Choose the best answer and write the corresponding letter in the blank.

_____ 21. Which of the following is a developmental task of infants and toddlers?
A. Developing good eating and sleeping habits.
B. Learning to relate to others.
C. Developing self-awareness.
D. All of the above.

_____ 22. At the time babies are weaned, they _____.
A. show greater interest in drinking from the bottle
B. learn how to eat with utensils
C. learn to drink from a container instead of from a bottle or from the mother's breast
D. are able to eat the same foods as other family members

_____23. Which of the following is NOT a developmental task of infants and toddlers?
A. Becoming aware of what the body can do.
B. Learning to express feelings and control actions.
C. Learning to relate to others.
D. Developing good eating and sleeping habits.

_____24. Which of the following is true of a school-age child?
A. At this age, children do not vary much physically.
B. They are not very competitive.
C. There is a close relationship between physical development and self-esteem.
D. Most of the development during this stage is physical, not intellectual.

_____ 25. Which of the following is NOT true about involving children in family decision making and responsibilities?
A. By having their opinions heard, children feel important to the group.
B. If children are involved in these activities, they will successfully assume each responsibility they are given.
C. When their ideas are treated with respect, children become more self-confident.
D. All of the above.

Essay Questions: Provide the answers you feel best show your understanding of the subject matter.

26. Explain what it means when infants are fed on a demand feeding schedule.

27. Explain why routines are important for preschoolers. Give three examples of specific helpful routines.

28. Explain how a child's self-esteem affects success in school.

29. Describe how a school-age child may benefit from assuming responsibilities in the home.

30. What is the most effective way for parents to influence their children's values? Give two examples to illustrate how this can be done.

8

Developmental Tasks from Adolescence Throughout Life

Objective

When students have completed this chapter, they will be able to

◆ relate the developmental tasks of adolescence, young adulthood, middle age, and late adulthood to their life goals.

Bulletin Boards

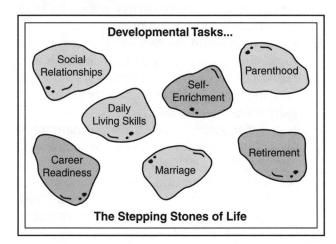

Developmental Tasks...

Social Relationships

Parenthood

Self-Enrichment

Daily Living Skills

Career Readiness

Marriage

Retirement

The Stepping Stones of Life

Title: *Developmental Tasks...The Stepping Stones of Life*

Select key words from the developmental tasks listed on the reproducible master 8-1. For example, *social relationships*, *self-enrichment*, *career readiness*, *marriage*, *parenthood*, *daily living skills*, or *retirement* could be labeled on the stepping-stones. Pictures could also be included on the bulletin board to emphasize the key developmental tasks.

Title: *Developmental Tasks Throughout Life*

Fill the bulletin board with pictures of people varying in age from infancy to aging. The people should be involved in a variety of activities alone or with others. In the center of the board, place a list of developmental tasks at the various stages of life. Have students use string and pushpins to connect the stages to pictures that apply.

Teaching Materials

Text, pages 134-155
  To Review
  To Challenge Your Thinking
  To Do with the Class
  To Do with Your Community
Student Activity Guide
  A. *Developmental Tasks*
  B. *Developmental Tasks of the Young Adult*
  C. *Developmental Tasks of Middle-Age Adults*
  D. *Developmental Tasks of Late Adulthood*
Teacher's Resources
  Developmental Tasks, transparency master 8-1
  My Evaluation...A Patterning Technique, reproducible master 8-2
  Chapter 8 Test
  The Road from Adolescence to Late Adulthood, color transparency CT-8

Introductory Activities

1. Prepare descriptions of the lives of about six different people to share with the class. The lives should be very different in terms of childhood and adult experiences. The descriptions may be true or fictitious. Read the descriptions to the class and have students discuss what may have influenced each person's life.

2. Divide the class into four groups and assign the students in each group to interview people in one of these categories: a friend, a person who has been out of college for less than five years, a person age 35 to 50, or a retired person. Students should ask people interviewed

what they consider to be important skills and responsibilities at their present age. Students should also ask what the people have needed to learn in recent years that was not as important in past years. Students should discuss their findings in class.

3. *The Road from Adolescence to Late Adulthood,* color transparency CT-8, TR. Ask students to give ideas about what a person might encounter on the road from adolescence to late adulthood. Write their responses on the blanks provided.

4. Panel discussion. As an introduction to the chapter, invite adults of various ages to discuss development as a lifelong process.

5. Panel discussion. Invite a clergy member, a social worker, a counselor, and/or any other individuals who work closely with a variety of people to discuss the importance of healthy social adjustment.

Instructional Concepts and Student Learning Experiences

Developmental Tasks of Adolescence

6. *Developmental Tasks*, transparency master 8-1, TR. Have each class member choose one task from the list to analyze. Each student should list ways in which family members might help influence the achievement of the task chosen. Students should discuss their ideas.

7. Have students discuss conflicting messages that they receive about sexual responsibility through media and other sources. Students should discuss how these messages make being sexually responsible difficult.

8. Guest speaker. Invite a representative from your high school guidance department to explain resources available through the school to guide young people on career choices.

9. Have students discuss levels of independence and responsibility parents give adolescents. Students should discuss how handling responsibilities properly affects the amount of independence that adolescents are given.

10. Have students identify ways in which parents and adolescents are dependent on each other physically, intellectually, and socially.

11. *Developmental Tasks,* Activity A, SAG. Have

students write questions designed to help a friend analyze their achievement in each of the developmental tasks listed.

12. *My Evaluation...A Patterning Technique,* reproducible master 8-2, TR. Have students use the patterning technique to evaluate their own progress regarding developmental tasks of adolescence. Students should include both positive and negative aspects of their development. Students should not be asked to share their responses to this activity. (Refer to Chapter 1 of the *Teacher's Resources* for an explanation of the patterning technique.)

Developmental Tasks of Young Adulthood

13. *Developmental Tasks of the Young Adult,* Activity B, SAG. For each of the tasks listed, have students list what they can do now to make later achievement of the tasks easier.

14. Have students discuss the importance of education in today's job market.

15. Panel discussion. Invite several young adults to discuss problems they have experienced related to consumer decisions, relationships, housing, etc., and resources they found to help solve those problems.

16. Panel discussion. Invite a clergy member, a financial counselor, a marriage counselor, and/or other qualified individuals to discuss readiness for marriage. Topics should include economics, physical compatibility, in-laws, religion, social and recreational interests, and household responsibilities.

17. Have students research training programs for displaced workers or homemakers and give an oral report on their findings.

18. Have students discuss how having too few or too many interests may affect personal development.

Developmental Tasks of Middle Age

19. *Developmental Tasks of Middle-Age Adults,* Activity C, SAG. For each of the tasks listed, have students talk with middle-age persons or generate ideas in small groups that can help achieve the tasks more smoothly and successfully.

20. Have students read articles about people who change occupations in the middle adult years and discuss their articles in class.

21. Guest speaker. Invite a physician to discuss health problems of middle-age people and ways to prevent or handle these problems.
22. Have students discuss the merits of the following suggestion: "The key to successfully coping with aging is to search out remaining strengths and build upon them."
23. Have students discuss ways that family mementos can be used to bridge the generation gap.

Developmental Tasks of Late Adulthood

24. *Developmental Tasks of Late Adulthood,* Activity D, SAG. Have students discuss what factors help or hinder adults in their later years. What earlier lifespan habits can help the tasks be easier and more developmentally successful in the later years?
25. Have students choose a myth of aging and find and present research that disproves the myth chosen.
26. Guest speaker. Invite a gerontologist or professional who works with older adults to discuss recreational programs for older adults. The guest should discuss types of programs, how programs are supported, and other aspects of the programs.

Answer Key

Text

To Review
1. (Student response.)
2. A, B, and C are true
3. (List four:) personal qualities, skills, capabilities, talents (Students may justify other responses.)
4. false
5. (List five:) trust, concern, respect, openness, a sense of responsibility
6. false
7. C
8. Menopause

9. Avocational interests give older adults a feeling of usefulness and stimulate and exercise their minds. These interests can fill up time constructively and provide opportunities for happiness and companionship.
10. denial, anger and resentment, depression, acceptance (Descriptions are student response.)

Teacher's Resources

Chapter 8 Test
1. B
2. E
3. G
4. I
5. H
6. F
7. C
8. A
9. T
10. T
11. F
12. F
13. T
14. F
15. F
16. F
17. T
18. F
19. B
20. A
21. D
22. C
23. C
24. B
25. (Student response.)
26. Couples need to keep their relationship strong as well as developing good relationships with their children. They can do so by participating in social and recreational interests together and by spending time alone together without the children. Developing the relationship beyond the children is important to the couple's ability to face future challenges together.
27. (Student response.)
28. (Student response.)

Transparency Master 8-1

Developmental Tasks

Developmental Tasks of Adolescence

To accept and manage your changing body
To be involved in a variety of social experiences
To assume more responsibility while moving toward greater independence
To develop personal resources helpful in reaching future goals
To continue to develop a healthy self-concept

Developmental Tasks of the Young Adult

To prepare for and become successfully involved in a career
To expand social relationships and assume social responsibilities
To exercise management skills related to daily living
To continue self-enriching pursuits
To assess readiness for marriage
To adjust to marriage
To assess readiness for parenthood
To assume responsibilities of parenthood
To develop a husband-wife relationship beyond the children

Developmental Tasks of Middle-Age Adults

To continue self-enriching vocational and avocational pursuits
To adjust to physiological changes
To continue family responsibilities
To further the growth of the husband-wife relationship
To manage daily living and prepare for later years

Developmental Tasks of Late Adulthood

To care for oneself physically
To continue self-enriching pursuits
To maintain family contacts and responsibilities
To adjust to retirement and changes in income and living arrangements
To adapt positively to the certainty of death

Reproducible Master 8-2

My Evaluation...A Patterning Technique

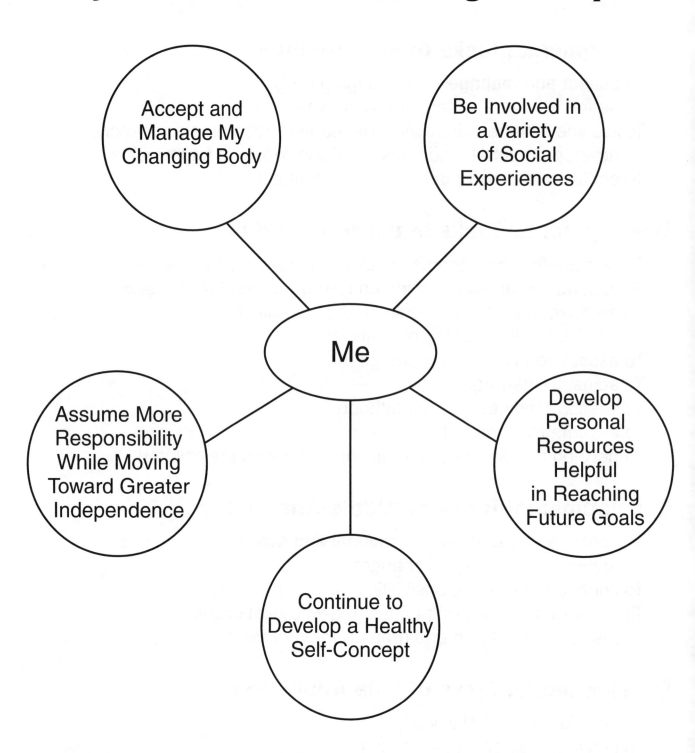

With the above illustration as your model, take out a separate sheet of paper and use the patterning technique to evaluate your progress regarding the developmental tasks of adolescence.

Developmental Tasks from Adolescence Throughout Life

Name _____

Date _____ Period _____ Score _____

Chapter 8 Test

Matching: Match the following terms and identifying phrases.

_____ 1. Physical and cultural expectations occurring at certain life stages.

_____ 2. The change in individuals as they move toward full development.

_____ 3. Includes physical health, mental health, and personality.

_____ 4. The process of understanding how to properly relate to others.

_____ 5. Requires careful thought and planning, especially with financial resources.

_____ 6. A physical change that has psychological implications.

_____ 7. Still a strong desire, even in late adulthood.

_____ 8. Time spent in activities that promote physical, social, emotional, and intellectual health and growth.

A. avocational interests

B. developmental tasks

C. independence

D. management

E. maturation

F. menopause

G. personal resources

H. retirement

I. socialization

True/False: Circle *T* if the statement is true or *F* if the statement is false.

T   F   9. Developmental tasks involve both biological and cultural expectations.

T   F   10. Close friendships help prepare adolescents for later adult relationships.

T   F   11. Parents who provide guidance and control rather than domination make the task of becoming independent more difficult for adolescents.

T   F   12. The only reason for adults to work is to earn a living.

T   F   13. Positive or negative factors at work can affect the success or failure of home life.

T   F   14. Lifestyle diseases usually do not begin until the later adult years.

T   F   15. The middle adult years find people in peak physical condition.

T   F   16. People in their middle adult years have little to offer their community.

T   F   17. People need to prepare and manage resources well early in life for better adjustment and well-being in the later adulthood years.

T   F   18. Flexibility in the various life stages is unimportant.

(Continued)

Name _____

Multiple Choice: Choose the best answer and write the corresponding letter in the blank.

_____ 19. Which of the following is NOT true about developmental tasks?
   A. When a task is achieved, the individual is ready to move on to the next developmental stage.
   B. Developmental tasks are determined only by cultural forces.
   C. Developmental tasks might be considered goals of growth.
   D. Human development can be examined through knowledge of developmental tasks.

_____ 20. Developmental tasks of adolescents involve all of the following EXCEPT _____.
   A. limiting opportunities to develop resources
   B. developing personal resources helpful in reaching future goals
   C. moving toward independence
   D. participating in a variety of social experiences

_____ 21. Which is true in order to assess a person's readiness for marriage?
   A. Respect and openness.
   B. Agreement on family planning.
   C. Effective communication.
   D. All of the above.

_____ 22. Poor reasons to have children include _____.
   A. wanting to share joys and responsibilities of guiding children
   B. having had positive family experiences and wish to continue the tradition
   C. relieving pressure from family and friends
   D. having become financially responsible

_____ 23. Which of the following is NOT a characteristic of most middle-age adults?
   A. Conflict between earlier dreams for the future and actual achievement in their careers.
   B. After child rearing, desire to return to work.
   C. Adjust to nursing home living.
   D. Need to redefine the marital relationship.

_____ 24. Developmental tasks of late adulthood include _____.
   A. assuming more responsibility while moving toward greater independence
   B. caring for the physical self
   C. assessing readiness for parenthood
   D. preparing for and becoming successfully involved in a career

Essay Questions: Provide the answers you feel best show your understanding of the subject matter.

25. Choose one developmental task of the adolescent. Explain how NOT completing this task might affect a person throughout life.

26. Explain what is meant by a husband-wife relationship beyond the children and why it is important.

27. List four developmental tasks that are related to building and maintaining a healthy self-concept. Explain how each task is related to self-concept.

28. Describe pressures that are usually experienced by men and women in their middle adult years.

Part Three
Understanding Relationships

Successful Relationships

Objectives

When students have completed this chapter, they will be able to
◆ analyze the importance of respect, trust, responsibility, and openness to successful relationships.
◆ examine the importance of relationships throughout life.
◆ identify the benefits of relationships within the family and relationships outside the family.

Bulletin Boards

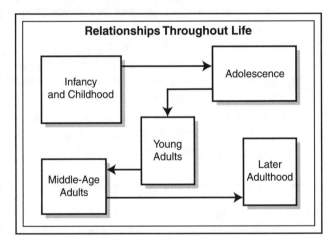

Relationships Throughout Life

Infancy and Childhood → Adolescence

Young Adults

Middle-Age Adults

Later Adulthood

Title: *Relationships Throughout Life*

Use different colored backgrounds or outlines to create five areas on the bulletin board, each labeled with a different stage of life. Connect the stages with arrows to show a normal life sequence. Display pictures of people relating to others in each stage.

Title: *The Basis of Good Relationships*

Make cutouts or drawings of building blocks stacked in a pyramid. Label the blocks in the bottom row with characteristics that form the basis of good relationships—respect, trust, responsibility, and openness. Label the blocks in the second row with examples of people with whom you might have functional relationships—teachers, employers, coworkers. Label the blocks in the top row with examples of people with whom you might have close personal relationships—parents, friends, dating/marriage partners, children.

Teaching Materials

Text, pages 157-168
To Review
To Challenge Your Thinking
To Do with the Class
To Do with Your Community
Student Activity Guide
A. *Describing Successful Relationships*
B. *The Basis of Good Relationships*
C. *Learning from Relationships*
D. *Relationships Throughout Life*
Teacher's Resources
Relationships...A Patterning Technique, reproducible master 9-1
Improving Relationships, reproducible master 9-2
Chapter 9 Test
Keys to Successful Relationships, color transparency CT-9

Introductory Activities

1. Have each student research periodical literature to find a current article about interpersonal relationships. Have students give brief oral reports on what they have read.
2. *Relationships…A Patterning Technique,* reproducible master 9-1, TR. Have students use the patterning technique to illustrate their relationships both within and outside the family. (Refer to Chapter 1 of the *Teacher's Resources* for an explanation of the patterning technique.)

Instructional Concepts and Student Learning Experiences

Characteristics of Positive Relationships

3. *Keys to Successful Relationships,* color transparency CT-9, TR. Use this master as a basis of discussion about how respect, trust, responsibility, and openness are vital to successful relationships at home, school, and work. Refer to the keys later by asking students to share examples of how they personally have used or could use these keys to improve personal and functional relationships.
4. Have students give two or three examples of each of the following in terms of relationships: lack of respect, lack of trust, irresponsibility, and unwillingness to communicate.
5. Have each student ask two people to define *respect* in their own words. Have students share and discuss their findings in class.
6. Ask students to keep a record for one day of examples of respect and lack of respect that they see in the relationships around them. Have students summarize their observations in a one-page written report.
7. Have students role-play situations in which stereotypes are used. Then discuss how using stereotypes shows a lack of respect for some individuals.
8. Review with students the basic human needs. Ask students to explain how a parent's ability or failure to meet these needs can affect a child's development of trust.
9. Ask students to jot down a list of people they trust. For each person on their lists, have students write down a couple of factors or situations that have caused that trust to develop. (This activity is for students' personal consideration. Students should not be required to share their responses with others.)
10. Divide the class into small groups. Assign each group a type of relationship, such as husband, wife, parent-child, brother-sister, etc. Have each group discuss the types of responsibilities that are usually assumed in that relationship.
11. Have students role-play situations showing how openness would benefit a relationship.
12. Have each student ask two people what they find most difficult about being open in a relationship. Have students discuss their findings in class.
13. Have students divide a sheet of paper into two vertical columns headed *sympathy* and *empathy.* Have them write parallel statements to compare and contrast these two concepts.
14. Have students give examples of class situations that might be improved by openness. Have them role-play some of these situations to practice being open without being rude or disrespectful.
15. *Describing Successful Relationships,* Activity A, SAG. Have students show their understanding of the significance of respect, trust, responsibility, and openness in relationships by developing descriptive situations.
16. *The Basis of Good Relationships,* Activity B, SAG. Have students answer the true/false questions to show their understanding of the basis of good relationships.
17. *Improving Relationships,* reproducible master 9-2, TR. Have students make a personal plan for improving their relationships with others.

The Importance of Relationships

18. Have students use library resources to research historical or literary instances in which special relationships have had a great effect on people's lives. Examples might include Queen Isabella and Christopher Columbus, Lewis and Clark, Romeo and Juliet, etc. Have students summarize their findings in two-page written reports.
19. Have each student write a one-page explanation of the statement "A person's happiness and success in life are closely related to his or her ability to form meaningful relationships with others."

20. Panel discussion. Invite a panel of qualified individuals, such as a psychologist, a pediatrician, and a member of the clergy, to speak to your class on the importance of developing relationships within the family.
21. Have students debate the statement "In today's society, other social institutions can better assume the responsibilities once fulfilled by the family."
22. Have students brainstorm a list of relationships people commonly form outside the family throughout a lifetime. Discuss why each of these relationships is important to people.
23. Have students discuss the meaning of the statement "The opportunity to know a variety of individuals is actually an opportunity to strengthen your self-concept."
24. Have each student read an article on the social development of young children and summarize the findings for the class.
25. Have students brainstorm a list of the various types of groups that might be considered adolescent peer groups. Discuss the varying benefits derived from these different groups.
26. Have each student find a periodical article on peer group influence. Then have students work in teams of two to compare and contrast the content of these articles. Have the teams present their conclusions in class.
27. Have students brainstorm a list of the benefits dating provides to members of both sexes.
28. Ask each student to write a log reviewing his or her dating history, noting events that were growth producing and events that were destructive to the self-concept and led to negative feelings about members of the opposite sex. (This activity is for students' personal consideration. Students should not be required to share their logs with others.)
29. Have students discuss how friends can help a person adjust to a different lifestyle after his or her spouse dies.
30. *Learning from Relationships*, Activity C, SAG. Have students describe situations to illustrate their understanding of relationships as human resources.
31. *Relationships Throughout Life*, Activity D, SAG. Have each student interview four people of differing ages to find out how their relationships have benefited them.
32. Field trip. Have students visit a child care center or nursery school to observe interactions between children. Ask students to record their observations and note how each interaction would benefit one or more of the children involved.

Answer Key

Text

To Review
1. A. false
   B. true
   C. true
2. (Student response. Give three examples.)
3. Trying to understand peoples' feelings without judging whether they are right or wrong.
4. (Student response. Describe three.)
5. Personal relationships are those that fulfill basic human needs such as the need to belong, to be cared for, and to be loved. Functional relationships involve everyday needs and interest. (Student response for examples.)
6. (Student response. Name three.)
7. peer
8. social
9. Dating
10. (Student response.)

Student Activity Guide

The Basis of Good Relationships, Activity B
1. F Respecting someone is not the same as liking them.
2. T
3. F Stereotyping usually indicates a lack of respect for the individual.
4. F Although trust develops slowly, it can be quickly destroyed.
5. T
6. F Being open involves a degree of risk, but the risk may be greater if you are not open.
7. F Acceptance does not mean agreeing with the other person.
8. T

Teacher's Resources

Chapter 9 Test

1. A
2. C
3. D
4. A
5. B
6. D
7. B
8. C
9. F
10. F
11. T
12. T
13. T
14. T
15. T
16. F
17. C
18. A
19. B
20. D
21. A
22. A
23. B

24. Young infants develop positive feelings when they are held closely. Young children develop positive feelings when brothers or sisters smile, talk, or play with them. Family members are teachers and models for children. They guide social behaviors and attitudes of children. Young children learn by observing how family members relate to one another and people outside the family. Modeling by family members strongly influences a child's skill at interpersonal relationships.

25. They learn what behaviors strengthen relationships and what behaviors cause problems. They learn much of this through trial and error. Children also learn how to behave in order to satisfy their own needs. They learn and practice relationship skills and become less self-centered.

26. Dating allows teens to improve communication skills as they share opinions, attitudes, values, and goals with others. It gives them an understanding of personalities and helps them develop an appreciation of respect, love, and caring from others.

Reproducible Master 9-1

Relationships...A Patterning Technique

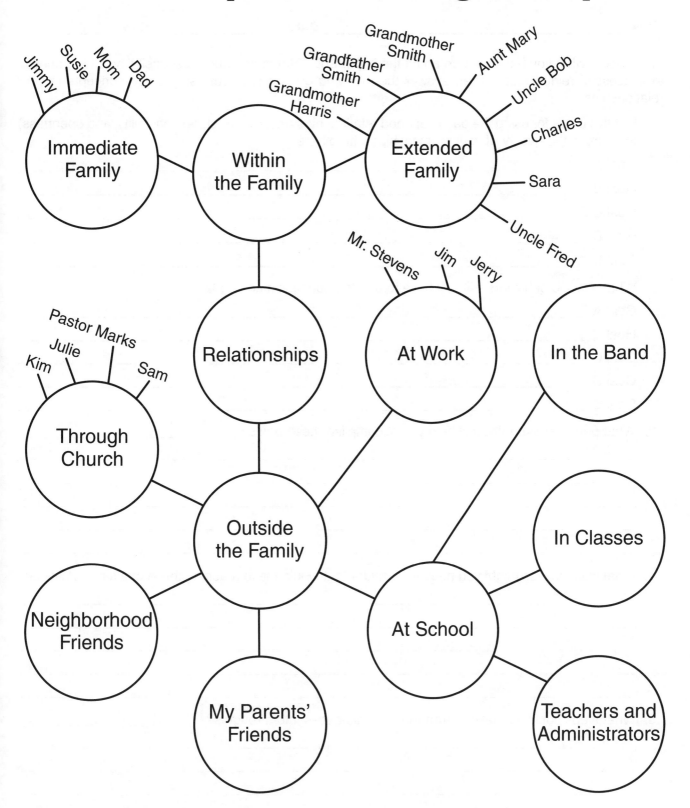

With the above illustration as your model, take out a separate sheet of paper and use the patterning technique to illustrate your relationships both within and outside the family.

Reproducible Master 9-2

Improving Relationships

Name _____ **Date** _____ **Period** _____

Think about what you have learned about the importance of respect, trust, responsibility, and openness to successful relationships. Then answer the following questions about using these concepts in your relationships.

1. List five goals for using the bases of good relationships (respect, trust, responsibility, and openness) to improve the quality of your relationships with others.

Goal A _____

Goal B _____

Goal C _____

Goal D _____

Goal E _____

2. What specific behaviors will you have to use to accomplish each goal?

Goal A _____

Goal B _____

Goal C _____

Goal D _____

Goal E _____

3. What personal strengths will help you accomplish these goals? _____

_____

_____

_____

_____

_____

4. What weaknesses might you need to consider that would make reaching these goals more difficult?

_____

_____

_____

_____

_____

5. What steps could you take to turn these weaknesses into strengths? _____

_____

_____

_____

_____

_____

Successful Relationships

Name _____

Date _____ Period _____ Score _____

Chapter 9 Test

Matching: Match the following descriptions with the characteristics of positive relationships. (Each letter will be used twice.)

_____ 1. Letting another person know your thoughts, opinions, and feelings.

_____ 2. Is closely related to trust.

_____ 3. This takes time to develop but is easily destroyed.

_____ 4. Is closely related to acceptance and empathy.

_____ 5. The feeling of human worth; a basic need of all people.

_____ 6. Believing that someone's word represents what he or she will do.

_____ 7. Stereotyping usually indicates a lack of this quality.

_____ 8. Being dependable, reliable, and accountable for your actions are indicators of this quality.

A. openness

B. respect

C. responsibility

D. trust

True/False: Circle *T* if the statement is true or *F* if the statement is false.

T F   9. A relationship with a family member is usually considered a functional relationship.

T F 10. Stereotyping is a positive step in developing relationships.

T F 11. Trust is difficult to develop, but it is easy to destroy.

T F 12. Relationships are important throughout life.

T F 13. Good relationships with others result in a more positive self-concept.

T F 14. The relationships a person develops outside the family have a great influence on happiness and quality of life.

T F 15. Close association with the peer group is normal during the process of growing up and establishing some independence from the family.

T F 16. Peer group relationships almost always have a negative effect on people.

(Continued)

Name _____

Multiple Choice: Choose the best answer and write the corresponding letter in the blank.

_____ 17. A situation that illustrates respect in a relationship would be _____.
    A. Jim knows his wife will remember to call him as planned
    B. Tim's father took him to get his vaccination
    C. Sue is not fond of Jenny's boyfriend, but she is happy that Jenny gets along with him so well
    D. All of the above.

_____ 18. _____ may involve taking a risk on hurt feelings, embarrassment, or insult.
    A. Openness
    B. Respect
    C. Responsibility
    D. Trust

_____ 19. An example of a relationship that would be considered more personal than functional would be _____.
    A. Sally and her employer at the restaurant
    B. Melinda and her two-year-old niece
    C. Jim and his chemistry teacher
    D. Mark and the clerk at the grocery store

_____ 20. Which of the following is NOT true about relationships?
    A. Successful relationships can contribute to development throughout life.
    B. Success in relationships can have a strong influence on the self-concept.
    C. Developing relationships teaches you about the differences that exist among people.
    D. Relationships are most important only during the young adult years.

_____ 21. Family relationships _____.
    A. are the first interpersonal relationships a child experiences
    B. are less important than relationships outside the family
    C. that are positive can eliminate the need for peer group relationships
    D. are basically functional relationships

_____ 22. Social experiences with other children are important for young children because _____.
    A. being with other children allows them to learn and practice relationship skills
    B. parents cannot serve as adequate role models
    C. these experiences help children develop deep, caring relationships
    D. these experiences help children become more self-centered

_____ 23. For young adults, relationships are _____.
    A. less important than they are to older adults
    B. often deeper and more caring than relationships were earlier in life
    C. usually more important to males than to females
    D. most likely to develop with people who have different interests from their own

Essay Questions: Provide the answers you feel best show your understanding of the subject matter.

24. Describe several ways in which the family teaches children about relationships.

25. Describe several ways a child develops socially when he or she is involved in a nursery school or child care center situation.

26. In what ways does dating or developing special relationships with persons of the opposite sex benefit teenagers?

Effective Communication

Objectives

When students have completed this chapter, they will be able to
- describe various communication skills.
- examine listening as an important step in communication.
- explain guidelines in conflict resolution.
- apply positive conflict resolution to their own lives.

Bulletin Boards

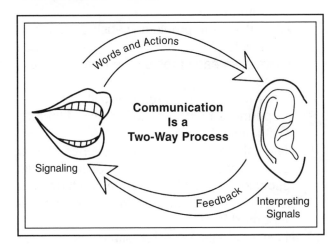

Title: *Communication Is a Two-Way Process*

Place a drawing or cutout of a large pair of lips on the left side of the bulletin board to represent signaling. Place a drawing or cutout of a large ear on the right side of the bulletin board to represent interpreting signals. Draw an arrow from the lips to the ear labeled, *Words and Actions*. Draw an arrow from the ear to the lips labeled, *Feedback*.

Title: *What Are They Saying?*

Display and label pictures illustrating gestures, facial expressions, posture, use of personal space, style of dress, and physical contact as examples of nonverbal communication.

Teaching Materials

Text, pages 169-181
 To Review
 To Challenge Your Thinking
 To Do with the Class
 To Do with Your Community
Student Activity Guide
 A. *Communication Skills*
 B. *Using "I" Messages*
 C. *Conflict Resolution*
 D. *Your Communication Skills*
Teacher's Resources
 Resolving Conflicts Constructively,
  reproducible master 10-1
 Avoiding Negative Communication,
  reproducible master 10-2
 Chapter 10 Test
 Conflict Resolution, color transparency
  CT-10

Introductory Activities

1. Instruct students to watch television for one hour, paying special attention to the way the characters communicate. Ask students to share what they observed with their classmates.
2. Have students play charades to introduce the function and importance of verbal and nonverbal communication.

Instructional Concepts and Student Learning Experiences

Types of Communication

3. Have each student write a description of a problem in a fictitious relationship that is caused by a lack of communication. Ask students to share what they have written and discuss what might have been done to avoid the problem.
4. For their personal benefit, ask students to spend a day really concentrating on communicating with themselves. Tell them to think carefully

about their feelings in various situations throughout the day. Instruct them to analyze what values are involved and think about whether or not they are reacting as they would really like to. Encourage students to use this experience to help them set goals for improvement. (Students should not be required to discuss this self-analysis with classmates.)

5. Have each student read an article on inner communication and share impressions in class.

6. Have students role-play situations in which they can practice being open and accepting of others.

7. Have students brainstorm a list of situations in which it is difficult to be honest with someone without hurting his or her feelings or being disrespectful.

8. *Communication Skills,* Activity A, SAG. Students are to write suggestions for openly communicating in a respectful manner in given situations.

Levels of Communication

9. Have each student design a mobile, model, or poster to illustrate the types of communication that occur at each of the three levels of full communication.

10. Have students look again at the descriptions of problems in relationships that they wrote in Learning Experience 3. Ask them to analyze the level at which communication was lacking in each fictitious situation. Discuss these analyses in class.

11. *Your Communication Skills,* Activity D, SAG. Students are to list six communication skills. Then they are to evaluate their own abilities related to each of the six skills and describe what steps they might take to improve those skills.

The Importance of Active Listening

12. Have students role-play situations that allow them to practice being good listeners and giving feedback.

13. Have each student write a story involving a situation in which a hidden message is used. Ask students to share their stories in class.

14. Guest speaker. Invite a psychologist to speak to your class about the importance of listening. Ask the speaker to give tips on how to listen and provide feedback.

Skill in Conflict Resolution

15. *Conflict Resolution,* color transparency CT-10, TR. Use this master as you work through an example of conflict resolution with students. Identify the elements of good communication in order to resolve conflict and reach a mutually beneficial goal. Ask students to share personal examples of when communication was successful.

16. Have students brainstorm a list of common conflict situations that occur in certain types of relationships, such as husband-wife, parent-child, etc.

17. Discuss with students the various conflict situations listed in Learning Experience 16. Ask students to analyze the situations to answer the following questions:
    • Are any of these conflicts caused by differing values? If so, what values are involved?
    • Are any of these conflicts caused by poor communication?
    • What are the problems causing the conflicts?
    • How can each problem be turned into a goal?
    • Are respect, trust, responsibility, or openness being violated in any of these situations?

18. Have students make up a puppet play to teach young children about positive conflict resolution. If possible, arrange for students to perform the puppet play for a preschool or kindergarten class.

19. Have students role-play situations to show the advantages of diagnosing the cause of a problem.

20. *Using "I" Messages,* Activity B, SAG. Students are to convert "you" messages into "I" messages.

21. *Conflict Resolution,* Activity C, SAG. Students are to apply the steps of positive conflict resolution to an interpersonal conflict situation.

22. *Resolving Conflicts Constructively,* reproducible master 10-1, TR. Create a role-play situation showing conflict between two people that includes the elements outlined on the master. Present the role-play for your class. Have students answer the questions on the handout based on what they see in the role-play.

23. Divide the class into groups. Ask each group to role-play a conflict situation in which the person, rather than the problem, is being attacked. Discuss each role-play and then have the group replay the situation using the more constructive approach of attacking the problem.
24. *Avoiding Negative Communication,* reproducible master 10-2, TR. Ask students to substitute positive messages and feelings for the negative ones resulting from the communication-blocking statements listed on the master.
25. Ask each student to find an article in a book or magazine about problem ownership. Ask students to summarize their articles for the class.
26. Ask students to give examples of situations illustrating a person assuming ownership of someone else's problem.

Answer Key

Text

To Review
1. inner
2. Open
3. At the informational level, you communicate thoughts, ideas, plans, beliefs, or stories. At the emotional level, you communicate feelings through nonverbal communication. At the behavioral level, you communicate by doing. When you communicate at all three levels, your message is more likely to be understood.
4. (Student response.)
5. Body language consists of your body movements, facial expressions, and posture. (Explanation is student response.)
6. (Student response. Give three examples.)
7. (Student response.)
8. Define the problem and find out what caused the conflict. Change the problem into a mutually acceptable goal. Work together to seek alternatives for reaching the goal. Evaluate each alternative and choose the most constructive one. Implement the plan. Evaluate the solution.
9. B, C, and E are true.
10. The person concerned or upset about the situation is said to own the problem.

Teacher's Resources

Chapter 10 Test
1. C
2. E
3. G
4. F
5. B
6. A
7. D
8. H
9. T
10. T
11. T
12. F
13. F
14. T
15. T
16. T
17. T
18. F
19. A
20. D
21. B
22. C
23. D
24. Communication is more than just talking. It involves sharing ideas and feelings with other people. People communicate verbally through speaking and writing, as well as nonverbally. Students may include a variety of specific methods of communication.
25. Communicating with yourself is called inner communication. It involves getting in touch with yourself and your feelings. In communicating with yourself, you learn to identify all the voices and feelings inside of you and set value priorities. Having skill in inner communication gives you more control over what you communicate to others.
26. Information level: Thoughts, ideas, plans, beliefs, or stories are communicated. Emotional level: Feelings are communicated through nonverbal communication. Behavioral level: Communication is expressed through actions.
27. "I" messages do not violate respect, trust, responsibility, or openness in relationships. They attack the problem rather than the person. They help the other person understand how you see the situation. They create a challenge for the other person in deciding what to do about your feelings.

Reproducible Master 10-1

Resolving Conflicts Constructively

Name _____ **Date** _____ **Period** _____

Complete this exercise as you view a role-play showing conflict between two people.

1. How would Person A define the problem? _____
   _____
   _____

2. How would Person B define the problem? _____
   _____
   _____

3. What behavior of Person A contributes to the problem? _____
   _____
   _____

4. What behavior of Person B contributes to the problem? _____
   _____
   _____

5. What event or events triggered the conflict? _____
   _____
   _____

6. What is the simplest way to define the problem?_____
   _____
   _____

7. What are the areas of difference or disagreement between Person A and Person B? _____
   _____
   _____

8. What are the areas of commonality or agreement between Person A and Person B? _____
   _____
   _____

9. What does Person A need to do in order to resolve the conflict? _____
   _____
   _____

10. What does Person B need to do in order to resolve the conflict? _____
    _____
    _____

11. How will Person A and Person B know if the conflict has been resolved? _____
    _____
    _____

Reproducible Master 10-2

Avoiding Negative Communication

Name _____ **Date** _____ **Period** _____

The italicized statements below block communication by communicating negative messages and producing negative feelings. Read the statements and answer the questions, focusing on positive communication.

1. *"Stop crying." "Try harder." "You must..."*

   Briefly describe a situation in which you might use one of these statements. _____
   _____
   _____
   _____

   These statements communicate directing, ordering, and commanding. What type of message are you really trying to communicate in the situation you just described? _____
   _____

   These statements often produce feelings of fright, defensiveness, resistance, resentment, vengeance, and rebellion. What feelings should you try to produce in this situation? _____
   _____

2. *"If you do that, you'll be..." "You'd better..."*

   Briefly describe a situation in which you might use one of these statements. _____
   _____
   _____
   _____

   These statements communicate threatening, warning, and punishing. What type of message are you really trying to communicate in the situation you just described? _____
   _____

   These statements often produce feelings of resentment, fear, anger, resistance, and rebellion. What feelings should you try to produce in this situation? _____
   _____

3. *"When you're older, you'll realize..." "The fact is,..."*

   Briefly describe a situation in which you might use one of these statements. _____
   _____
   _____

   These statements communicate lecturing, arguing, and persuading. What type of message are you really trying to communicate in the situation you just described? _____
   _____

   These statements often produce feelings of defensiveness, anger, and resistance to openness. What feelings should you try to produce in this situation? _____
   _____

(Continued)

Name _____

4. *"You never..." "You always..."*

   Briefly describe a situation in which you might use one of these statements. _____

   _____

   _____

   These statements communicate criticizing and blaming. What type of message are you really trying to communicate in the situation you just described? _____

   _____

   These statements often produce feelings of lowered self-esteem, guilt, resentment, and resistance to openness. What feelings should you try to produce in this situation? _____

   _____

5. *"Oh sure, you're always right." "I bet. "*

   Briefly describe a situation in which you might use one of these statements. _____

   _____

   _____

   These statements communicate teasing and sarcasm. What type of message are you really trying to communicate in the situation you just described? _____

   _____

   These statements often produce feelings of anger, frustration, resentment, and rejection. What feelings should you try to produce in this situation? _____

   _____

6. *"No, not now." "I won't discuss it anymore."*

   Briefly describe a situation in which you might use one of these statements. _____

   _____

   _____

   These statements communicate avoiding, withdrawing, and diverting. What type of message are you really trying to communicate in the situation you just described? _____

   _____

   These statements often produce feelings of frustration, lack of respect, and anxiety. What feelings should you try to produce in this situation? _____

   _____

Effective Communication

Name _____

Date _____ Period _____ Score _____

Chapter 10 Test

Matching: Each of the statements or situations listed below is an example of a communication term. Write the letter of the correct communication term in the blank.

_____ 1. "Don't you have anything but jeans to wear?"

_____ 2. "I'm angry that my parents won't let me go to the party tonight, yet I'm somewhat relieved since I have to be at work at 7:30 in the morning."

_____ 3. "I'm wondering why you smoke so often when it is evident that smoking makes you more susceptible to cancer, heart disease, and other illnesses."

_____ 4. Jim throws his helmet to the ground as the other team scores a touchdown.

_____ 5. Beaming with pride, Roberta's father hugs her and congratulates her for winning the award.

_____ 6. "What I hear you saying, Sarah, is you are afraid you will not pass the math course."

_____ 7. "I feel uneasy and concerned when you do not arrive home by the time you say you will."

_____ 8. "You are so irresponsible. You should never have left the car windows down last night when you knew it was going to rain."

A. feedback

B. full communication

C. hidden message

D. "I" message

E. inner communication

F. nonverbal communication

G. open communication

H. "you" message

True/False: Circle *T* if the statement is true or *F* if the statement is false.

T   F   9. A good relationship is likely to exist if respect, trust, responsibility, and openness are communicated to the other person over time.

T   F   10. If you communicate effectively, the message you send is the same as the messages received.

T   F   11. Effective inner communication involves setting value priorities.

T   F   12. Communication takes place on four levels: the informational level, the hidden message level, the emotional level, and the behavioral level.

T   F   13. In an "I" message, the person asks questions and repeats what he or she feels has been said.

T   F   14. Presence of conflict in relationships is normal, natural, and inevitable.

(Continued)

Name _____

T F 15. In interpersonal conflict situations, it is helpful to first pinpoint the issue that is causing the conflict.

T F 16. "I" messages help the other person understand how you perceive the situation.

T F 17. When an "I" message is used, the other person is challenged to decide what to do about your feelings.

T F 18. If another person's behavior is bothering you, it is that person's problem.

Multiple Choice: Choose the best answer and write the corresponding letter in the blank.

_____ 19. Verbal communication relates to_____.
    A. both speaking and writing
    B. eye contact
    C. your thoughts and opinions about what others say and do
    D. All of the above.

_____ 20. When you learn to communicate with yourself, you _____.
    A. are more likely to communicate effectively with others
    B. learn to identify all the voices and feelings inside of you
    C. are learning to set value priorities
    D. All of the above.

_____ 21. Which of the following illustrates communication at the emotional level?
    A. Having a surprise birthday party for your brother.
    B. Giving a friend a hug.
    C. Telling your sister that you want to borrow her favorite sweater.
    D. Going to a school dance.

_____ 22. "I" messages _____.
    A. tell the other person what you don't like about him or her
    B. tend to attack the other person
    C. are your feelings about the situation and a statement of the behavior or situation that bothers you
    D. are more destructive than helpful when used in conflict resolution

_____ 23. Which of the following usually occurs in conflict resolution when persons work together to seek alternatives?
    A. Evaluation of alternatives.
    B. Negotiation.
    C. Compromise.
    D. All of the above.

Essay Questions: Provide the answers you feel best show your understanding of the subject matter.

24. Define communication and describe ways in which people communicate.

25. Describe what is meant by communicating with yourself.

26. Full communication takes place at three levels. Name and describe these three levels.

27. State reasons why the use of "I" messages can be helpful in resolving conflicts.

11

The Family Today

Objectives

When students have completed this chapter, they will be able to

- explain why the family survives as an institution.
- describe ways families meet basic human needs.
- analyze challenges the family faces due to social and technological changes.
- cite the characteristics of a functional family.
- describe crises that can have major effects on a family.
- describe resources available to families.

Bulletin Boards

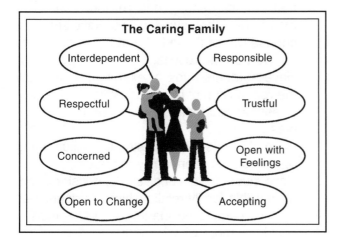

The Caring Family

Interdependent · Responsible · Respectful · Trustful · Concerned · Open with Feelings · Open to Change · Accepting

Title: *The Caring Family*

Cut out three pictures of several types of families and place in the center of the board. Place colored circles around the pictures with the characteristics of caring families written in each circle as shown.

Title: *The Family—Meeting Human Needs*

Divide the board into five sections and give each section one of the following labels: *Physical Needs, Love and Acceptance, Recognition, Self-Worth, Respect*. Have students fill each section with pictures that show families satisfying the appropriate need.

Teaching Materials

Text, pages 183-194
   To Review
   To Challenge Your Thinking
   To Do with the Class
   To Do with Your Community
Student Activity Guide
   A. *Families—Meeting Human Needs*
   B. *Change and Families*
   C. *A Family Who Cares*
   D. *Family Crises*
Teacher's Resources
   What Is a Family? reproducible master 11-1
   Chapter 11 Test
   Change Is Constant for Today's Family, color
      transparency CT-11

Introductory Activities

1. Have students write a brief paper titled *Why My Family Is Important to Me*. Students should share their ideas with others in the class.
2. *What Is a Family?* reproducible master 11-1, TR. Have students read the definitions of family and use the questions that follow to evaluate the definitions. Have students discuss their responses in class.

Instructional Concepts and Student Learning Experiences

The Importance of Families

3. Have students discuss the strengths and weaknesses of various family forms.
4. Have students examine the four family forms listed in Chart 11-2 found in the text and brainstorm a list of factors that all four forms of families have in common.
5. *Families—Meeting Human Needs,* Activity A, SAG. Have students write situations to illustrate how the family can meet each of the listed basic needs for children and for parents.
6. Have students write a fictional story about a person in a culture where families as they are known in our culture do not exist. The story should focus on how the person's needs would be met.
7. *Change Is Constant for Today's Family,* color transparency CT-11, TR. Use this transparency to identify influences that challenge today's families. Discuss how these influences can be positive or negative.
8. *Change and Families,* Activity B, SAG. Have students list five changes, either societal or technological, that have occurred. Then describe how these changes have affected their families either positively or negatively.
9. Have students compare the functions of families of the past to functions of families today.
10. Have students research to find societal trends pertaining to economics, occupations, education, religion, laws, and health care. Students should try to project how these trends will affect families.
11. Have students discuss how government action and changes in laws affect families. Actions to be discussed might include changes in income tax structures, equal opportunity laws, laws regarding welfare, changes in policies regarding mass transportation, and changes in policies that affect housing opportunities.
12. Panel discussion. Invite people with various areas of expertise to talk about trends within their area and effects of these trends on the family. Guests might include lawyers, stockbrokers, consumer product specialists, and government officials.

The Functional Family

13. Have students work together as a class to identify ways in which family members depend on each other physically, intellectually, emotionally, and socially.
14. Have students write a short paper giving examples of how interdependence in the family requires a cooperative use of resources.
15. Have students discuss dependency. Students should cite instances when dependency is healthy and when it may hamper a person's own growth and ability to be independent when needed.
16. Divide the class into small groups for a discussion. Have each group discuss how the irresponsible actions of one family member might affect other family members. Each group should choose one example and plan and perform a skit based on that example.
17. Have students react to the statement "Your privileges are in direct relationship to the responsibilities you assume."
18. Panel discussion. Invite three parents of teenagers and their teenage children to discuss trust and responsibility in the family. Students should prepare questions in advance for the panelists.
19. Have students discuss the idea that trust is hard to build up but easy to destroy.
20. Have students make a list of specific ways that they can show concern and respect for members of their own families. Have students choose two of these to try at home and write a report on the results.
21. Have students think of examples that show the recognition of individual worth in the family setting. Students should share their examples with the class.
22. Have students role-play situations illustrating openness between family members.
23. Have students list conditions that foster openness within family relationships. Students may start by completing the following statement: I could talk more with _____ if...
24. Guest speaker. Invite a communications specialist to discuss how to be open and accepting, not offending, when communicating with family members.

25. Have students discuss how families can help members prepare for changes in societal thinking. For instance, society once felt strongly that competition was the highest value in becoming successful. Families therefore needed to teach their children to compete if the children were to succeed. Emerging today in society is the idea that cooperation is the highest value in becoming successful. Therefore, families need to teach their children to negotiate and cooperate to become successful. How can parents who were raised with one ideal help prepare children for the new ideal?

26. Have students divide into small groups and discuss changes that families and family members have to face. Students should discuss possible effects of not being willing to accept these changes.

27. *A Family Who Cares,* Activity C, SAG. Have students fill in the chart provided with ways that a teenager and a parent could promote each characteristic of a caring family.

Families in Crises

28. *Family Crises,* Activity D, SAG. Have each student find an article in a newspaper or periodical related to family crises and share interesting information from the article with others in the class.

29. Role-play situations that might occur in families experiencing any of the crises included in this chapter.

Resources for Families

30. Working in groups, investigate resources that might be available to people in your community that deal with various family crises. Report your findings to the class.

31. Collect brochures, pamphlets, and other information from various support or resource groups within the community. Have students work in pairs or groups to briefly share the main focus and key information that can be used to help families.

32. Guest speaker. Invite a representative from a family counseling agency to speak on the importance of family members being open to change.

Answer Key

Text

To Review
1. Nuclear
2. Single-parent
3. Blended
4. Extended
5. (Name four:) love, acceptance, feelings of self-worth, respect, recognition from others, room to grow and develop capabilities, food, shelter, clothing
6. false
7. Family members are interdependent. Family members are responsible and trustful. Family members show respect and concern. Family members openly express and accept feelings. Family members are open to change.
8. (List four:) Protecting the child. Providing discipline that guides the child toward self-control. Providing opportunities to express feelings. Providing opportunities to develop. Helping their children learn to cope with problems effectively.
9. leveling
10. (Describe three:) Family violence, child abuse and neglect, substance abuse, divorce, suicide, and other answers may be considered.

Teacher's Resources

Chapter 11 Test
1. B
2. D
3. A
4. C
5. T
6. T
7. F
8. F
9. F
10. F
11. F
12. T
13. D
14. D
15. A
16. A
17. (Student response.)
18. (Student response.)
19. (Student response.)
20. (Student response.)

Reproducible Master 11-1

What Is a Family?

Name _____ **Date** _____ **Period** _____

Read the following information about the definition of family and answer the questions that follow. Discuss your answers in class.

The American Association of Family and Consumer Sciences (AAFCS) provides a general definition of family that applies to most family systems:

→ A family is two or more people who share resources, share responsibility for decision making, share values and goals, and have commitment to one another over time.

People also define the family in other ways:

→ Parents and their children.

→ Parents, their children, and relatives.

→ People related by blood, marriage, or adoption who share common experiences and mutual concerns.

→ Two or more people who have mutual relationships of care or concern.

→ Two or more people living together in a household, exchanging resources, and maintaining a commitment over time.

Many people accept one or more of the definitions of family listed above. However, some types of families do not fit every definition. The definition provided by AAFCS best describes most family forms.

1. Which of the definitions above most closely fits your definition of *family*? _____

   _____

   _____

2. Are there any definitions listed above that you do not accept? If so, explain which one and why.

   _____

   _____

   _____

   _____

3. Write your own definition of *family*. _____

   _____

   _____

   _____

   _____

The Family Today

Name _____

Date _____ Period _____ Score _____

Chapter 11 Test

Matching: Match the following terms and identifying phrases.

_____ 1. Events that affect one family often affect each of
the other family members.

_____ 2. Being dependable and reliable.

_____ 3. Having a special interest in what happens in the
lives of others.

_____ 4. Letting others know how you feel about them
and their behavior.

A. concern

B. interdependence

C. leveling

D. responsible

True/False: Circle *T* if the statement is true or *F* if the statement is false.

T   F   5. A caring family is able to meet the basic human needs of family members.

T   F   6. Many factors outside the home influence children's lives.

T   F   7. Because the family unit is so strong, the actions of individual family members do not
affect the unit as a whole.

T   F   8. Responsibility and trust have no relationship to each other.

T   F   9. Until a child is old enough to assume family responsibilities, that child is not entitled to
respect from others.

T   F   10. The three components of open expression are sharing, leveling, and conceding.

T   F   11. Members of a caring family hide their negative feelings.

T   F   12. Caring families prepare family members to deal with change and look at change as an
opportunity for personal growth.

Multiple Choice: Choose the best answer and write the corresponding letter in the blank.

_____ 13. Interdependence in a caring family is shown by the fact that _____.
A. events that affect one family member often have some effect on the others
B. many services are performed by one family member for another
C. behavior of individual family members often affects the success of the family
as a unit
D. All of the above.

_____ 14. Which of the following is true about trust?
A. Responsibility breeds trust.
B. Trust develops as basic needs are met within the family.
C. Unless a person is given a certain degree of trust, that person cannot practice
responsibility.
D. All of the above.

(Continued)

Name _____

_____ 15. Which of the following is true about respect?
A. Every family member is entitled to respect.
B. Respect means agreeing and approving of another person's opinions or feelings.
C. A child cannot expect to be respected by his or her parents when he or she makes mistakes.
D. All of the above.

_____ 16. Open expression is promoted by all of the following except letting others know _____.
A. their feelings are unacceptable
B. how you feel about their behavior
C. how good you feel about them
D. if you disagree with some of their ideas

Essay Questions: Provide the answers you feel best show your understanding of the subject matter.

17. List and describe three family forms.

18. Describe several challenges to the family that exist today and did not exist many years ago.

19. Describe three characteristics of a caring family.

20. Describe a type of family crisis and explain what organizations are available to help the family experiencing that crisis.

The Marriage Relationship

Objectives

When students have completed this chapter, they will be able to
- explain the factors that influence marital success.
- analyze the importance of mutual expectations in a marriage.
- recognize marriage adjustments commonly made throughout married life.
- explain the advantage of anticipating adjustments and of mutual efforts in solving problems.

Bulletin Boards

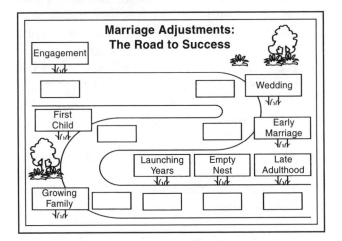

Title: *Marriage Adjustments: The Road to Success*

Draw a curving road on the bulletin board. Place signs along the road with the following labels: *engagement, wedding, early marriage, first child, growing family, launching years, empty nest, late adulthood.* If possible, get pictures of the same couple at each of these stages of their married life to place on the road.

Title: *Marriage Commitment???*

Have students collect magazine and newspaper articles related to marriage and divorce to post on the bulletin board.

Teaching Materials

Text, pages 195-205
    To Review
    To Challenge Your Thinking
    To Do with the Class
    To Do with Your Community
Student Activity Guide
    A. *Success Through the Years*
    B. *Marriage Adjustments*
    C. *Maturity and Marriage*
    D. *Mutual Expectations About Marriage*
Teacher's Resources
    Maturity Characteristics Related to Marriage, transparency master 12-1
    Adjustments Early in Marriage, reproducible master 12-2
    Chapter 12 Test
    Marital Success, color transparency CT-12

Introductory Activities

1. *Success Through the Years,* Activity A, SAG. Have students interview four couples who have been married for 20 or more years, asking them to tell why they feel their marriages have been a success. (*Marriage Adjustments,* Activity B in the *Student Activity Guide,* involves a second interview with the same four couples. You may wish to have students complete this activity now and save it for discussion later in the chapter.)
2. Have students brainstorm a list of factors that they feel affect the quality of relationships between husbands and wives. As students study the chapter, ask them to note which of the items they listed are discussed in the text.

Instructional Concepts and Student Learning Experiences

Factors Influencing Marital Success

3. *Marital Success,* color transparency CT-12, TR. Use this transparency as a basis of discussion about how to attain marital success. Ask students to define and share examples in each of the areas of maturity, cultural and family influences, shared interest, and mutual expectations.

4. Provide telephone books for students. Ask them to use the Yellow Pages to identify the variety of resources available in their community to assist people in planning and preparing for marriage. (Students should focus more on counseling and guidance resources than on resources related to the wedding ceremony.) Ask them to also identify resources available to assist couples after marriage.

5. *Maturity and Marriage,* Activity C, SAG. Have students complete a chart describing a mature person and an immature person as related to different types of maturity.

6. Ask students to identify and analyze problems that often occur in youthful marriages.

7. Have students discuss the meaning of the statement, "We do not fall in love...but instead, we grow in love."

8. *Maturity Characteristics Related to Marriage,* transparency master 12-1, TR. Use the transparency to stimulate discussion of how immaturity characteristics might weaken a marital relationship and maturity characteristics might strengthen it.

9. Have each student write a two-page essay about ways that love can be expressed in everyday living.

10. Ask students to identify personal values that might influence marital success. Have them use their lists to discuss problems that might arise in marriages where values are in conflict.

11. Have students write their reactions to the statement "All marriages are mixed marriages."

12. Ask students to discuss the effects of cultural upbringing on individual attitudes toward marriage and childbearing.

13. Ask students to write about childhood experiences that influenced their attitudes and expectations about marriage and family living. (Students should not be required to share their papers with others.)

14. Have students debate the topic, "You marry an individual, not his or her family."

15. Have each student interview a couple who has been married a number of years. Ask students to find out what interests they shared before marriage and what mutual interests they developed after marriage.

16. Have students brainstorm a list of reasons for marrying. Ask them to discuss weak and strong points of each reason. Then have them identify those reasons that might be given by a person who is committed to the goal of a successful marriage.

17. Ask students to explain what criteria they use for measuring marital success.

18. Have students role-play situations in which a husband and wife have conflicting role expectations. Repeat each role-play to show how the conflict may be logically resolved.

19. Have students brainstorm a list of the many roles both husbands and wives might assume.

20. Have students make a list of three areas that they think should be discussed before marriage. The list might include financial goals, handling finances, desire for children, views on disciplining children, household responsibilities, etc. Ask them to write paragraphs describing their positions on each area.

21. Panel discussion. Invite a married couple, a member of the clergy, and a marriage counselor to discuss the importance of sharing future expectations with your partner before marriage.

22. *Mutual Expectations About Marriage,* Activity D, SAG. Have students complete the chart by listing two contrasting attitudes for each type of expectation.

Mutual Adjustments in Marriage

23. *Adjustments Early in Marriage,* reproducible master 12-2, TR. Ask students to evaluate how they would handle some adjustments that are common to all newlyweds. Have students discuss their answers with a partner.

24. Have students debate the statement "The ideal marriage has no need for adjustment."

25. Have each student read an article about a social force that is impacting marriage relationships in today's society. Ask students to write reports summarizing what they have read. Ask them to also give their opinions on why these social forces did not have as much impact on marriages in the past.

26. Ask students to explain why husband-wife relationships may be strained during middle age.
27. Discuss with students how marital adjustments associated with the birth of a child may be less traumatic for couples who have had time to make earlier adjustments in their marriage relationships.
28. Discuss with students why agreeing about child discipline and training is important for couples. Have students predict the results if husbands and wives do not agree on this issue.
29. Have students list physical and psychological characteristics associated with aging. Ask students to discuss what effects any of these characteristics might have on husband-wife relationships.
30. *Marriage Adjustments,* Activity B, SAG. Have students interview the same four couples they interviewed for Activity A, *Success Through the Years.* Have students ask the couples about adjustments they have made during various periods of their married lives.
31. Guest speaker. Invite someone from a family service agency to speak to your class about the kinds of adjustments that bring people in for counseling.

Answer Key

Text

To Review
1. false
2. Social
3. Emotional
4. Intellectual
5. (List five:) Are comfortable with themselves. Recognize their abilities and accept their shortcomings. Are independent. Have an increased awareness and concern about others. Understand and control their emotions. Can express emotions in appropriate ways. Able to learn from daily experiences and to adapt to new situations.
6. Promising to work to bind the marriage together throughout life.
7. Lifestyle refers to the way people live their lives. It includes their possessions and their patterns of living.

8. (Student response.)
9. (Student response.)
10. (List two reasons for each stage of life. Student response.)

Teacher's Resources

Chapter 12 Test
1. D
2. G
3. E
4. C
5. B
6. A
7. F
8. F
9. T
10. T
11. T
12. F
13. T
14. T
15. T
16. B
17. C
18. D
19. B
20. Mature people have learned to be comfortable with themselves. They recognize their abilities and accept their shortcomings. When you can accept yourself as you really are, you are more likely to be able to develop and maintain a relationship with another person. This is particularly so in a commitment such as marriage. You will find it difficult to respect, trust, and care for another person if you are not comfortable with yourself.
21. In today's world, the decision to marry is only one of several options. Whether or not a person stays married is a matter of choice. One person might feel that marriage is a lifelong commitment, while another person feels it is a temporary arrangement. It is helpful if both partners agree on marriage as a commitment. Marital adjustments would be very challenging if one partner believed in traditional commitment and the other saw marriage as only a temporary arrangement.
22. (Student response.)
23. (Student response.)
24. (Student response. Describe three.)

Transparency Master 12-1

Maturity Characteristics Related to Marriage

Immaturity

→ Moody and erratic. Imposes moods on spouse.

→ Is competitive and aggressive. Tries to have own way.

→ Tends to belittle spouse.

→ Is rigid, cannot admit mistakes, must always be right and thinks spouse is wrong.

→ Makes snap judgments, acts on impulse.

→ Does not face problems constructively, then blames spouse for results.

→ Lives for today. Does not look ahead except in a "dream world."

→ Tends to use defense mechanisms to hide the truth about own weaknesses.

→ Is irresponsible in use of money, spends impulsively.

→ Depends on parents rather than consulting spouse about important decisions.

→ Relies heavily on spouse to make everyday decisions.

→ Considers own wants and needs more important than the wants and needs of spouse.

→ Is easily hurt and shows jealousy.

Maturity

→ Is not moody, and uses constructive ways to work out feelings.

→ Deals with spouse in a cooperative way.

→ Recognizes spouse's weaknesses and emphasizes spouse's strengths.

→ Is flexible, accepts blame when it is due, analyzes situations fairly.

→ Is reasonably cautious in making decisions.

→ Uses problem-solving approach, analyzing possible consequences for self and spouse.

→ Is realistic about expectations and goals.

→ Has a healthy self-concept including a complete and realistic understanding of self.

→ Makes responsible decisions related to the earning and spending of money.

→ Is reasonably independent of parents, involves spouse in decision-making process.

→ Acts independently in handling daily tasks.

→ Can sacrifice personal preferences for the good of spouse.

→ Is self-confident, secure in the relationship, trusting of spouse.

Reproducible Master 12-2

Adjustments Early in Marriage

Name _____ **Date** _____ **Period** _____

Answer the following questions to help you evaluate how you would handle some adjustments that are common to all newlyweds. Then discuss your answers with a partner.

Day-to-Day Situations

1. What habits do you have that your spouse might need to adjust to? _____

   _____

2. What habits do you think you would have trouble adjusting to in a spouse? _____

   _____

Division of Responsibilities

Make up a plan for dividing household responsibilities fairly between you and a spouse. List specific tasks in each of the following areas that you might do and that your spouse might do.

3. Meal planning and preparation.
   You: _____

   Spouse:_____

4. Clothing care.
   You: _____

   Spouse:_____

5. Housekeeping.
   You: _____

   Spouse:_____

6. Home maintenance and repairs.
   You: _____

   Spouse:_____

7. Car maintenance and repairs.
   You: _____

   Spouse:_____

8. Bill payment and record keeping. (This refers to performing tasks such as writing checks and maintaining accounts. Deciding who's earnings will be used for which expenses will be covered in a later section.)
   You: _____

   Spouse:_____

(Continued)

Name _____

Social Life

9. What types of interests do you have that your spouse might not share? _____

_____

10. What types of interests might your spouse have that you would not share? _____

_____

Financial Responsibilities

11. Who do you anticipate will work to generate income for your household?

_____ You _____ Spouse _____ Both

12. If both you and your spouse would be generating income, how do you think you would divide expenses? (These expenses would include rent or mortgage payments, car payments, insurance premiums, medical care, food and other grocery items, clothing, utilities, transportation, entertainment, gifts and contributions, and savings.) For instance, maybe you and your spouse would evenly split some or all expenses. You might split expenses in proportion with your earnings. Perhaps you would cover certain expenses and your spouse would cover others. In the space below, make up a plan for sharing financial responsibilities fairly with your spouse.

_____

_____

_____

_____

_____

13. Why do you think it might be important to discuss the items on this worksheet with your partner before you get married? _____

_____

_____

_____

_____

_____

The Marriage Relationship

Name _____

Date _____ Period _____ Score _____

Chapter 12 Test

Matching: Match the following terms and identifying phrases.

_____ 1. Involves abilities related to communicating, solving problems, and reasoning.

_____ 2. Indicates moving from a dependent self to a more independent self and becoming less self-centered and more concerned about others.

_____ 3. The way people live their lives—including their possessions and their pattern of living.

_____ 4. Involves the ability to understand and control emotions.

_____ 5. Exists when a couple share similar interests and enjoy doing activities together.

_____ 6. Similar to a pledge or promise.

_____ 7. Each person cares about the well-being of the other person, and they realistically accept each other for their positive characteristics along with those characteristics that are not as desirable.

A. commitment

B. companionship

C. emotional maturity

D. intellectual maturity

E. lifestyle

F. mature love

G. social maturity

True/False: Circle *T* if the statement is true or *F* if the statement is false.

T F   8. Age and maturity are the same.

T F   9. Being able to express anger in appropriate ways is an indication of emotional maturity.

T F   10. Unhealthy dependency on parents of one of the marriage partners often puts a strain on the marriage.

T F   11. Common interests are a bond that holds husband and wife together.

T F   12. The women's liberation movement and the increased number of women in the workforce have made role expectations more clearly defined.

T F   13. Lifestyle and career choices are closely related.

T F   14. Throughout married life, there are specific stages that almost always require adjustments.

T F   15. It is important to the success of a marriage that the husband and wife develop and maintain a relationship beyond their children.

(Continued)

Name _____

Multiple Choice: Choose the best answer and write the corresponding letter in the blank.

_____ 16. For a husband and wife to live together successfully, _____.
   A. each of the marriage partners must accept all of the other person's values
   B. both husband and wife must accept some values that differ from their own
   C. one of the marriage partners must be willing to take on all of the other person's values
   D. each of the partners should maintain their own separate sets of values and not discuss them

_____ 17. An example of a positive factor in marriage success would be _____.
   A. Jim's father was the patriarch of the family, and what he said was what was done
   B. Jim is outgoing, while Jackie is rather shy
   C. Jim and Jackie enjoy bowling together
   D. Jackie has two brothers and three sisters, while Jim is an only child

_____ 18. Which of the following statements about lifestyle is true?
   A. With various lifestyles come advantages and disadvantages.
   B. No one lifestyle is right or wrong.
   C. Two people who have very different lifestyle goals must be willing to adjust, or marriage will be very difficult.
   D. All of the above are true.

_____ 19. Which of the following statements about adjustments in marriage is true?
   A. Retirement is such a joyous occasion that few adjustments are needed.
   B. The birth of the first child usually causes adjustments for both husband and wife.
   C. Making adjustments at the time the children leave home is a very minor problem for most couples.
   D. All of the above are true.

Essay Questions: Provide the answers you feel best show your understanding of the subject matter.

20. Briefly describe how maturity influences a person's chances for success in a marriage.

21. Describe differing views on marriage as a commitment.

22. Briefly explain problems related to role expectations that could occur between two people considering marriage.

23. Describe a husband and wife whose expectations related to their lifestyle differ.

24. Describe three common marital adjustments throughout life and some of the reasons that each of these adjustments is necessary.

Parenting

Objectives

When students have completed this chapter, they will be able to
- describe responsibilities of parents to their children.
- explain how parental responsibilities influence the parent-child relationship.
- describe the stages of dependency children pass through as they mature.

Bulletin Boards

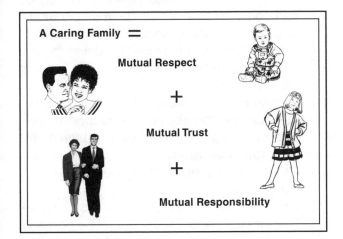

A Caring Family =

Mutual Respect

+

Mutual Trust

+

Mutual Responsibility

Title: *A Caring Family*

Put the wording *A Caring Family = Mutual Respect + Mutual Trust + Mutual Responsibility* on the bulletin board. Then put either drawings or pictures of parents on one side and children on the other.

Title: *Meeting Children's Needs*

Divide the bulletin board into two sections. Label one section *Meeting Physical Needs*. Label the other section *Meeting Psychological Needs*. Find pictures that illustrate these needs being met at various life stages.

Teaching Materials

Text, pages 206-215
   To Review
   To Challenge Your Thinking
   To Do with the Class
   To Do with Your Community
Student Activity Guide
   A. *Assuming Parental Responsibilities*
   B. *Parent-Child Communication*
   C. *Conflicting Views*
   D. *Changes in Dependency*
Teacher's Resources
   Meeting Children's Needs, reproducible
      master 13-1
   Trading Places, reproducible master 13-2
   Chapter 13 Test
   Parenting: Rewards and Responsibilities,
      color transparency CT-13

Introductory Activities

1. Have each student read an article on parent-child relationships from a popular magazine. Ask students to give brief oral reports summarizing the articles and giving their opinions of the information they read.
2. Have students brainstorm a list of parental characteristics that positively affect the quality of their relationships with their children.

Instructional Concepts and Student Learning Experiences

Rewards and Responsibilities of Parenting

3. *Parenting: Rewards and Responsibilities,* color transparency CT-13, TR. Use this transparency as an introductory activity to show that parenting has its rewards, but also responsibilities. Ask students to share what specific responsibilities are necessary in order to experience the rewards of parenting.

4. Have students develop a survey about how failure to fulfill each of the parental responsibilities discussed in the chapter could affect a parent's relationship with his or her child. Ask each student to use the survey to interview two parents.

5. Ask each student to interview a friend that has an excellent relationship with his or her parents. Have students ask the interviewees whether or not they feel their parents assumed each of the responsibilities discussed in the chapter.

6. *Assuming Parental Responsibilities,* Activity A, SAG. Have students use the worksheets to list examples of two specific ways parents might assume responsibilities related to meeting the psychological needs of teenagers.

7. Have students brainstorm a list of the many ways that parents meet the physical needs of their children each day.

8. *Meeting Children's Needs,* reproducible master 13-1, TR. Have students match situations with the parental responsibilities they describe.

9. Have students discuss the meaning of the statement "The home acts as a small world to which the child relates."

10. Have students discuss the effects that frequent criticism from parents can have on children.

11. Guest speaker. Invite a child care teacher or child care worker to speak to your class about how to show respect and acceptance for children through both verbal and nonverbal communication.

12. Have each student write a short story about a parent-child relationship that is strengthened through the parent's verbal or nonverbal show of caring for the child. Ask students to share and discuss their stories in class.

13. Have students draw a time line showing the life of a child from birth to age 18. Ask students to mark events along the time line through which parents might influence the development of the child's self-esteem.

14. Ask each student to write about an experience involving one or both parents that had a positive effect on his or her self-esteem. Ask volunteers to share their experiences with the class.

15. Have students debate the statement "People appreciate and value most those things that they work for, earn, or feel they really deserve."

16. Have students brainstorm a list of home and family responsibilities that people assume. Write student responses on the chalkboard.

17. Ask students to do a self-analysis on the positive values they have learned from their parents. (Students should not be required to share this analysis with their classmates.)

18. Divide the chalkboard into four sections headed *physical growth, social growth, emotional growth,* and *intellectual growth.* Have students brainstorm ways parents can encourage or provide experiences for each type of growth for their children.

19. Divide the class into five groups. Assign each group one of the following experiences: taking a walk in the park, spending an afternoon fishing, helping clean the basement, helping with the grocery shopping, going to an art fair. Ask each group to make a list of the ways a child could benefit from their assigned experience.

20. Ask students to discuss how clearly defined and consistently maintained limits contribute to a child's sense of security and direction.

21. Have a group of students develop and present a panel discussion on gaining self-discipline.

22. *Trading Places,* reproducible master 13-2, TR. Ask students to write positive responses parents could use when replying to statements often made by teens.

23. Have students read an article on a child's right to fail.

24. Guest speaker. Invite a psychologist to speak to your class about the therapeutic power of love in repairing psychological and physical damage.

25. Ask each student to write about a personal growth experience that occurred as the result of a failure. Ask volunteers to share their experiences with the class.

Changes in Dependency

26. Have students brainstorm a list of situations throughout life in which people are dependent on others.

27. Have each student write about a situation that illustrates negative dependence. Ask students to share their illustrations in class.

28. Discuss with students why independence is a necessary step in development.

29. Have students discuss ways in which parents might actually inhibit their child's independence.
30. *Parent-Child Communication,* Activity B, SAG. Students are to give examples of how teenagers could communicate feelings of respect, trust, openness, and a sense of responsibility to their parents. Also give examples of how parents might communicate these same feelings to their children.
31. *Conflicting Views,* Activity C, SAG. Have the students list four issues on which teens and parents often seem to have differing views. Considering what they have read in this chapter about parent-child relationships, have the students suggest ways that each might work to eliminate these differences.
32. *Changes in Dependency,* Activity D, SAG. Have students give examples of dependence, independence, and interdependence their friends have experienced with their families.
33. Panel discussion. Invite a panel of parents and teenagers to discuss how rapid social change has put an additional strain on parent-child relationships.

Answer Key

Text

To Review
1. independence, dependence
2. (Name four:) providing warmth, providing shelter, providing food, providing clothing, providing safety, feeding the child, dressing the child, providing a place to sleep, providing a place to play
3. (Student response. List six.)
4. dependent
5. independent
6. false
7. true
8. (Student response.)
9. (Student response.)
10. Interdependence

Teacher's Resources

Meeting Children's Needs,
reproducible master 13-1
1. G
2. D
3. I
4. A
5. C
6. H
7. B
8. F
9. E

Chapter 13 Test
1. D
2. C
3. F
4. A
5. B
6. E
7. T
8. F
9. T
10. T
11. F
12. F
13. F
14. F
15. B
16. C
17. A
18. B
19. (Student response. Name and give an example of four.)
20. When young adults become independent, they are able to make choices based on what they feel is right or wrong. For this independence to be established, there may be a period of withdrawal and separation from their parents. To become fully mature, young people must separate physically and emotionally from their parents.
21. Ideally there is a balance between freedom and responsibility in families. This balance is called interdependence. Family members work together and share each other's resources. A sense of give-and-take exists, yet family members maintain their own identities.

Reproducible Master 13-1

Meeting Children's Needs

Name _____ **Date** _____ **Period** _____

Beside each situation, write the letter of the parental responsibility it describes.

_____ 1. Dan's parents agreed to let him sign up for the baseball clinic.

_____ 2. Everyone complimented 12-year-old Molly on the delicious dinner she had prepared for the family.

_____ 3. Chou's father encouraged him to finish his science project without any help from his parents.

_____ 4. Baby Todd seems happier after his mother changes his dirty diaper.

_____ 5. Even though he lost the race, the pat on the back from his father made Frank feel a little better.

_____ 6. Rosa's parents insisted that she call them if, for some unexpected reason, she was going to be late getting home.

_____ 7. Mother and Dad did not laugh when little Tatum suggested he could sell his pet rabbit so that they might have more money to buy a new car they needed.

_____ 8. The church service on New Year's Eve was always very special to Carlos and his parents.

_____ 9. Sam's father felt that now that he was old enough to understand the importance of safe use of the power mower, he could take over much of the care of the lawn.

A. meeting physical needs

B. respecting each child

C. letting the child know someone cares about him or her

D. helping the children feel good about themselves

E. providing opportunities for responsibilities

F. transmitting values

G. providing opportunity for growth

H. guiding and disciplining

I. encouraging independence

Reproducible Master 13-2

Trading Places

Name _____ **Date** _____ **Period** _____

Below is a list of statements that some teenagers use when trying to sway a parent's opinion. Put yourself in the parent's place and write positive responses you could use in reply to each statement.

Teen	**Parent**
1. Everybody's doing it.	_____ _____ _____ _____
2. You want me to be weird.	_____ _____ _____ _____
3. But we can afford it.	_____ _____ _____ _____
4. You're treating me like a child.	_____ _____ _____ _____
5. Don't you want me to be part of the group?	_____ _____ _____ _____
6. You're old-fashioned.	_____ _____ _____ _____

(Continued)

Name _____

Teen	Parent

7. You don't trust me.

_____

_____

_____

_____

8. You hate my friends.

_____

_____

_____

_____

9. Susan's parents are letting her go.

_____

_____

_____

_____

10. How am I ever going to grow up if you don't let me make my own decisions?

_____

_____

_____

_____

11. Kids are different now from the way they were when you were a kid.

_____

_____

_____

_____

12. I need my privacy.

_____

_____

_____

_____

Parenting

Name _____

Date _____ **Period** _____ **Score** _____

Chapter 13 Test

Matching: Match the following terms and identifying phrases.

_____ 1. Working together and sharing each other's resources.

_____ 2. Making a choice of action and then taking full responsibility for the results.

_____ 3. The needs that relate to mental well-being and sense of worth.

_____ 4. Relying on others to satisfy your needs.

_____ 5. A process that guides children in the direction of independence and self-discipline.

_____ 6. The needs for warmth, shelter, food, clothing, and safety.

A. dependence

B. discipline

C. independence

D. interdependence

E. physical needs

F. psychological needs

True/False: Circle *T* if the statement is true or *F* if the statement is false.

T F   7. The quality of the parent-child relationship is extremely important to children.

T F   8. Children depend on their parents for psychological needs, such as food, clothing, and shelter.

T F   9. Parents play the most important role in providing the nurturing and stimulation that is required for early brain development.

T F   10. Parents can communicate caring to their children by being available when their children need them.

T F   11. Parents have little influence on their child's self-image.

T F   12. Discipline is a process of punishment.

T F   13. Independence means working together and cooperating in the use of each other's resources.

T F   14. It is important for parents to protect their children from failure.

Multiple Choice: Choose the best answer and write the corresponding letter in the blank.

_____ 15. Which of the following is NOT true?
   A. Young people need to know their parents care about them even when their actions have been negative.
   B. For children to know that they have been accepted, that acceptance must be given verbally.
   C. Parents can let their children know they care about them by respecting them as people.
   D. Knowing that their parents accept and respect them helps young people grow to maturity.

(Continued)

Name _____

_____ 16. The atmosphere in the home _____.
    A. has little or no influence on the development of children
    B. affects male children more than females
    C. influences the values children develop
    D. is more important to parents than to their children

_____ 17. Which of the following statements about limits is true?
    A. Limits help children learn appropriate behaviors.
    B. Limits are used to penalize children for their mistakes.
    C. Limits should be vaguely stated.
    D. Limits that are set when a child is very young will always stay the same.

_____ 18. Which of the following is NOT true?
    A. Overprotection takes away the child's independence.
    B. Children learn little through mistakes.
    C. It is important for parents to allow their children to fail.
    D. All of the above are NOT true.

Essay Questions: Provide the answers you feel best show your understanding of the subject matter.

19. Name four parental responsibilities and give an example of each responsibility.

20. Describe the importance of independence to mature development.

21. Explain the relationship between freedom and responsibility in a caring family.

Family Management

Objectives

When students have completed this chapter, they will be able to

◆ explain the factors that affect family management.

◆ list the steps in family decision making.

◆ describe challenges to making family decisions.

◆ recognize the importance of sharing family responsibilities.

◆ discuss guidelines for sharing family responsibilities.

Bulletin Boards

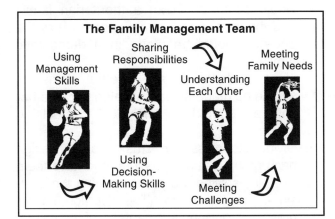

The Family Management Team

Using Management Skills

Sharing Responsibilities

Understanding Each Other

Meeting Family Needs

Using Decision-Making Skills

Meeting Challenges

Title: *The Family Management Team*

Draw or cut out the shapes of basketball players and a basketball hoop as shown. Place the following labels near the players: *Understanding Each Other*, *Using Management Skills*, *Meeting Challenges*, *Sharing Responsibilities*, and *Using Decision-Making Skills*. Place the label *Meeting Family Needs* above the basketball hoop.

Title: *Sharing Responsibilities*

Develop a chart that might be used by a family to indicate a division of family responsibilities on a daily basis. Place a large sample of the chart on the board. Fill in spaces with pictures showing people fulfilling the responsibilities listed on the chart.

Teaching Materials

Text, pages 216-228
To Review
To Challenge Your Thinking
To Do with the Class
To Do with Your Community

Student Activity Guide
A. *Factors Affecting Family Management*
B. *Assuming Management Responsibilities*
C. *Sharing Family Management*
D. *A Family Management Plan*

Teacher's Resources
Helps and Harms in Sharing Family Responsibilities, transparency master 14-1
Guidelines for Sharing Family Responsibilities, transparency master 14-2
Chapter 14 Test
The Family Life Cycle Stages, color transparency CT-14

Introductory Activities

1. Have students discuss families that are shown in popular television programs. Students should discuss whether the families spend realistic amounts of time on family responsibilities.

2. Have students brainstorm lists of human and nonhuman resources that families can use in managing their daily activities.

Instructional Concepts and Student Learning Experiences

Factors Affecting Family Management

3. Have students discuss each of the factors affecting family management listed in the text. Students should give examples illustrating how each factor can affect family management.

4. *Factors Affecting Family Management,* Activity A, SAG. Have students read each of the situations described and write explanations of factors in each situation that are likely to affect home and family management.

5. Guest speaker. Invite an adult who has experienced a major change in his or her family circumstance to speak with the class. The change may be loss of a family member, economic change, career change, etc. The speaker should discuss how the change affected the management of his or her family.

6. Have students discuss how family management would be different in a household with six children and in a household with one child.

7. Have students develop and perform a skit in which parents whose children are two and six compare family management with parents whose children are fourteen and eighteen.

8. Have students write a paper contrasting family management in a household with three children and one parent and in a household with three children and two parents.

9. *The Family Life Cycle Stages,* color transparency CT-14, TR. Use this transparency to introduce the various stages of the family life cycle. Ask students to share examples of roles and responsibilities in each of the stages.

10. Have students work together to develop a list of demands on the family in each stage of the family life cycle.

11. Divide the class into five groups. Have each group develop a list of resources that would be helpful in one of the five stages of the family life cycle. Have the class compare their lists.

12. Have students interview couples in their late adult years who have been through the five stages of the family life cycle. Students should ask them about the challenges they confronted along the way and how they were able to cope with those challenges. Have students discuss their findings in class.

13. Have students develop and perform skits that illustrate some of the friction resulting from differences in ideas about role expectations.

14. Invite a panel of people ranging in age from 20 to 60 to discuss the changing concepts of male and female roles.

15. Have each student make a list of his or her role expectations for various family roles. Students should compare their lists and try to identify factors that influenced various role expectations.

16. Have students role-play situations illustrating how family members can work together to clarify their values and goals. Students should discuss how doing this can avoid future conflict.

17. Have students write short stories illustrating standards that a family shares.

18. Guest speaker. Invite a family counselor to discuss how instability within the family affects the management of family lives.

19. As a class, have students make a list of typical family management problems. Discuss ways to turn those problems into goals.

Family Decision Making

20. Have students research what is meant by authoritarian family and democratic family. Have two groups role-play a family decision. One group should portray how the decision would be made in an authoritarian family and the other group should portray how the decision would be made in a democratic family.

21. Have students debate whether decisions should be made by parents alone or whether children should be included in decision making.

22. Divide the class into small groups. Assign each group a family problem, and have them role-play solving the problem using the decision-making process. (The decision-making process is outlined in Chapter 1 of the text.)

23. Select a group of students to role-play various barriers to family decision making. Have observing class members determine what barriers are causing problems and determine how the problems could be solved.

24. Have a group of students portray different family members whose personal goals conflict with those of other family members. Each family member should present his or her point of view to the class. Then have the class determine priorities for the family's goals.

Sharing Family Management Responsibilities

25. *Helps and Harms in Sharing Family Responsibilities,* transparency master 14-1, TR. Have students discuss why each item is listed as an item that may help the family in sharing management responsibilities or as an item that will not help the family.
26. Guest speaker. Invite an efficiency expert to discuss skills that are helpful in managing daily living.
27. Have students list benefits to the individual and to the family from sharing family management responsibilities.
28. Guest speaker. Invite a retired person to discuss division of family responsibilities when he or she was a child. Students should use information from the speaker to compare current division of family responsibilities to those when the speaker was a child.
29. Have each student make a list of family responsibilities that he or she has assumed. The student should choose three of the responsibilities listed and write explanations of how he or she has benefited from those experiences.
30. *Assuming Management Responsibilities,* Activity B, SAG. Have students analyze the responsibilities listed and write explanations of how having these responsibilities as a teen could benefit that person in the adult years.
31. Divide the class into groups. Have each group develop a list of tasks related to one aspect of the family. For instance, one group might develop a list of tasks related to the kitchen and family meals. Another group might work on tasks related to clothing. Combine the group work into one master list. Have students analyze the tasks to determine which family members could handle the responsibilities involved with each task.
32. *Guidelines for Sharing Family Responsibilities,* transparency master 14-2, TR. Have students discuss each guideline, giving examples of how the guideline could be used in family situations.
33. Have students react to the statement "There are no family responsibilities that must be done by only a male or only a female."
34. Have students describe some situations in which it would be unrealistic for a responsibility to be given to one family member.

35. *Sharing Family Management,* Activity C, SAG. Have students answer the questions provided about sharing family management responsibilities.
36. Have students interview families to find out the methods they use to divide management responsibilities among family members. Students should discuss their findings in class.
37. *A Family Management Plan,* Activity D, SAG. Have students develop plans for sharing management responsibilities within their own families. Students may develop the plan for another family or a fictitious family if they wish.

Answer Key

Text

To Review

1. (Name four:) family composition, life stages of the family, family stability, role expectations, change in family circumstances, management skills
2. beginning stage, expanding stage, developing stage, contracting stage, later years
3. The relationship greatly influences family management. Couples who have a positive relationship and communicate openly help the family to succeed in reaching their goals. In contrast, reaching family goals will be more difficult for couples who have a strained, angry relationship.
4. (List six:) understanding values, setting priorities, communicating effectively, having flexible standards, using resources wisely, having organizational skills, managing time and energy, having decision-making and problem-solving skills
5. problem, goal
6. false
7. true
8. (Student response.)
9. standards
10. (Describe four:) Develop a team effort attitude in assuming responsibilities. Give family members realistic responsibilities. Guide family members in doing tasks. Be flexible. Develop mutual standards. Avoid sexist division of responsibilities.

Student Activity Guide

Sharing Family Management, Activity C
1. Sharing family responsibilities meets the need for a feeling of self-worth, and children become self-confident. They develop skills and become self-reliant. Sharing responsibilities also increases family bonds.
2. When given realistic responsibilities, family members gain a sense of security and accomplishment. If responsibilities are too difficult, frustration and failure may result.
3. The responsibility should be appropriate for the person. Some family members may need guidance for doing a task. Family members should agree on standards for doing a task, but those standards may need to be relaxed for young children. Families should avoid sexist divisions of responsibilities.

Teacher's Resources

Chapter 14 Test
1. D
2. E
3. C
4. B
5. A
6. T
7. F
8. F
9. T
10. T
11. F
12. T
13. T
14. A
15. D
16. B
17. B
18. (Student response.)
19. (Student response.)
20. (Student response.)

Transparency Master 14-1

Helps and Harms in Sharing Family Responsibilities

May Help the Family

humor
fun
compromising
common goals
commitment
cooperation

respect
flexibility
sensitivity
trust
accepting responsibility

Will Not Help the Family

not listening
unclear issues
no defined goals
impatience
being afraid to speak
rejecting others' ideas
    without hearing them out

self-interest
rigid standards
unclear roles
lack of confidence
dependence

Transparency Master 14-2

Guidelines for Sharing Family Responsibilities

→ Develop a team effort attitude in assuming responsibilities.

→ Give family members realistic responsibilities.

→ Guide family members in doing tasks.

→ Be flexible.

→ Develop mutual standards.

→ Avoid sexist division of responsibilities.

Family Management

Name _____

Date _____ Period _____ Score _____

Chapter 14 Test

Matching: Match the following terms and identifying phrases.

_____ 1. The number of people in the family and the spacing in age of the children.

_____ 2. Behaviors expected in certain positions of responsibility.

_____ 3. Basic activity of the family group that is often used to solve problems and reach goals.

_____ 4. When one person must give in completely.

_____ 5. When each person gives up some things in order to reach the best decision.

A. compromise

B. concession

C. decision making

D. family composition

E. role expectations

True/False: Circle *T* if the statement is true or *F* if the statement is false.

T F 6. A larger family requires more resources for daily living than a small family.

T F 7. When a couple marry and establish a home, they are in the expanding stage of life.

T F 8. The type of relationship a husband and wife develop has little effect on family management.

T F 9. Families are likely to manage better when roles are clearly defined.

T F 10. The more values are understood, the more families are able to make choices directed toward their goals.

T F 11. Family decision making is usually easier than personal decision making because there are more people to help with the decision.

T F 12. In family decision making, compromise is often necessary.

T F 13. Two people may use different methods to complete a task and yet achieve similar results.

Multiple Choice: Choose the best answer and write the corresponding letter in the blank.

_____ 14. Which of the following illustrates organizational skills in family management?
   A. Jim decides to carry the boxes upstairs for his father early in the day while he is fresh and full of energy.
   B. Because Shari enjoys being outdoors, gardening chores are pleasant for her.
   C. Mr. Pantaleone liked his old lawn mower better than the new one, but decides he will learn to cope with the new one.
   D. All of the above illustrate organizational skills.

(Continued)

Name _____

_____ 15. Which of the following is true about family decision making?
     A. Not every decision needs to be a group decision.
     B. Caring families make an effort to involve all family members in the decision-making process in some way.
     C. Being able to speak your own opinion and know you will be listened to with respect builds self-confidence.
     D. All of the above.

_____ 16. Which of the following is NOT true about the benefits of assuming family responsibilities?
     A. Through assuming family responsibilities, you can meet the human need for a feeling of self-worth.
     B. Most family responsibilities are important enough that they must be assumed by adults.
     C. Each time a task is repeated, a person develops greater skill and a feeling of self-confidence in relation to that skill.
     D. Developing skills in all areas of daily living is just as important for adults as for children.

_____ 17. Performing a task for the first time may be very challenging for a young child. Therefore, _____.
     A. a child should always be reprimanded for doing a task wrong
     B. standards for doing a task often have to be relaxed
     C. the parents should ignore what the child has done
     D. a child should not share in family responsibilities until at least the age of eight

Essay Questions: Provide the answers you feel best show your understanding of the subject matter.

18. Describe the five life stages as discussed in the text.

19. Describe three of the factors that affect family management.

20. Describe a family management task you could assume as a teenager that would help you later in life.

Combining Family and Workplace Roles

Objectives

When students have completed this chapter, they will be able to
◆ describe trends related to family and work.
◆ identify ways family and work influence each other.
◆ explain ways that employers, governments, and communities are responding to family needs.
◆ describe skills helpful in successfully combining family and workplace roles.

Bulletin Boards

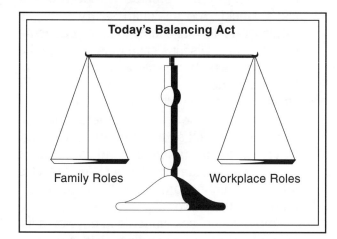

Title: *Today's Balancing Act*

Draw a large scale on the bulletin board. Place the words *Family Roles* on one side of the scale and *Workplace Roles* on the other side. Ask students to list the responsibilities involved with family roles and the responsibilities involved with workplace roles. Discuss the challenges of keeping the scale in balance. As the chapter is studied, point out techniques that can be used to keep the scale in balance.

Title: *Child Care Options*

Develop a bulletin board on local child care options in your community. List the following three categories of child care on the bulletin board: *Child Care Options Provided by Local Employers, Community Child Care Centers,* and *Home-Based Child Care.* Have the students research and identify local programs offered in their community and list these under the appropriate categories. Refer to this bulletin board as you discuss the advantages and disadvantages of each option.

Teaching Materials

Text, pages 229-251
   To Review
   To Challenge Your Thinking
   To Do with the Class
   To Do with Your Community
Student Activity Guide
   A. *Work Patterns*
   B. *Impact of Family and Work on Each Other*
   C. *Responses to Family Needs*
   D. *Skills Helpful in Combining Family and Work*
Teacher's Resources
   Who Keeps House? transparency master 15-1
   Family and Medical Leave Act, transparency master 15-2
   Chapter 15 Test
   Combining Family and Work, color transparency CT-15

Introductory Activities

1. To help students begin to think about family and workplace roles, have them complete the following sentences:
   • Both parents should/should not work because…
   • Children whose parents both work…
   • Husbands should/should not do an equal amount of housekeeping chores when the wife works because…

- Employers are more/less concerned about working parents today as evidenced by...

Ask volunteers to share some of their sentences with the class.

2. Have students write papers describing how their daily lives are affected by their parents' employment. Ask them not to sign their names. Read some of the papers to the class so that students will begin to think about the impact of work on family. Save these papers for later use.

Instructional Concepts and Student Learning Experiences

Trends—Family and Work

3. Have students research current statistics on dual-career families, single parents who work, the number of women in the workforce, etc. Report findings to the class.

4. Ask each student to interview five women who are employed outside the home and find out the reasons they work. Share the results of the survey with others in the class and discuss the implications.

5. Have students role-play situations representing the various reasons women choose to work outside the home. For instance, a woman who works for a tailor may enjoy her work because she receives a great deal of personal satisfaction when a garment she has worked on is worn by the customer.

6. *Work Patterns,* Activity A, SAG. Students are to list pros and cons of various work patterns. They are to then select the pattern they would most likely choose and explain why.

7. Have students think of individuals they know and describe the work patterns they have followed. Ask students to share these work patterns with the class so students understand the many possible variations.

8. Discuss the importance of both men and women preparing for careers even though they may not work immediately following their schooling. Point out the importance of single parents having job skills in the event of a family crisis, such as a divorce or death of one parent.

The Impact of Family and Work

9. As a class, have students form two lists on the chalkboard: ways employment of both parents or a single parent outside the home impacts the parents and ways it impacts the children. Keep a copy of the list for later use.

10. *Impact of Family and Work on Each Other,* Activity B, SAG. Students are to describe how possible events might affect a particular family and their work.

11. Panel discussion. Invite several women who are employed outside the home to present to the class what they see as the advantages and disadvantages of their employment. Try to include a single parent in the group. Ask the women what work patterns they have followed and if they feel that the patterns they chose were the best ones for them.

12. Have students list expenses involved when parents seek employment—child care, transportation, new wardrobe, etc. Assign a small group to research the actual costs involved in each category and prepare a report for the class. Decide the minimum salary a parent would need to make employment economically feasible. Discuss situations in which the decision for both parents to work might not be a wise one.

13. Have students write their own definitions of a "superparent." Use these to generate discussion of the impact of dual careers on parents.

14. Have students research and develop a checklist for evaluating quality child care. Use the information to form a pamphlet that could be distributed to working parents.

15. In small groups, ask students to develop a list of parents' needs regarding child care services. Then have them develop a list of children's needs related to quality child care services. Have the groups share their lists with the class.

16. Have students research the latest information on children in self-care. Work together as a class to compile a report on the self-care phenomenon.

17. Have the class break into small groups to develop a list of concerns related to children in self-care. Share the lists with the entire class. Then develop a list of suggestions for preparing children for self-care. Research community services that are available locally to assist parents and their children in self-care.

18. Invite several husbands who are actively involved in parenting and housekeeping to share their feelings and ideas about sharing these responsibilities with their wives.

19. *Who Keeps House?* transparency master 15-1, TR. Use this transparency as you discuss the sharing of household tasks when wives and mothers work full-time. Discuss the implications of these statistics.

20. Have the students think of examples of how having working parents has had a positive impact on their lives. Ask volunteers to share their examples with the class.

21. Invite a caregiver from a child care center to present ways in which children can benefit from their contact with other children and adults through the child care arrangements.

22. Ask students what they think employers really want from their employees. List these on the chalkboard. Then ask students to consider how each of these factors might impact dual-career and single-parent families.

Employers, Governments, and Communities—Responding to Family Needs

23. *Responses to Family Needs,* Activity C, SAG. Students are to explain how various responses by employers, governments, and communities might be helpful to families.

24. Panel discussion. Have a panel of business persons present their views on how dual-career and single-parent families impact the workplace.

25. Have each student interview five people to see if any of them are involved in flexible work situations such as flextime, job sharing, or flexplace. Report to the class on the variety of situations found. Total the responses from all of the students. What conclusions can students draw from the results of their interviews?

26. Divide the class into small groups. Have each group write a description of a fictitious family situation. Have the groups exchange their descriptions with other groups. Then have the groups develop a plan involving flexible work arrangements that would help meet the needs of each family situation.

27. Research to find information on, or actual individuals involved in, paternity leave situations. Share this information in a class discussion.

28. Have students react to the following statement: "As more men take advantage of paternity leave, society will move closer to accepting child rearing as a 'parental' issue, rather than a 'women's' issue."

29. Have students contact the larger businesses in your community to inquire about the educational and support programs they offer their working parents. Report back to the class.

30. Guest speaker. Invite a qualified individual to speak to the class on "Family Friendly Policies of Business and Industry."

31. Guest speakers. Invite personnel managers or human resource managers from several local companies to speak about new trends in flexible personnel policies and work arrangements.

32. Invite one or more qualified individuals from local businesses to explain benefit package options that are typically offered by employers.

33. *Family and Medical Leave Act,* transparency master 15-2, TR. This master provides more detailed information concerning the Family and Medical Leave Act. Use as the basis for a class discussion.

34. Divide the class into groups and have each group develop a poster or chart on one of the ways government has responded to family needs.

35. Have each student research a child care service in your community. The student should report on the type of service, characteristics of the service, the caregivers, and the environment. Identify the ages of children served, the programs offered, any food service provided, and the type of license held or required.

36. Provide telephone books for students. Ask them to use the Yellow Pages to identify the variety of resources available in your community to assist in various aspects of child care.

37. Guest speaker. Invite a speaker to report on state regulations and licenses for family child care services and group child care centers.

38. Research what is being done in your community through schools and community groups to help with the problem of children in self-care.

39. As a class, analyze the various child care options, discussing advantages and disadvantages of each.

Successfully Combining Family and Work

40. *Combining Family and Work,* color transparency CT-15, TR. Use this transparency to illustrate the importance of good management skills in combining family and work. Discuss each of the success factors and relate each to the material in the text.
41. Panel discussion. Invite a group of mothers and fathers to answer questions about why they work, their work patterns, and how they balance work demands and family needs.
42. *Skills Helpful in Combining Family and Work,* Activity D, SAG. Students are asked to respond to specific family situations, explaining which skill would be most helpful in each situation.
43. Ask students to role-play various situations that illustrate the various skills helpful in successfully combining family and work.
44. Using the situations and lists developed in learning experiences 2 and 9, have the class decide which skills would be helpful in handling each situation.
45. Divide the class into groups and have students practice using the decision-making process in some of the situations from the previous activity.

Answer Key

Text

To Review

1. (List four:) because of economic necessity, to assure financial stability for their children and themselves, for their own personal self-actualization, because they enjoy the challenge and stimulation, for a greater sense of independence, for a sense of identity (Students may justify other responses.)
2. (Describe two:) Some women choose a full-time career, deciding not to have children. Others start work when they leave school and work until they marry or have children, at which time they quit their jobs. Many women work full-time after leaving school, and then leave their jobs when children are born. Later, they return to the work world.

3. (List two. Student response.)
4. (Describe two. Student response.)
5. Flextime permits employees to determine their own working hours within certain guidelines and limits. Flextime does not usually reduce the total number of hours of the work week. Job sharing occurs when two people share the responsibilities of one full-time job. One might work mornings and the other person work in the afternoons.
6. Paternity leave is time allowed for a father to be absent from his job immediately following the birth of his child.
7. (Describe two. Student response.)
8. Family and Medical Leave Act
9. A. true
   B. false
   C. false
10. (Student response.)

Teacher's Resources

Chapter 15 Test
1. D
2. C
3. H
4. A
5. E
6. G
7. B
8. I
9. F
10. T
11. F
12. F
13. T
14. F
15. T
16. F
17. F
18. T
19. T
20. C
21. D
22. C
23. A
24. D
25. (Student response.)
26. (Student response.)
27. (Student response.)

Transparency Master 15-1

Who Keeps House?

The results of a poll of 3,000 working women yielded the following statistics:

→ They spent an average of 63 hours a week working.

38 hours in paid employment

25 hours on home maintenance and cooking

→ 92% do the laundry regularly

→ 67% vacuum regularly

→ 77% prepare dinner regularly

Transparency Master 15-2

Family and Medical Leave Act
1993

Employers affected: Employers who employ 50 or more people each working day during each of 20 or more calendar workweeks in the current or preceding calendar year.

Employees covered: Employees are eligible for benefits if they have been employed for at least 12 months, during which they worked at least 1,250 hours.

Reasons for leaving: Birth and care of a child, adoption, or foster-care placement; care of a seriously ill relative (child, parent, or spouse); a serious health condition that prevents the employee from working.

Giving notice: Employees must give at least 30 days' notice, or as much as is feasible, before taking leave.

Duration of leave: Employees are entitled to 12 workweeks of unpaid leave during a given 12-month period.

Returning to work: Employees have the right to be reinstated to the position held prior to leave or to a comparable position.

Pay and benefits: Employees are not entitled to pay during the leave, but preexisting health benefits must be maintained as they were during employment. If employees do not return to work following leave, they may be asked to reimburse the employer for insurance premiums. An employer may require that vacation or personal time be used for part of the leave.

State laws: Individual states may offer more extensive provisions for leave than required under the FMLA.

Combining Family and Workplace Roles

Name _____

Date _____ Period _____ Score _____

Chapter 15 Test

Matching: Match the following terms and identifying phrases.

_____ 1. Child care provided in a private home other than the child's own home.

_____ 2. A way of getting what you want by exchanging goods or services instead of spending money.

_____ 3. Provides a tax credit for child care expenses.

_____ 4. Guarantees same employee benefits for pregnant employees.

_____ 5. A father takes time off from work to be with his newborn

_____ 6. Programs in which counselors assess employee problems and refer workers to outside help.

_____ 7. A leave of absence for a mother to care for her newborn child.

_____ 8. Another name for telecommuting.

_____ 9. Law that allows unpaid leave from work for child care or health reasons.

A. Pregnancy Discrimination Act

B. maternity leave

C. bartering

D. family child care

E. paternity leave

F. Family and Medical Leave Act

G. EAPs

H. Child and Dependent Care Tax Credit

I. flexplace

True/False: Circle *T* if the statement is true or *F* if the statement is false.

T F 10. Most mothers and fathers work because of economic necessity.

T F 11. The proportion of households headed by a single adult has declined over the past decade.

T F 12. Most permanent part-time workers receive company benefits just as full-time workers do.

T F 13. If a corporation establishes a child care center to improve worker productivity, then company supplied startup and operating costs are fully deductible business expenses.

T F 14. An advantage of family child care is that parents do not have to worry about the caregivers becoming ill or quitting.

T F 15. Learning to recognize your resources is an important management skill.

T F 16. Bartering involves trading money for services.

(Continued)

Name _____

T F 17. Infant care is common in most child care centers.

T F 18. Some corporations subsidize child care services that are licensed whether in homes or centers.

T F 19. Most family child care consists of unregulated providers who operate informally and independently of any regulatory system.

Multiple Choice: Choose the best answer and write the corresponding letter in the blank.

_____ 20. Children in self-care are _____.
A. found in decreasing numbers in recent years
B. often under the age of six
C. sometimes referred to as latch-key children
D. All of the above.

_____ 21. When both parents are employed, _____.
A. men are more likely to be involved in the child care
B. children are more likely to have contact with other children and adults through child care arrangements
C. family members can benefit from sharing home management tasks
D. All of the above.

_____ 22. Flextime does NOT _____.
A. permit employees to determine their own working hours within certain guidelines and limits
B. give options in the number of days the employee works each week
C. usually reduce the number of hours in the employee's workweek
D. allow for a 40-hour workweek in four days

_____ 23. Which of the following is true?
A. Most families do not need dual insurance coverage.
B. Part-time workers usually receive full company benefits.
C. Maternity leaves are unpaid leaves.
D. More job transfers are taking place today due to the increase in dual-career families.

_____ 24. Child care centers in or near the business location _____.
A. aid in recruitment
B. reduce absenteeism and tardiness
C. usually provide care for toddlers and preschoolers, but not for infants
D. All of the above.

Essay Questions: Provide the answers you feel best show your understanding of the subject matter.

25. Describe three ways children benefit when their parents work outside the home. Also describe three concerns parents have about their children when they must work.

26. Describe three ways family-friendly policies and programs can benefit businesses.

27. Describe three specific practices that could help dual-career and single-parent families better manage their at-home tasks. Explain how each of these would be helpful.

Physical and Mental Wellness

Objectives

When students have completed this chapter, they will be able to
◆ explain how good eating habits, physical activity, and rest affect a person's health.
◆ analyze good mental health and the healthful use of defense mechanisms.
◆ identify lifestyle decisions that affect a person's health.

Bulletin Boards

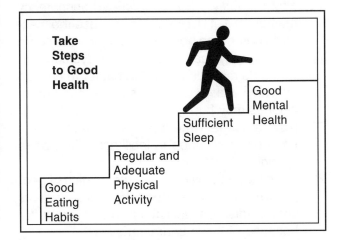

Title: *Take Steps to Good Health*

Draw a set of four steps and place the following labels on them: *Good Eating Habits, Regular and Adequate Physical Activity, Sufficient Sleep,* and *Good Mental Health.* Place a picture or drawing of one or more healthy-looking teens at the top of the steps.

Title: *Lifestyle Choices*

Place pictures of people involved in both positive and negative lifestyle choices on the board. At the bottom of the board, place the question, "How do each of these lifestyle choices affect a person's health?"

Teaching Materials

Text, pages 253-277
To Review
To Challenge Your Thinking
To Do with the Class
To Do with Your Community
Student Activity Guide
A. *Improving Health Habits*
B. *Factors Leading to Good Health*
C. *Researching Health Issues*
Teacher's Resources
Physical Activity Burns Calories,
transparency master 16-1
Dietary Guidelines for Americans,
transparency master 16-2
Check Your Diet for Starch and Fiber,
reproducible master 16-3
Chapter 16 Test
Are You on Target? color transparency CT-16

Introductory Activities

1. Have students find articles on wellness, fitness, and health and bring them to class. Have students give brief oral reports on their articles.
2. As a class, have students list adjectives they would use to describe a healthy person. Encourage students to list adjectives describing both physical and mental health.

Instructional Concepts and Student Learning Experiences

Factors that Contribute to Good Health

3. *Are You on Target?* color transparency CT-16, TR. Use this transparency to illustrate what students can do to target good health. Ask them to describe how good eating habits, regular and adequate physical activity, and sufficient sleep contribute to good health.

4. Have students react to the following statement: "Good health is not so much a goal in itself as a resource that can be used to reach other goals."

5. Have students recall their activities of the last few days and evaluate whether the activities and choices influenced their health. Students should discuss some of their choices.

6. *Improving Health Habits,* Activity A, SAG. Using the form provided, have students evaluate their mental health and health habits and write suggestions for improving mental health and health habits.

7. Have students describe situations that illustrate the relationship between physical and mental health. For instance, having a bad cold makes studying for a test difficult.

8. Have students keep a record of their eating habits for three days. Students should evaluate the number of servings eaten from each of the five food groups listed in the text. Students should determine whether they need to increase their intake of some food groups and list ways that they could do this.

9. Panel discussion. Invite a doctor, nurse, social worker, counselor, and/or other qualified professionals to discuss the relationship between physical and mental health.

10. Guest speaker. Invite a dietitian to discuss how to categorize foods in terms of the MyPyramid. Also have the dietitian discuss how poor nutrition and fad diets can affect health.

11. Have students develop a poster or public service announcement promoting good nutrition.

12. Have students find recipes for snacks that are low in salt, fat, and sugar. Choose some recipes and have students prepare and sample the snacks in class.

13. Guest speaker. Invite a certified aerobics instructor to demonstrate proper techniques for warming up, aerobic physical activity, toning muscle groups, and cooling down. Have the instructor talk about the importance of each phase. If possible, have students try some of the techniques.

14. Guest speaker. Invite a doctor to talk about the relationship between physical activity and heart disease.

15. Have students write a short report on the specific benefits of one type of physical activity. Students should share their reports in class.

16. Have students make a list of excuses people use for not being physically active. Then have students make suggestions for physical activity programs that address the problems expressed in the excuses. For instance, one excuse is that health clubs and sports equipment are too expensive. Taking up jogging or jumping rope would solve this problem.

17. Have students write a jingle or public service announcement designed to motivate students to become physically active. Make arrangements for the students to present the jingle or announcement over the school public address system.

18. *Physical Activity Burns Calories,* transparency master 16-1, TR. Have students use the master to determine how many calories they burn through physical activity in a typical day. Students may also use the master to choose activities that will increase the number of calories they burn.

19. Have students write a research paper on the importance of sleep in facilitating the body's biological functions.

20. Have students discuss characteristics of people who do not get enough sleep. Students should discuss activities that may suffer because of these characteristics.

21. Have students work together to develop a list of suggestions for people who have trouble sleeping.

22. Have students choose a quality of a mentally healthy person from the text and write six suggestions for ways to improve that quality.

23. Have students role-play using each of the defense mechanisms listed in the text.

24. *Factors Leading to Good Health,* Activity B, SAG. Students are to indicate which statements are true and which are false, and to correct the false statements.

Factors Affecting Good Health

25. Have each class member write a description of fictitious family members and their activities that clearly illustrates their lifestyles. Select a few contrasting descriptions to read to the class. Have students discuss how the differences might affect each family's health.
26. Have students compare modern society to society in the 1800s. Students should determine lifestyle factors that might have led to better health in the past and lifestyle factors that might have led to poorer health.
27. *Dietary Guidelines for Americans,* transparency master 16-2, TR. Use this master as you introduce the Dietary Guidelines for Americans to the students.
28. *Researching Health Issues,* Activity C, SAG. Have students research one of the listed lifestyle issues and write a report on their findings.
29. Have each student research dietary habits in a country other than the United States. Students should report their findings to the class, comparing U.S. diet and health to the diet and health of the country researched.
30. *Check Your Diet for Starch and Fiber,* reproducible master 16-3, TR. Have students record the foods they eat for one week. Then distribute the master and have students evaluate their diets for starch and fiber.
31. Guest speaker. Invite a doctor to speak about the symptoms and problems of bronchitis and emphysema.
32. Have students write a research report on how drug use affects the body's metabolism and other biological functions.
33. Have students discuss how over-the-counter and prescription drugs can be harmful if taken improperly.
34. Have students research a birth defect that is caused by drug or alcohol abuse. Students should give an oral report on their findings.
35. Have each student write a report on the causes, symptoms, and treatment of a sexually transmitted disease.
36. Guest speaker. Invite a representative of an alcohol or drug rehabilitation program to discuss the link between drugs, mental and physical health, and disease.

Answer Key

Text

To Review
1. (Student response.)
2. protein, carbohydrates, fats, vitamins, minerals, water
3. (List and explain three. Student response.)
4. (List four:) feel comfortable about themselves, are able to balance independence and dependence on others, can control their emotions, are able to love, are realistic, are able to accept and adapt to change
5. false
6. preventive health care
7. (Describe four. Student response.)
8. reduces life expectancy by 10 to 12 years; may cause scaring or hardening of the liver; may damage the heart; may cause cancers of the mouth, throat, and liver; may cause birth defects in infants; may be the cause of crime, accidents, and divorce
9. true
10. (Describe two:) The person rarely becomes noticeably ill when diseases are in their earliest stages. Many people are afraid to seek treatment for fear of what others will think. People may be too ashamed to tell their sexual partners they are infected.

Student Activity Guide

Factors Leading to Good Health, Activity B
1. T
2. T
3. F; Vitamins are also a nutrient.
4. T
5. F; The heart, liver, brain, and lungs all benefit from physical activity.
6. T
7. F; Body temperature falls, breathing slows, blood pressure and pulse rate fall.
8. T
9. F; The first period of sleep is the deepest and most refreshing.
10. T
11. F; They get angry, but not violent, because they control their emotions.
12. F; Only overuse of defense mechanisms indicates poor mental health.

13. F; Compensation occurs when a person counteracts a weakness by emphasizing a desirable characteristic.
14. T
15. F; Displacement shifts the blame for an undesirable act to someone else.

Teacher's Resources

Chapter 16 Test

 1. F
 2. C
 3. B
 4. A
 5. E
 6. D
 7. F
 8. F
 9. T
10. T
11. F
12. F
13. T
14. T
15. D
16. B
17. D
18. C
19. B
20. B

21. Physical and mental health go hand-in-hand. If you are physically ill, your mental health is affected. You may be in a bad mood. If you have an emotional problem, your physical health may be affected. You may develop a headache. The factors that influence physical and mental health are closely related. Understanding these factors can help you make wise decisions about both physical and mental health.
22. (Student response. List and describe four.)
23. Defense mechanisms help people deal with real-life situations and adjust to frustrations. They can reduce tensions, protect self-esteem, and maintain emotional stability.
24. (Student response. Describe three.)

Transparency Master 16-1

Physical Activity Burns Calories

Activity	Calories Used Per Hour
Light Activity Sitting Driving a car Standing Office work (filing, typing)	100-150
Moderate Activity Light housework Leisurely walking Gardening Canoeing Golf Lawn mowing Rowing	150-250
Swimming Dancing Tennis Softball Heavy housework Horseback riding Volleyball Walking rapidly Skating	250-350
Vigorous Activity Mini trampoline jumping Shoveling Wood chopping Bicycling Tennis Aerobic dancing	350-450
Dancing (fast) Cycling Jogging Downhill skiing Running Soccer Skipping rope Racquetball	450-600

Transparency Master 16-2

Dietary Guidelines for Americans

Adequate Nutrients Within Calorie Needs

◆ Consume a variety of nutrient-dense foods and beverages within and among the basic food groups. Choose foods that limit the intake of saturated and trans fats, cholesterol, added sugars, salt, and alcohol.

◆ Meet recommended intakes within energy needs by adopting a balanced eating pattern, such as the USDA Food Guide.

Weight Management

◆ To maintain body weight in a healthy range, balance calories from foods and beverages with calories expended.

◆ To prevent gradual weight gain over time, make small decreases in food and beverage calories and increase physical activity.

Physical Activity

◆ Engage in regular physical activity and reduce sedentary activities to promote health, psychological well-being, and a healthy body weight.

◆ Achieve physical fitness by including cardiovascular conditioning, stretching exercises for flexibility, and resistance exercises or calisthenics for muscle strength and endurance.

Food Groups to Encourage

◆ Consume a sufficient amount of fruits and vegetables while staying within energy needs. Two cups of fruit and 2 1/2 cups of vegetables per day are recommended for a reference 2,000-calorie intake, with higher or lower amounts depending on the calorie level.

◆ Choose a variety of fruits and vegetables each day. In particular, select from all five vegetable subgroups (dark green, orange, legumes, starchy vegetables, and other vegetables) several times a week.

◆ Consume 3 or more ounce-equivalents of whole-grain products per day, with the rest of the recommended grains coming from enriched or whole-grain products. In general, at least half the grains should come from whole grains.

◆ Consume 3 cups per day of fat-free or low-fat milk or equivalent milk products.

Fats

◆ Consume less than 10 percent of calories from saturated fatty acids and less than 300 mg/day of cholesterol. Keep trans fatty acid consumption as low as possible.

◆ Keep total fat intake between 20 to 35 percent of calories, with most fats coming from sources of polyunsaturated and monounsaturated fatty acids, such as fish, nuts, and vegetable oils.

◆ When selecting and preparing meat, poultry, dry beans, and milk or milk products, make choices that are lean, low-fat, or fat-free.

◆ Limit intake of fats and oils high in saturated and/or trans fatty acids, and choose products low in such fats and oils.

(Continued)

Carbohydrates

◆ Choose fiber-rich fruits, vegetables, and whole grains often.
◆ Choose and prepare foods and beverages with little added sugars or caloric sweeteners.
◆ Reduce the incidence of dental caries by practicing good oral hygiene and consuming sugar- and starch-containing foods and beverages less frequently.

Sodium and Potassium

◆ Consume less than 2,300 mg (approximately 1 teaspoon of salt) of sodium per day.
◆ Choose and prepare foods with little salt. At the same time, consume potassium-rich foods, such as fruits and vegetables.

Alcoholic Beverages

◆ Alcoholic beverages should not be consumed by some individuals, including those who cannot restrict their alcohol intake, women of childbearing age who may become pregnant, pregnant and lactating women, children and adolescents, individuals taking medications that can interact with alcohol, and those with specific medical conditions.
◆ Alcoholic beverages should be avoided by individuals engaging in activities that require attention, skill, or coordination, such as driving or operating machinery.

Food Safety

◆ To avoid microbial foodborne illness:
◆ Clean hands, food contact surfaces, and fruits and vegetables. Meat and poultry should not be washed or rinsed.
◆ Separate raw, cooked, and ready-to-eat foods while shopping, preparing, or storing foods.
◆ Cook foods to a safe temperature to kill microorganisms.
◆ Chill (refrigerate) perishable food promptly and defrost foods properly.
◆ Avoid raw (unpasteurized) milk or any products made from unpasteurized milk, raw or partially cooked eggs or foods containing raw eggs, raw or undercooked meat and poultry, unpasteurized juices, and raw sprouts.

Reproducible Master 16-3

Check Your Diet for Starch and Fiber

Name _____ **Date** _____ **Period** _____

Starch and fiber are important in the diet. Foods high in starch provide energy, vitamins, and minerals. Foods high in fiber help keep the digestive system working properly. Most foods high in starch and fiber are low in fat. Use a one-week record of your food intake to take the test below. Then check the bottom of the page to see how you did.

How often do you eat	Seldom or never	1 or 2 times a week	3 or 4 times a week	Almost daily
1. Several servings of breads, cereals, pasta, or rice?	☐	☐	☐	☐
2. Starchy vegetables like potatoes, corn, peas, or dishes made with dry beans or peas?	☐	☐	☐	☐
3. Whole-grain breads or cereals?	☐	☐	☐	☐
4. Several servings of vegetables?	☐	☐	☐	☐
5. Whole fruit with skins and/or seeds (berries, apples, pears, etc.)?	☐	☐	☐	☐

Before You Choose Foods...

Think about the form of the food. The form affects the amount of fiber:

Apple juice, 3/4 cup:
0.2 g fiber

Applesauce, 1/2 cup:
2.1 g fiber

Whole apple with peel:
3.6 g fiber

How Did You Do?

The best answer for all of the questions above is Almost Daily. To increase the amounts of starch and fiber in your diet, choose the following foods:

Foods high in starch:

Breads
Breakfast cereals
Pasta, such as spaghetti and noodles
Rice
Dry beans and peas
Starchy vegetables such as potatoes, corn,
   peas, lima beans

Foods high in fiber:

Whole-grain breads
Whole-grain breakfast cereals
Whole-wheat pasta
Vegetables, especially with edible skins,
   stems, seeds
Dry beans and peas
Whole fruits, especially with skins or seeds
Nuts and seeds

Physical and Mental Wellness

Name _____

Date _____ **Period** _____ **Score** _____

Chapter 16 Test

Matching: Match the following diseases to their descriptions.

_____ 1. Infections that are almost always transmitted by intimate sexual contact.

_____ 2. Disease of the heart and blood vessels.

_____ 3. A progressive disease that involves loss of control over drinking alcoholic beverages.

_____ 4. Virus that breaks down the immune system and leaves the body vulnerable to diseases a healthy body could resist.

_____ 5. Diseases that are more closely related to a person's behavior than to infectious agents.

_____ 6. High blood pressure.

A. HIV

B. alcoholism

C. cardiovascular disease

D. hypertension

E. lifestyle diseases

F. STDs

True/False: Circle *T* if the statement is true or *F* if the statement is false.

T F 7. No evidence suggests that lack of physical activity is related to cardiovascular disease.

T F 8. Mentally healthy people are never dependent upon others.

T F 9. Excessive use of defense mechanisms may indicate mental illness.

T F 10. Statistics indicate that obesity is associated with chronic disorders.

T F 11. Low-fiber diets are linked with the risk of developing lung cancer.

T F 12. Cigarette smoke is not harmful to nonsmokers.

T F 13. Sexually transmitted diseases are some of the most widespread diseases in the United States.

T F 14. A person can carry the AIDS virus, HIV, without actually having the disease.

(Continued)

Name _____

Multiple Choice: Choose the best answer and write the corresponding letter in the blank.

_____ 15. Which of the following is true about good health?
  A. Good health helps you reach other valuable goals.
  B. Good health means more than just the absence of disease.
  C. Good health is influenced by heredity and the environment.
  D. All of the above are true.

_____ 16. Which of the following is NOT true about sufficient sleep?
  A. During sleep, many of the physical functions of the body slow down.
  B. All adults need six hours of sleep.
  C. During sleep, the body repairs itself, and living cells of the body are replaced.
  D. New skin cells are created about twice as fast during sleep as in waking hours.

_____ 17. Which of the following is true?
  A. Heart attacks, strokes, and cancer are often referred to as lifestyle diseases.
  B. People today tend to be less physically active than they should be.
  C. Preventing disease is becoming a matter of changing habits and customs.
  D. All of the above are true.

_____ 18. Which of the following is NOT true?
  A. An overweight person can expect a shorter life than a person of ideal weight.
  B. Obesity means added risks during pregnancy and childbirth.
  C. Obese people are usually happier than people who are thin.
  D. Loneliness and lack of self-esteem are possible hazards of obesity.

_____ 19. Markus, a member of the state championship hockey team, wears his hockey letter jacket as often as possible. The defense mechanism illustrated by this example is _____.
  A. displacement
  B. identification
  C. rationalization
  D. regression

_____ 20. Albert, who had just had an argument with his father, snapped at his friend as he came out of the house to go to school. The defense mechanism illustrated by this example is _____.
  A. compensation
  B. displacement
  C. projection
  D. regression

Essay Questions: Provide the answers you feel best show your understanding of the subject matter.

21. Describe the relationship between physical health and mental health.

22. List and briefly describe four factors that contribute to good health.

23. Explain how defense mechanisms may be helpful to a person.

24. Describe three cautions or suggestions related to the link between diet and disease.

Objectives

When students have completed this chapter, they will be able to
- identify the nutrients the body needs and explain the importance of each.
- describe the functions of food in the body.
- describe the importance of the food guidance system, MyPyramid.
- identify special nutritional needs of people at various stages in the life cycle.
- plan diets that meet food guide requirements.
- develop menu plans based on various meal patterns.
- list resources that can help them make wise choices in selecting nutritious foods.
- follow guidelines in selecting nutritious foods when eating out.
- identify and explain factors that influence food choices.

Bulletin Boards

```
+------------------------------------------+
|          Current News on                 |
|             Nutrition                    |
|  _____  _____  _____            |
|  _____  [ food   _____            |
|  _____   images] _____            |
|  _____  _____  _____            |
|  _____  _____  _____            |
|  _____  _____  _____            |
|  _____  _____  _____            |
+------------------------------------------+
```

Title: *Current News on Nutrition*

Cut out stylized letters for the title. Place the title on the bulletin board to look like the masthead of a newspaper. Have students bring in articles on nutrition topics from newspapers and magazines. Place the articles in the "columns" of the bulletin board newspaper.

Title: *Special Foods for Special Times*

Place 12 monthly calendar pages on the bulletin board. On each page, place pictures of foods used to celebrate the special days in that month (hot dogs on July 4th, turkey on Thanksgiving, etc.).

Teaching Materials

Text, pages 278-303
> *To Review*
> *To Challenge Your Thinking*
> *To Do with the Class*
> *To Do with Your Community*

Student Activity Guide
> A. *The Functions of Food*
> B. *Watching Your Diet*
> C. *Eating Out*
> D. *Positive Influences on Eating Habits*

Teacher's Resources
> *Protein Planning Guide,* transparency master 17-1
> *Nutrition Label Analysis,* reproducible master 17-2
> Chapter 17 Test
> *MyPyramid,* color transparency CT-17

Introductory Activities

1. Discuss with students the value of being aware of what they are eating. Ask students to begin keeping a three-day record of all the foods they eat. This record will be used in activities throughout the chapter.
2. Ask students to name nutrition topics and food trends that are currently receiving a lot of press. Have several articles on current food and nutrition topics on hand to spark or support student ideas.

Instructional Concepts and Student Learning Experiences

Basic Concepts of Nutrition

3. Have the class develop a nutrition information file. The file should include any nutritional materials the students are able to gather. It should also include a listing of resource persons, places, and organizations from which additional nutritional materials and information might be obtained.

4. Have students use a chart listing the nutritive values of foods to compare the nutritive values of two types of meats, vegetables, fruits, dairy products, and bread products. Then have students compare their findings with classmates.

5. Divide the class into six groups. Have each group develop a poster on one of the six basic nutrients. The posters should show how the nutrient is used in body metabolism and be illustrated with pictures of food sources.

6. *Protein Planning Guide,* transparency master 17-1, TR. Use the master to show students how incomplete proteins can be combined to form complete proteins. Ask students to give examples of foods that would illustrate each combination.

7. Have students develop a bulletin board, poster, or display contrasting pictures of high-calorie and low-calorie foods.

8. *The Functions of Food,* Activity A, SAG. Have students answer the questions to show their understanding of the functions of food.

9. Panel discussion. Invite an obstetrician, pediatrician, geriatrician, and dietitian to discuss varying nutritional needs throughout life.

Food Guides and Eating Patterns

10. Have students give suggestions for nutritious snacks made from foods from each of the MyPyramid food groups.

11. Guest speaker. Invite a dietitian to speak to the class on recent nutrition research findings that might affect people's eating habits.

12. *Watching Your Diet,* Activity B, SAG. Have students list all the foods they have eaten for the last three days according to the groups of MyPyramid. Then ask them to analyze their eating habits to determine which food groups they may be lacking and give suggestions for improvement.

13. Guest speaker. Invite someone from another country to talk to your students about food habits and eating customs in his or her country.

14. Have students research other food guides that are used to help people select nutritious foods. Have them compare these guides with the MyPyramid in brief oral or written reports.

15. Have students develop a display showing what constitutes a serving of various foods according to the MyPyramid.

16. Give students a list of a variety of foods. Have them practice placing the foods in the different groups in MyPyramid. Discuss the correct answers in class.

17. *MyPyramid,* color transparency CT-17, TR. Use this transparency as you introduce MyPyramid. Ask students to determine whether their diets follow the recommendations.

18. Write basic breakfast, lunch, and dinner meal patterns on the chalkboard. Have students discuss how these patterns might be adjusted to provide for light, moderate, and heavy food intake.

19. Have students use the meal patterns written on the chalkboard for Learning Experience 18 to plan menus for one day.

20. Have students visit the MyPyramid Web site at www.MyPyramid.gov. Ask them to enter their age, gender, and physical activity level to determine what they should eat from the MyPyramid food groups. Ask them to explore the Web site and prepare a report about the experience.

21. Guest speaker. Invite a psychologist specializing in eating disorders to speak to your class about the ways in which individuals reveal psychological needs through eating behaviors.

Selecting Nutritious Foods

22. Have students contact a consumer food manufacturer to find out how they obtain the nutritional information they list on their product labels.

23. Have students bring in examples of food packages or labels that make nutritional claims. Discuss why manufacturers put these claims on their products.

24. *Nutrition Label Analysis,* reproducible master 17-2, TR. Have each student mount a nutrition information label on the worksheet. Ask students to use the information on their labels to answer the questions on the worksheet.
25. Have students discuss how they could use nutrition labeling when planning, shopping for, and preparing meals.
26. Have students prepare a bulletin board in one of the school's main traffic areas explaining the various information found on nutrition labels.
27. Bring in several food packages showing product dating. Ask students to determine which type of date is displayed on each package.
28. Have students discuss how they could use product dating when shopping for and preparing food.
29. Have students brainstorm a list of guidelines for selecting nutritious foods.
30. Have students prepare a brochure on guidelines for selecting nutritious foods. The brochure should explain how to use nutritional labels and product dating as well as giving a number of specific food selection tips. Have students distribute the brochure throughout the school.
31. *Eating Out,* Activity C, SAG. Students are to list a variety of foods an individual might select at a fast-food restaurant in certain situations and explain why they are good choices for that particular individual.

Factors That Influence Food Choices

32. Have students brainstorm a list of factors that influence food choices. Write student responses on the chalkboard. Then discuss how and why each factor has an effect on the foods people choose to eat.
33. Have each student write an essay about a food practice in his or her family that reflects a tradition, custom, or religious influence. Ask volunteers to share their essays in class.
34. Ask each student to select a region of the United States and identify three foods that are typical of that region. Then have students research the cultural origins of those foods. Have students summarize their findings in oral reports.

35. Have students discuss how each of the following American lifestyle trends influence food choices and eating patterns: increasing family income, dual-career families, less home food production, growth of urban areas.
36. Have students give examples of prejudices and superstitions associated with food that might affect food choices.
37. Have each student describe five specific situations that would influence food choices or habits. Then indicate whether these are positive or negative influences on food choices or habits and explain why.
38. Have students discuss the relationship between the planning of family meals and the shaping of family food habits and choices.
39. Have each student list all the members in his or her household on a sheet of paper. Then have students list ways that each member could assume some responsibility in the planning and preparation of family meals. Ask students to share these suggestions with their families. Have volunteers report the reactions of family members in class.
40. Ask students to discuss how the texture of a food could affect its appeal. Have students give examples of foods they reject because of texture.
41. Have students find menus in magazines or cookbooks. Ask students to analyze these menus in terms of color, flavor, and texture.
42. *Positive Influences on Eating Habits,* Activity D, SAG. Have students describe how given situations would positively influence the eating habits of family members.

Answer Key

Text

To Review
1. E, D, F, B, A, C
2. Complete proteins are protein foods that contain an adequate amount of all the essential amino acids. These are the amino acids that the body cannot produce in an amount large enough to meet its needs. If a protein food lacks one or more of the essential amino acids, it would not meet the growth needs of the body and would be called an incomplete protein.

3. (Describe four:) is part of the blood; is part of the cells; is present in special tissues; brings digested substances through the digestive tract and through the intestinal wall into the blood; helps transport nutrients throughout the body; carries away waste products
4. (Student response.)
5. building and maintaining physical structure, controlling and coordinating body processes, providing energy for activity and warmth (Students may justify other responses.)
6. Grains; Vegetables; Fruits; Milk; Meat and Beans; Oils (Examples are student response.)
7. true
8. calcium and iron
9. (List four:) serving size; servings per package; number of calories per serving and amount of calories per serving from fat; nutrients contained in the product; percent Daily Values based on a 2,000-calorie diet
10. (Student response)

Student Activity Guide

The Functions of Food, Activity A
1. building and maintaining physical structure, controlling and coordinating body processes, providing energy for activity and warmth.
2. body protein
3. calcium and phosphorus
4. protein, minerals, and other nutrients
5. digestion, absorption, metabolism
6. Food is chemically or mechanically reduced so it can pass through the intestinal wall into the bloodstream.
7. Enzymes are proteins found in digestive juices. They help break down foods so the body can use them.
8. Nutrients are absorbed through the walls of the intestine and into the bloodstream.
9. processes that help build, maintain, and repair body cells; processes that break down waste products that are eliminated by the body; processes that transform modified foods into energy and heat
10. Hemoglobin carries oxygen to the tissues and carries some of the carbon dioxide from the tissues back to the lungs.
11. carbohydrates, fats, proteins
12. calories

Teacher's Resources

Chapter 17 Test
1. E
2. J
3. F
4. H
5. A
6. B
7. D
8. I
9. G
10. C
11. T
12. T
13. T
14. F
15. F
16. F
17. F
18. T
19. F
20. T
21. A
22. A
23. D
24. D
25. B
26. Grains; Vegetables; Fruits; Milk; Meat and Beans; Oils (Examples are student response.)
27. Meal patterns make meal planning easier. They provide a framework for planning nutritious meals. They help you avoid omitting essential foods.
28. (List and explain three. Student response.)
29. Color: Variety in color is pleasing to the eye and to the appetite. Flavor: A variety of foods can be combined to create a pleasant combination of flavors. Textures: Meals are more enjoyable when there are varied textures. Type of preparation: Meals are more pleasing when a variety of preparation techniques is used.

Transparency Master 17-1

Protein Planning Guide

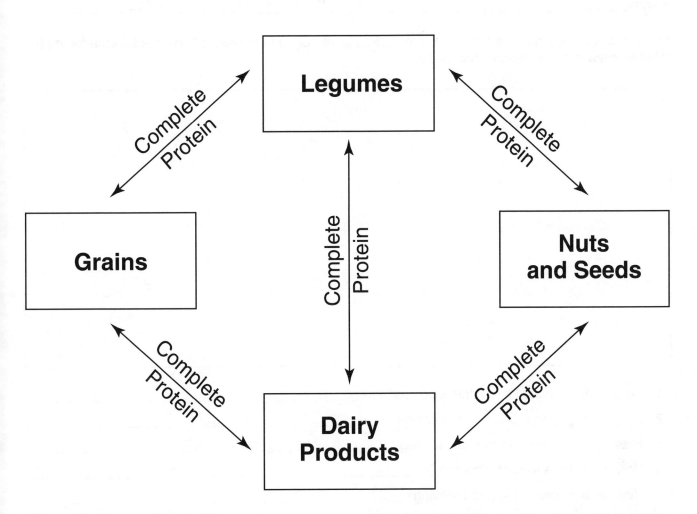

Sources of Complete Protein:

eggs

dairy products

meat

seafood

poultry

Sources of Incomplete Protein:

grains—wheat, barley, rice, oats , corn, rye

legumes—dried beans, dried peas, lentils, soybeans

nuts—peanuts, walnuts, cashews, almonds

seeds—sesame seeds, sunflower seeds

Reproducible Master 17-2

Nutrition Label Analysis

Name _____ **Date** _____ **Period** _____

In the space below, mount a nutritional information label from a food product. Use the information on the label to answer the questions that follow.

1. What is the serving size of this food product? _____

2. How many servings are in this container? _____

3. How many calories are in each serving? _____

4. How much fat is in each serving?_____

5. How much sodium is in each serving?_____

6. What percentage of the U.S. RDA for protein does one serving supply? _____

7. Would this product be a good source of vitamin C? _____

8. What percentage of the U.S. RDA for calcium does one serving supply? _____

9. For which nutrients, if any, does this product provide less than 2 percent of the U.S. RDA? _____

10. Does this label list any nutrients that are not required by law? If so, which ones? _____

11. Is this food product required to have a nutrition label? If so, why? If not, why do you think the manufacturer chose to put a nutrition label on the product? _____

    _____

    _____

12. How could you use nutrition labeling as a resource to help you plan healthful and satisfying meals?

    _____

    _____

Healthful Eating

Name _____

Date _____ Period _____ Score _____

Chapter 17 Test

Matching: Match the following terms and identifying phrases.

_____ 1. Process that modifies and reduces foods mechanically and chemically so they can pass through the intestinal wall into the bloodstream.

_____ 2. Examples are corn and safflower oil; they are usually liquid at room temperature.

_____ 3. Protein foods that lack one or more of the essential amino acids; most plant foods are examples.

_____ 4. Substances supplied by the diet that the body needs to function.

_____ 5. Process that absorbs nutrients through the wall of the intestine and into the bloodstream.

_____ 6. Units that indicate the amount of energy burned.

_____ 7. Protein foods that contain an adequate amount of all essential amino acids; many foods from animals are examples.

_____ 8. Found in meats and dairy products, contains the most hydrogen, and are usually solid at room temperature; a diet high in these may cause high cholesterol.

_____ 9. The processes that help build, maintain, and repair body cells after food compounds have been absorbed into the bloodstream.

_____ 10. Protein foods that, when combined, meet the body's growth needs; one food provides the amino acids that are missing in the other.

A. absorption

B. calories

C. complementary proteins

D. complete proteins

E. digestion

F. incomplete proteins

G. metabolism

H. nutrients

I. saturated fats

J. unsaturated fats

True/False: Circle *T* if the statement is true or *F* if the statement is false.

T   F   11. No single food contains all the nutrients the body needs.

T   F   12. Carbohydrate, protein, and fat are all potential sources of body fat.

T   F   13. The amount of stored fat in the body reflects the total amount of food that has been eaten in excess of energy needs.

T   F   14. Fat-soluble vitamins need to be supplied to the body daily.

(Continued)

Name _____

T   F   15. When a person is fully grown, protein in the diet is no longer necessary.

T   F   16. In the process of digestion, metabolism occurs first, then absorption into the bloodstream.

T   F   17. Cellulose, a protein in the blood, carries oxygen to the tissues.

T   F   18. The more calories in a food, the more energy it can supply.

T   F   19. Dating of food products is not legally required by federal, state, or local governments.

T   F   20. When selecting fresh vegetables, crisp, ripe vegetables are best.

Multiple Choice: Choose the best answer and write the corresponding letter in the blank.

_____ 21. Which of the following is true?
   A. For good nutrition, it is important to choose a variety of foods from within each food group.
   B. A good diet contains a great deal of refined carbohydrates.
   C. A good diet avoids all oils.
   D. All of the above.

_____ 22. MyPyramid provides an estimate of what and how much food you should eat from the different food groups based on all EXCEPT your _____.
   A. genetics
   B. age
   C. gender
   D. physical activity level

_____ 23. Which of the following is NOT true?
   A. Whole grain and enriched breads and cereals are important sources of B-vitamins.
   B. Vegetables tend to be low in fat and high in fiber.
   C. The milk group provides protein, vitamins, and minerals.
   D. The oils found in fish and vegetable oils raise LDL (bad) cholesterol levels in blood.

_____ 24. Availability of foods is determined by _____.
   A. climate conditions
   B. production and marketing systems
   C. the economic situation
   D. All of the above.

_____ 25. A woman's pleasant childhood memories of eating her grandmother's homemade brownies come to mind whenever she eats a brownie. This is an example of _____.
   A. economic influences on eating habits
   B. personal experiences and associations that influence eating habits
   C. societal and cultural influences on eating habits
   D. lifestyle influences on eating habits

Essay Questions: Provide the answers you feel best show your understanding of the subject matter.

26. List the food groups of MyPyramid and give an example of a serving from each group.

27. What are the benefits of using meal patterns in meal planning?

28. List and explain three influences on food choices.

29. List and explain four different ways variety occurs in a well-balanced menu.

Coping with Stress

Objectives

When students have completed this chapter, they will be able to
- explain what stress is and describe common reactions to stress.
- describe the causes of stress.
- apply the problem-solving process to stressful situations in their lives.
- analyze personal skills for effective stress management.

Bulletin Boards

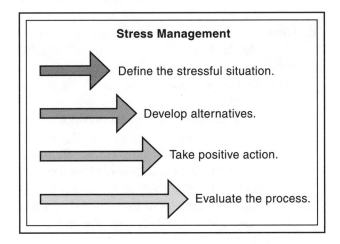

Title: *Stress Management*

Use colored arrows to emphasize the steps in managing stress as shown. Place the following steps on the board: *Define the Stressful Situation*, *Develop Alternatives*, *Take Positive Action*, and *Evaluate the Process*.

Title: *What Is Stressful to You?*

Cut shapes from construction paper and distribute them to students. Have students write about situations that are stressful to them on their papers. Arrange the papers on the bulletin board. As you discuss the chapter, use situations from the board as bases for discussion topics in the student learning experiences.

Teaching Materials

Text, pages 304-318
  To Review
  To Challenge Your Thinking
  To Do with the Class
  To Do with Your Community
Student Activity Guide
  A. *Stress in Your Life*
  B. *Managing Stress*
  C. *Personal Skills for Coping with Stress*
  D. *Understanding Coping Skills*
Teacher's Resources
  What Causes You Stress? reproducible
    master 18-1
  *Using the Problem-Solving Process to
    Manage Stress,* transparency
    master 18-2
  Chapter 18 Test
  Link Up with Stress Management Skills!
    color transparency CT-18

Introductory Activities

1. *What Causes You Stress?* reproducible master 18-1, TR. Have students use the master to determine what events they find stressful in their lives. Each student should choose one event and explain why it causes stress and what can be done to reduce the stress. Students should save their responses and evaluate them after studying the chapter.
2. Have students write questions that they have about stress and submit them to you. Develop a master sheet of questions and have students fill out answers as they study the chapter. If some questions are still unanswered, assign students to research and find the answers.
3. *Stress in Your Life,* Activity A, SAG. Have students list five situations that caused them stress in the past week. Students should then describe their physical reactions to, and possible causes of, the stresses listed.

Instructional Concepts and Student Learning Experiences

Understanding Stress

4. Have students research to find various definitions of stress. Students should share and discuss their findings in class.

5. Have students discuss the meaning of the statement, "Stress indicates a need to adapt."

6. Make two columns on the chalkboard: physical demands and psychological demands. Have students give situations that cause stress and list them under the appropriate headings. (Some items may be listed in both columns.)

7. Have each student make a list of several stressful situations that he or she has experienced in the past month. Students should jot down their reactions to each situation listed. Have students look over their lists to determine if there is any pattern to their reactions.

8. Have students discuss differences in perceptions as related to stress in the following situations:
   - Receiving a traffic ticket
   - The death of a grandparent
   - Being laid off of a job
   - Having an argument with a parent
   - Going to the dentist to have a tooth filled

9. Have students refer to the list of stressful situations developed in Learning Experience 7 and list these activities according to the intensity of stress, from the most intense to the least intense.

10. Using the list from Learning Experience 7, have students list the situations in order of duration, from those that continued for the longest amount of time to those that were the shortest duration.

11. Have students make a series of cartoons that illustrate how different people might react to the same stressful situation in different ways.

12. Develop a series of note cards with descriptions of different stressful situations on them. Have each student select a situation and discuss what he or she feels could have been the cause or condition contributing to the stress.

13. Have students choose one of the life conditions listed in the text and give an oral or written research report on how the condition contributes to stress.

Managing Stress

14. *Link Up with Stress Management Skills!* color transparency CT-18, TR. Use this transparency as a basis of discussion about how to manage stress. Each skill could be further defined and examples given to illustrate the use of each in a real-life situation.

15. Select some scenes from popular movies or television shows that depict stressful situations and show them to the class. Have students identify physical and mental signs of stress in the characters.

16. Have students discuss reasons why defining a stress situation may be difficult even if a person recognizes that he or she is reacting to stress.

17. Have students choose one of the following crisis situations and list all of the possible factors that can cause stress in that situation: moving to a new state, having a family member lose a job, a death in the family, or having a family member or close friend who is an alcoholic.

18. Choose a stressful situation and have students brainstorm as many alternative solutions as possible. Then have students evaluate the positive and negative aspects to each solution.

19. Have the class choose a solution from Learning Experience 18 and develop a plan for carrying out the alternative. Students should determine possible ways that the plan may need to be modified as it is carried out.

20. Have students develop a list of questions that could be used to evaluate the problem-solving process.

21. *Managing Stress,* Activity B, SAG. Have students choose a stressful situation from Activity A and use the form provided to use the problem-solving process to cope with the stress.

22. *Using the Problem-Solving Process to Manage Stress,* transparency master 18-2, TR. As a class, have students choose a stressful situation and work through a solution using the problem-solving process. Record class input on the transparency.

Personal Skills for Effective Coping

23. Have students begin a diary of sensations experienced when under stress. Students should begin by recalling reactions to previous situations. Students should then add to the list shortly after they have been in new stressful situations. After two weeks, have students write a short, confidential report on what they learned by keeping the diary.
24. Discuss why people who suffer stress-related illness may not even realize that they are under stress. Discuss ways that this problem may be avoided.
25. Set up a two-day period in which classmates are to observe each other whenever possible during and outside of class. Students should look for negative responses from classmates to stressful situations. The student who sees the response should make a note of it and let the other student know what was observed as soon as possible. (For instance, if a response is noted in another class, the student should wait until the end of the class to talk to the other student.) The two students should then discuss and record alternative, positive responses to the situation. Have students share their findings in class at the end of the two-day period.
26. Have each student give two examples of pressures that can be turned into positive challenges.
27. Divide the class into four groups. Have each group develop and perform a skit illustrating how one of the following four emotions is helpful in dealing with stress: cheerfulness, courage, optimism, and a sense of humor.
28. Have students write two anecdotes. One should depict a person with a negative outlook dealing with a stressful situation. The other should depict a person with a positive outlook dealing with the same stressful situation.
29. Have students choose common stressful events and discuss how the situations might be anticipated. Students should suggest steps that could be taken to reduce or avoid each stressful event discussed.
30. Have each student choose a stressful situation that he or she will probably encounter in the near future. Each student should write a plan to help prepare for the situation.

31. Have students discuss how clarifying values and prioritizing goals can help reduce stress.
32. Have students give examples of stressful situations that can cause a person to reexamine their standards. Students should discuss how having flexible standards helps reduce stress in these situations.
33. Have students develop and perform skits to demonstrate how being organized helps a person deal with stressful situations.
34. Have students choose a stressful event such as a prom or finals. Ask them to develop a time management plan that will help reduce the stress often associated with the event.
35. Have students review the guidelines for good communication given in Chapter 10. Discuss how following these guidelines can help reduce stress in relationships.
36. Have students develop skits illustrating how miscommunication can result in unnecessary stress in relationships.
37. Have students research current literature to find information on relaxation techniques such as meditation. Give oral reports on their findings.
38. Have students write down three activities that they find relaxing and turn them in anonymously. Read the activities aloud and have students discuss why so many different activities might be used by different people to relax.
39. Guest speaker. Invite a counselor or psychologist to discuss and demonstrate relaxation techniques.
40. Have students develop a list of quick relaxation techniques that can be used just before or during stressful situations.
41. *Personal Skills for Coping with Stress,* Activity C, SAG. Have students make a list of stressful situations in which they have been involved. Students should use the chart provided to analyze which personal skills for coping can help in dealing with each situation listed.
42. *Understanding Coping Skills,* Activity D, SAG. Have students write thorough explanations of each of the coping skills listed.
43. Guest speaker. Invite a qualified representative of a fitness program to discuss the advantages of exercise in reducing stress.

Answer Key

Text

To Review

1. (List three:) divorce; death of a family member; job loss (Students may justify other responses.)
2. (List three: Student response.)
3. (List four:) increased heartbeat, faster pulse rate, muscle tenseness, increased perspiration, headaches, irritability, emotional outbursts, indigestion
4. an understanding of stress, a process for managing stress, personal skills for effective coping
5. A. self-imposed stress
   B. situational stress
   C. situational stress
   D. self-imposed stress
6. A. false
   B. true
   C. false
7. physical, psychological, reaction
8. (List three:) being positive, having a healthy attitude toward yourself, behaving assertively but not aggressively, developing healthy emotions, having an open attitude toward change
9. Organizational, time management
10. (List three: Student response.)

Teacher's Resources

Chapter 18 Test

1. F
2. D
3. A
4. B
5. C
6. G
7. E
8. F
9. T
10. T
11. T
12. F
13. T
14. F
15. T
16. T
17. F
18. A
19. D
20. B
21. D
22. A
23. (Student response.)
24. (Student response.)
25. (Student response.)
26. (Student response.)

Reproducible Master 18-1

What Causes You Stress?

Name _____ **Date** _____ **Period** _____

For the situations listed below, indicate the amount of stress they cause you by checking the appropriate category.

	Extremely stressful	Very stressful	Moderately stressful	Slightly stressful	Not stressful
Taking a test					
Giving a speech					
Meeting a person for the first time					
Going to a dance					
Participating in a sports-oriented activity					
Asking someone for a date					
Getting yelled at					
Arguing with a friend					
Arguing with a parent					
Asking permission to do something your parent objects to					
Cleaning your room					
Being late for an event					
Losing something of yours					
Losing something that you borrowed					

Choose one of the items listed above that causes you stress and explain how you react when in that situation. _____

_____

_____

_____

_____

What do you think causes you to feel stress in the above situation? _____

_____

_____

_____

_____

_____

Transparency Master 18-2

Using the Problem-Solving Process to Manage Stress

Define the Stress Situation:

Turn the Problem into a Goal:

Develop Alternative Solutions:

Take Positive Action:

Evaluate the Process:

Coping with Stress

Name _____

Date _____ Period _____ Score _____

Chapter 18 Test

Matching: Match the following terms and identifying phrases.

_____ 1. Skills that allow you to learn how your body and mind react to stress.

_____ 2. Include skills in clarifying values, prioritizing goals, planning ahead, and controlling use of time.

_____ 3. May eliminate the cause of the stress, reduce the stress, or help you to accept the cause of the stress.

_____ 4. Any response to a stressful situation that helps prevent, avoid, or control physical or emotional stress.

_____ 5. Developing healthy emotions, such as cheerfulness, courage, optimism, and a sense of humor.

_____ 6. Feeling tense, irritable, and suffering from nervous indigestion are examples of these.

_____ 7. Skills that include the ability to communicate effectively and the ability to listen attentively, interpreting and responding to what others say.

A. alternative solutions

B. coping

C. attitude skills

D. personal management skills

E. relationship skills

F. self-observation skills

G. stressful reactions

True/False: Circle *T* if the statement is true or *F* if the statement is false.

T   F   8. All stress is negative and undesirable.

T   F   9. Different people may react to the same stressful situation in different ways.

T   F   10. You can develop personal skills in stress management to improve the way you react to stress.

T   F   11. Breaking a crisis situation into smaller, more manageable problems makes problem solving less difficult.

T   F   12. Trying to develop healthy emotions, such as courage and optimism, is part of developing relationship skills.

T   F   13. Creative activities can provide an outlet for excess tension.

T   F   14. By being aware of situations that might cause stress and preparing for those situations, you are practicing the skill of self-observation.

T   F   15. Being able to clarify your values and make choices directed toward your goals are personal management skills.

(Continued)

Name _____

T   F   16. People who have flexible standards tend to experience less stress than people who are
            not willing to adapt their standards to a situation.

T   F   17. Yoga is an example of a momentary relaxation skill.

Multiple Choice: Choose the best answer and write the corresponding letter in the blank.

_____ 18. Which of the following is NOT true about stressful situations?
               A. Almost all stressful situations are the result of major life events.
               B. Stressful situations can have a great impact on a person's health and happiness.
               C. Over half of all diseases are related to stress.
               D. If your goals are unreasonable, you may experience frustration and stressful situations.

_____ 19. Self-imposed stress _____.
               A. results from a person's own thought processes
               B. often results from unrealistic expectations
               C. often results from self-imposed obligations
               D. All of the above.

_____ 20. Situational stress _____.
               A. involves conditions inside a person
               B. often occurs as a result of change
               C. is seldom related to basic human needs
               D. All of the above.

_____ 21. Which of the following is true about the use of the problem-solving process in
               managing stress?
               A. Being able to recognize signs of stress is important when defining the stress
                  situation.
               B. Alternative solutions may eliminate the cause of the stress, reduce the stress, or
                  help you to accept the cause of the stress.
               C. Evaluating the process each time you use it can help you solve problems in the future.
               D. All of the above are true.

_____ 22. Which of the following is true about personal skills for effective coping?
               A. Most pressures can be converted into positive challenges.
               B. Learning organizational skills means learning how your body and mind react to
                  stressful situations.
               C. Skills in deep relaxation will prevent stressful situations from occurring.
               D. All of the above are true.

Essay Questions: Provide the answers you feel best show your understanding of the subject matter.

23. Describe a situation when a teenager might experience self-imposed stress.

24. Describe a situation in which change might cause stress to occur.

25. Name and describe each step of the problem-solving process as used in dealing with stress.

26. Explain why skills in personal health and relaxation are important in dealing with stress and describe
    three of these skills.

19

Environmental Responsibility

Objectives

When students have completed this chapter, they will be able to

◆ recognize environmental conditions that are hazardous to their health and safety.
◆ identify actions they can take to protect the enironment.
◆ identify preventive techniques that will help them stay safe and healthy.

Bulletin Boards

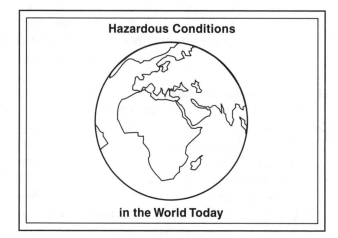

Hazardous Conditions

in the World Today

Title: *Hazardous Conditions in the World Today*

Draw a large globe in the center of the board. Place a collage of pictures depicting air pollution, water pollution, noise pollution, pollution from solid waste material, pollution by radiation, accidents, fire injuries and deaths, and poisonous substances around the globe.

Title: *Stay Healthy Through Preventive Techniques*

List and illustrate each of the following steps in prevention: routine medical exams, medical health records, vaccinations, awareness of warning signals of illness and disease, and emergency care of sick or injured.

Teaching Materials

Text, pages 319-339
To Review
To Challenge Your Thinking
To Do with the Class
To Do with Your Community
Student Activity Guide
A. *Hazardous Conditions*
B. *Resources for a Safer Environment*
C. *Staying Healthy*
Teacher's Resources
Handling Hazardous Waste at Home, reproducible master 19-1
Home Safety Checklist, reproducible master 19-2
Chapter 19 Test
Home Safety, color transparency CT-19

Introductory Activities

1. Develop a set of answers for which students must compete to state the questions in a game-show format. Answers should focus on global, national, community, and home concerns related to health hazards. Allow the class to work in teams to find the questions.
2. Develop a display of pictures, pamphlets, and books on hazardous conditions and prevention of health hazards. Allow students to view the display and discuss their reactions to the display.

Instructional Concepts and Student Learning Experiences

Hazardous Environmental Conditions

3. Have students research current information on concerns regarding the world's food supply in relation to increasing population. Have students share their findings with the class.

4. Have students discuss the effect of population density on the quality of life.

5. In small groups, have students develop plans for making areas with high population density more pleasant places to live. Students should display and discuss their plans in class.

6. Have students work as a class to develop a chart listing items that are considered air pollutants. For each item on the list, students should give the effects of the pollutant and ways to keep the substance from polluting the air.

7. Have students write a research report on the link between chronic lung disease and air pollution.

8. Have students interview an official from your community's sewage treatment plant to find out how effective sewage treatment is in preventing water pollution. Students should write an article based on their findings.

9. Have students discuss how water is used at home, either for essential or nonessential purposes. Ask them to suggest ways to eliminate or reduce waste of water.

10. Divide the class into three groups for a panel discussion. One group should present information on how industry contributes to pollution. A second group should present information on efforts being made—either through public policy or private industry—to reduce industry pollution. The third group should prepare questions for the panelists.

11. Have students work as a class to develop a list of noises that could be considered noise pollutants.

12. Have students discuss ways that noise can cause both physical and psychological problems.

13. Guest speaker. Invite a doctor who specializes in hearing problems to discuss types of jobs in which noise pollution is especially harmful.

14. Have students discuss ways that individuals can help control solid waste pollution.

15. Invite a representative from your city government to discuss what is being done in your community to help relieve solid waste disposal problems.

16. Have students give an oral report on recycling programs designed to control pollution from solid waste.

17. *Handling Hazardous Waste at Home,* reproducible master 19-1, TR. Have students research to find the appropriate procedures for disposing of each of the items listed.

18. Have students research to find natural sources of radiation. Students should discuss their findings in class.

19. Guest speaker. Invite an X-ray technologist to discuss the pros and cons of X rays.

20. Panel discussion. Invite qualified individuals to discuss the advantages and disadvantages of using herbicides and pesticides when growing foods. Speakers might include farmers, representatives of produce associations, government representatives, and consumer advocacy group representatives.

21. Guest speaker. Invite a pharmacist to speak on the responsible use of drugs.

22. *Resources for a Safer Environment*, Activity B, SAG. Have each student find a recent article related to food and drug concerns or accidents. Each student should write a brief summary of the article and explain how people might use information in the article as a resource to help make the environment safer.

23. Have students make posters that highlight ways to prevent food contamination.

24. Have students debate the following topic: "Food Additives—Harmful or Helpful?" Students should be prepared to back their arguments with research.

25. Have students write to the National Safety Council and other safety-related organizations to request literature on accident prevention. Students should organize the information received into a fact file.

26. Have students plan a presentation in which they demonstrate proper methods of storing cleaning supplies, medicines, insecticides, and poisons in the household. Invite parents of young children to view the demonstration.

27. *Home Safety,* color transparency CT-19, TR. Use this transparency as an introduction to home safety. Ask students to share examples of how to prevent accidents and ensure security at home. List their examples on the transparency.

28. Have students make a videotape on home safety. Students could show common hazards in the home and ways to correct or improve those situations. Make arrangements for members of the community to view the tape at school or at a local business that is willing to run the tape.
29. *Home Safety Checklist,* reproducible master 19-2, TR. Have students use the checklist to evaluate the safety of a home. Each student may evaluate his or her own home or the home of another family willing to have their home inspected.
30. Guest speaker. Invite a law enforcement official to discuss motor vehicle accidents. The guest should focus on ways to prevent accidents.
31. *Hazardous Conditions,* Activity A, SAG. Have students complete the chart by giving three steps a person could take to make the environment safer and healthier for each of the items listed.

Prevention Techniques

32. *Staying Healthy,* Activity C, SAG. Have students answer the questions related to preventing health problems.
33. Guest speaker. Invite a doctor or nurse to discuss symptoms in children and adults that indicate a need to see a doctor.
34. As a class, have students identify various medical conditions that can be detected in regular physicals. Students should list these conditions in a chart. Beside each condition, students should place an explanation of how early detection can lessen the severity of the condition.
35. Have students interview a dentist about changes in dentistry over the years. Students should write an article based on the interview.
36. Have students develop a chart that can be used to keep family health records up-to-date. Include the chart in a school district newsletter or mailing to parents.
37. Have students research to find information on new vaccinations that are still in the experimental stages. Students should discuss their findings in class.
38. Have students write a research report on a disease that is currently preventable through vaccinations. Students should include information on the prevalence and severity of the disease before the vaccine was developed.

39. Have students make posters informing people of health signs that indicate a need to visit a doctor.
40. Have students interview a professional from a mental health clinic to find out about signs of poor mental health. Students should report their findings to the class.
41. Have students conduct a survey to find out whether people know who to contact in case of a medical emergency. Have students use information from the survey to develop an informational pamphlet about contacting emergency medical help. Distribute the pamphlet throughout the school and/or community.
42. Have students develop a list of community resources for learning first aid procedures.
43. Demonstration. Invite a paramedic or doctor to demonstrate first aid for cuts and burns.

Answer Key

Text

To Review
1. (Student response.)
2. (Student response.)
3. Recycling is taking a used product and turning it back into something that can be used again.
4. Heavy taxes might be imposed on any product or wrapping designed to be thrown away rather than returned or recycled. Laws could prohibit the manufacture of products that are neither biodegradable nor recyclable. Large deposits could be required for beverage cans to encourage the return of these containers.
5. (Name two:) increases a person's chances of cancer, may do damage to reproductive cells, can cause radiation sickness
6. harmful bacteria, chemical contamination
7. A. false
   B. true
8. (List six:) blood type, allergies, drug sensitivities, serious illnesses, immunizations, surgeries
9. Vaccinations can prevent many serious diseases or make them less serious. The vaccination stimulates a person's body to build up resistance to a disease.
10. (List five:) change in bowel or bladder habits; a sore that does not heal; unusual bleeding or discharge; thickening or lump in breast or elsewhere; indigestion or difficulty in swallowing; obvious change in wart or mole; nagging cough or hoarseness

Student Activity Guide

Staying Healthy, Activity C

1. information about the health of close relatives, previous illnesses, related health problems, immunizations
2. Some people question whether the cost of the exam is worth the doctor's time and the patient's money.
3. blood pressure test, standard blood and urine test, Pap smear for women (People with special concerns may need other tests.)
4. To clean the teeth and remove deposits of tartar, food, and other matter. This process helps prevent gum disease and tooth decay.
5. They periodically take X rays of the teeth.
6. Children—before starting school and at puberty. Adults—periodically until age 40; then every two or three years.
7. A small amount of dead or weakened bacteria or virus is given by mouth or by injection. It stimulates the body to build up resistance to the disease.
8. change in bowel or bladder habits, a sore that does not heal, unusual bleeding or discharge, thickening or lump in the breast or elsewhere, indigestion, nagging cough or hoarseness
9. (List three:) depression, sudden changes in behavior, inability to feel pleasure, not enjoying life, overuse of defense mechanisms
10. To help a victim until he or she can get to a doctor.

Teacher's Resources

Chapter 19 Test

1. D
2. F
3. C
4. G
5. E
6. A
7. B
8. H
9. F
10. F
11. T
12. T
13. T
14. T
15. F
16. T
17. T
18. F
19. B
20. D
21. C
22. B
23. B
24. (Name three:) increase in population, altering the environment, food contamination, drug use, accidents (Student response for explanations.)
25. salmonellosis, staph poisoning, botulism (Student response for descriptions.)
26. (List four:) speed, alcohol, emotions, fatigue, lack of preparedness, failure to drive defensively, or a combination of factors (Student response for descriptions.)
27. (List four:) change in bowel or bladder habits, a sore that does not heal, unusual bleeding or discharge, thickening or lump in breast or elsewhere, indigestion or difficulty in swallowing, obvious change in wart or mole, nagging cough or hoarseness

Reproducible Master 19-1

Handling Hazardous Waste at Home

Name _____ Date _____ Period _____

Many home products can become hazardous if they are not disposed of properly. Research to find the proper ways to dispose of the products listed below and complete the chart.

Hazardous Waste in the Home	Proper Disposal Methods
Lead-based paints	
Paint thinner/turpentine	
Paint or varnish stripper	
Varnish/shellac/stains	
Pesticides	
Disinfectants	
Mothballs	
Wood preservatives	
Waste oil	
Antifreeze	
Batteries	
Brake fluid	
Contaminated gasoline	
Medicine	
Detergents	
Bleach	
Ammonia-based cleaners	
Aerosol cans	
Pest control poisons	

Reproducible Master 19-2

Home Safety Checklist

Name _____ **Date** _____ **Period** _____

Evaluate the safety of a home using the checklist below.

	Yes	No
Are smoke alarms installed and working?	❑	❑
Are smoke alarms tested regularly?	❑	❑
Are handrails and banisters secure?	❑	❑
Are electrical outlets in good condition? (They do not smoke, spark, make unusual intermittent noises, or have warm or hot spots in or around them?)	❑	❑
Is a fireplace screen used whenever a fire is burning in the fireplace?	❑	❑
Is the chimney flue clean?	❑	❑
Are kitchen appliances unplugged when not in use?	❑	❑
Do bathtubs and showers have slip-proof surfaces?	❑	❑
Are shower doors made of safety glazed materials?	❑	❑
Are hair dryers, shavers, and other appliances unplugged when not in use?	❑	❑
Are there no more than two plugs connected to any one outlet?	❑	❑
Are cords on lamps, TVs, radios, and other devices safely routed out of traffic patterns?	❑	❑
Are cords in good condition, not frayed, taped, with loose plugs, or stapled or nailed to the floor or walls?	❑	❑
Do the plug prongs on the device's cord or extension cord match the outlet's openings?	❑	❑
Do all heavy-duty appliances such as window air conditioners, washers, and dryers operate on their own circuits?	❑	❑
Are all small kitchen appliances listed as approved by Underwriters Laboratories or another recognized testing organization?	❑	❑

	Yes	No
Do all large appliances such as dishwashers, washers, dryers, and TVs have Underwriters Laboratories or another appropriate organization's safety label?	❑	❑
Are all appliances used in the kitchen, bathroom, and laundry areas fitted with three-pronged, grounding plugs?	❑	❑
Do all doors close and lock securely? Are the entryway and front hall well lit?	❑	❑
Are rugs, runners, or mats secure so they don't slip or slide?	❑	❑
Are power tools unplugged when not in use?	❑	❑
Are all tools stored out of children's reach?	❑	❑
Is gardening and maintenance equipment cleaned and hung out of children's reach?	❑	❑
Are flammables kept in sealed containers in the garage?	❑	❑
Is garage storage neat and clear of all doors?	❑	❑
Are automatic garage door opening devices kept out of children's reach?	❑	❑
Are all appliances and electrical equipment used away from sinks, bathtubs, showers, and other wet areas?	❑	❑
Are medicines and cleaning products kept out of children's reach?	❑	❑
Are antidotes for cleaning products and other poisons posted where poisonous items are stored? Do you review them periodically?	❑	❑
Are flammable paints, glues, varnishes, and sprays stored outside living areas?	❑	❑
Are infants' and toddlers' furnishings up to federal and ASTM standards including stability and strength of construction?	❑	❑

Environmental Responsibility

Name _____

Date _____ **Period** _____ **Score** _____

Chapter 19 Test

Matching: Match the following terms and identifying phrases.

_____ 1. Occurs when a person's genes are damaged or altered.

_____ 2. The wastes that are responsible for polluting the environment.

_____ 3. The rarest and deadliest type of food poisoning, which is most commonly caused by inadequately processed home canned food.

_____ 4. Type of food poisoning caused by the most common disease-producing bacteria that can be transmitted through food, people, insects, rodents, or pets.

_____ 5. Additives that are generally recognized as safe.

_____ 6. Is linked with lung cancer, emphysema, bronchitis, and other respiratory ailments.

_____ 7. The wastes that can be broken down into useful substances by natural processes.

_____ 8. A small amount of dead or weakened bacteria or virus given by mouth or injection to stimulate a person's body to build up resistance to a disease.

A. air pollution

B. biodegradable

C. botulism

D. genetic mutation

E. GRAS list

F. nonbiodegradable

G. salmonellosis

H. vaccine

True/False: Circle *T* if the statement is true or *F* if the statement is false.

T F 9. Although noise pollution is unpleasant, it cannot be physically harmful to a person.

T F 10. All radiation is manufactured.

T F 11. Foods on the GRAS list are generally recognized as safe to human health.

T F 12. Although sodium nitrite is suspected of being cancer-producing, the government allows permissible levels to be used as a preservative.

T F 13. Accidents are among the four leading causes of death for people of all ages.

T F 14. Statistics show that wearing seat belts has helped save many lives.

T F 15. The majority of poisoning deaths are among young children.

T F 16. A fever usually indicates illness or infection.

T F 17. A person who is untrained in first aid could cause serious injury if attempting to help someone who has been involved in a bad accident.

T F 18. It is recommended that people have dental examinations once every two years.

(Continued)

Name _____

Multiple Choice: Choose the best answer and write the corresponding letter in the blank.

_____ 19. The increase in population in the United States is due largely to _____.
A. a decrease in the standard of living
B. improved nutritional standards
C. improved birth control measures
D. All of the above.

_____ 20. Which of the following is NOT true about botulism?
A. It is considered a deadly kind of food poisoning.
B. It occurs when home canned foods are not heated to a high enough temperature to kill the bacterial spores.
C. Fish, fruits, and vegetables may carry the organism that causes botulism.
D. It frequently occurs in commercially processed foods.

_____ 21. Which of the following is NOT true about vaccinations?
A. Vaccines against infectious diseases have played a major role in preventing illness and death at a young age.
B. Polio, tetanus, measles, and mumps are examples of diseases vaccines can prevent.
C. All vaccines are 100 percent effective.
D. Some vaccinations are occasionally accompanied by adverse reactions.

_____ 22. Which of the following statements is true in relation to medical and health records?
A. Your medical records should include only information about yourself
B. Families should keep their own accurate family health records.
C. Information about your medical history is usually not very helpful to a doctor in making a diagnosis.
D. All doctors are willing to release medical histories directly to their patients.

_____ 23. Which of the following is true about first aid care?
A. After first aid treatment, the victim should not need to see a doctor.
B. Because first aid can mean the difference between life and death, only competent people should perform it.
C. Skill in first aid procedures can be learned by reading brief written instructions.
D. First aid is always helpful to the victim.

Essay Questions: Provide the answers you feel best show your understanding of the subject matter.

24. Name three hazardous conditions of the environment and briefly explain why they are threats.

25. List three types of food poisoning by harmful bacteria and briefly describe each.

26. List and briefly describe four common causes of motor vehicle accidents.

27. List four warning signs of cancer.

20

Financial Management

Objectives

When students have completed this chapter, they will be able to

◆ describe financial challenges at various stages of life.
◆ explain the reasons for various paycheck deductions.
◆ manage a checking account.
◆ describe records and papers to keep for financial planning.
◆ explain the importance of a budget.
◆ demonstrate the steps in developing a budget.

Bulletin Boards

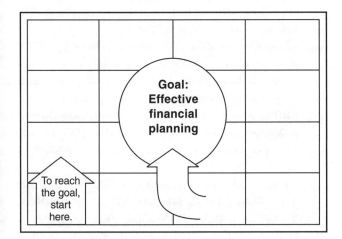

Title: *Goal: Effective Financial Planning*

Divide the board into squares to give the appearance of a board game. Place the words *To reach the goal, start here* in the corner square as shown. In each box, place an example of a type of record or form used in financial planning, such as

bank statements and canceled checks, insurance records, a budget, etc.

Title: *Save or Spend? Manage Your Money Wisely*

Place the words *Save or Spend* at the top of the board. At the bottom of the board place the words *Manage Your Money Wisely*. Construct or find a picture of an owl to place on the board. Surround the owl and fill in the background with dollar signs. These could be drawn directly on the background or cut from paper.

Teaching Materials

Text, pages 341-358
   To Review
   To Challenge Your Thinking
   To Do with the Class
   To Do with Your Community
Student Activity Guide
   A. *Keeping Track of Your Records*
   B. *A Monthly Budget*
   C. *Cash Spending*
Teacher's Resources
   Recording Checking Transactions,
      reproducible master 20-1
   Family Business Information, transparency
      master 20-2
   Chapter 20 Test
   Check It Out! color transparency CT-20

Introductory Activities

1. Develop a skit that exaggerates some of the problems caused when a person does not keep financial records or plans. Present the skit with another faculty member. Problems in the skit should focus on financial problems

that are relevant to teens. For instance, a teen may not be able to go to a concert with friends because he or she just bought four CDs and has no money left. Have students discuss how financial record keeping and planning can help avoid the problems presented in the skit.

2. Develop a display of materials available to help with record keeping. Have students examine the materials and discuss how they might be helpful.

Instructional Concepts and Student Learning Experiences

Financial Management Throughout Life

3. Have students survey persons of their own age, young adults, middle adults, and older adults. The students could develop preliminary questions to ask about the challenges and priorities with regard to the management of finances in the various stages of life. Have students report their findings to the class.

4. Divide the class in groups, with each group selecting a specific stage of life. Have the students collect pictures and make a collage of the spending habits related to the various stages. Students could share with the class their views on financial management throughout the life cycle.

5. Have students collect and share articles from the newspapers, magazines, or the Internet related to consumer habits and spending throughout the life cycle. The articles could also be specific to a certain stage of life.

6. Guest speaker. Invite a family or marriage counselor to discuss how misunderstandings related to money and financial planning can affect marriages.

Understanding Your Paycheck

7. Display a variety of checkbook and paycheck formats. Have the class compare them and discuss their differences, advantages, and disadvantages.

8. Invite a guest speaker to discuss occupations in which deductions are not taken from the worker's paycheck and what this means in terms of that individual's income tax and social security payments.

9. *Recording Checking Transactions,* reproducible master 20-1, TR. Have students use the information given to record the transactions in the given check register.

Basic Banking

10. Develop through class activity a bulletin board showing the various types of checking accounts.

11. Invite a representative from a local bank to make a presentation on managing a checking account and answer questions from the class.

Record Keeping

12. *Keeping Track of Your Records,* Activity A, SAG. Have students develop and describe a record keeping system that would work well.

13. *Cash Spending,* Activity C, SAG. Have students use the form provided to plan and evaluate a system to account for the cash that they spend.

14. Guest speaker. Invite a financial counselor to discuss the importance of good record keeping in financial planning.

15. Have students interview an insurance agent to find out what kinds of records people should keep for insurance purposes. Students should write an article based on their findings.

16. *Check It Out!* color transparency CT-20, TR. Use this transparency as you explain the proper way to write a check.

17. *Family Business Information,* transparency master 20-2, TR. Have students discuss the types of information included on the form and why the information might be needed.

18. Panel discussion. Invite an insurance agent, a banker, and a lawyer to discuss how important papers and records may be needed in various life situations.

19. Have students interview an adult about the system that he or she uses to keep records. Students should share their findings in class.

20. Guest speaker. Invite a representative of a bank or savings and loan to explain the procedure in renting and using a safe deposit box and to give reasons why people rent safe deposit boxes.

21. Have students evaluate a home safe found at a local retail or office supply store. Students should report to the class on the safe's features and price.

Developing a Budget—
A Spending Plan

22. Have students plan and present commercials "selling" the advantages of having a budget.

23. Have students interview couples to find suggestions they have for making financial plans work. Students should compare their suggestions in class and develop a list of suggestions based on class input.

24. Have students discuss reasons why family income might vary from month to month.

25. Have students develop a list of common family expenditures. Students should then indicate whether each expenditure is fixed or flexible.

26. Have students develop a survey form to find out how students spend their money. Arrange to have the survey filled out in a few other classes. Students should analyze the results and write an article on them to be printed in the school newspaper.

27. Have students interview young adults who are living on their own or are sharing an apartment with another person to find what categories of spending they experience each month and approximately how much they spend in each category.

28. Have students list five short-term goals and five long-term goals. Students should write explanations of how each of the goals listed might affect a person's budget.

29. Have students debate whether children should be included in family budget planning.

30. *A Monthly Budget,* Activity B, SAG. Have students use the form provided to develop and evaluate a monthly budget.

31. Have students brainstorm a list of reasons why a family may not be able to follow their budget. Students should discuss how families may need to adjust spending in other categories to compensate for changes in spending.

Answer Key

Text

To Review

1. (Name at least two:) Social security or FICA, federal income tax, state income tax, retirement fund contributions, insurance premiums, union dues

2. (Give three:) You can avoid carrying a lot of cash. It provides a record of spending and receipts of payment. It provides a safe place to keep cash. It's a convenient way to buy goods and services and pay bills by mail.

3. Decide which records and papers to keep. Make decisions about the method of keeping those records. Decide where the records should be kept.

4. financial records, property records, personal records

5. The household inventory is a list of personal property including household furniture, furnishings, and equipment. The date of purchase and the purchase price or appraised value are included. This is an important document to have to prove ownership and value in case of fire or theft.

6. A. true
   B. true

7. (List five. Student response.)

8. Fixed expenses stay the same or nearly the same each month. Rent or house payments and loan payments are fixed expenses. Some fixed expenses are periodic rather than monthly. Certain bills, such as taxes and insurance, are fixed expenses, but may be paid once or twice a year. Flexible expenses vary both in amount and frequency of occurrence. They include items such as food, clothing, transportation, and personal expenses.

9. Saving part of your income is an important spending goal, even if it is a small monthly amount. It is helpful to have some type of "cushion" amount in case of emergencies. The amount in savings can be earning interest. Putting a set amount in savings each month is a good plan for saving.

10. You may need to make adjustments if your actual spending and planned spending do not come out nearly the same.

Teacher's Resources

Recording Checking Transactions,
reproducible master 20-1

See illustration below.

Chapter 20 Test
1. J
2. A
3. F
4. I
5. G
6. E
7. C
8. D
9. H
10. B
11. N
12. L
13. M
14. K
15. F
16. F
17. F
18. T
19. F
20. T
21. T
22. F
23. T
24. F
25. B
26. D
27. D
28. C
29. C
30. (Student response.)
31. (Student response.)
32. (Student response.)
33. They can either reduce their expenses or generate additional income. They may be able to reduce their fixed expenses more easily than their flexible expenses. They could generate additional income by changing jobs or by having two adults in the family work.

NUMBER	DATE	CHECKS ISSUED TO OR DESCRIPTION OF DEPOSIT	(–) AMOUNT OF CHECK		✓ T	(–) CHECK FEE (IF ANY)	(+) AMOUNT OF DEPOSIT		BALANCE	
		PLEASE BE SURE TO DEDUCT ANY PER CHECK CHARGES OR SERVICE CHARGES THAT MAY APPLY TO YOUR ACCOUNT							705	83
		TO/FOR Citizen's Electric							21	73
823	4/19	April electric bill	21	73				BAL	684	10
		TO/FOR Bell Phone							35	83
824	4/19	April phone bill	35	83				BAL	648	27
		TO/FOR Pleasentview Apartments							215	00
825	4/30	May rent	215	00				BAL	433	27
		TO/FOR deposit							295	73
	5/5						295	73 BAL	729	00
		TO/FOR Charge – Amay Company							113	57
826	5/7	April credit card bill	113	57				BAL	615	43
		TO/FOR							BAL		

Reproducible Master 20-1

Recording Checking Transactions

Name _____ **Date** _____ **Period** _____

Use the check register below to record the transactions indicated by the checks and deposit ticket on this page.

PLEASE BE SURE TO DEDUCT ANY PER CHECK CHARGES OR SERVICE CHARGES THAT MAY APPLY TO YOUR ACCOUNT

NUMBER	DATE	CHECKS ISSUED TO OR DESCRIPTION OF DEPOSIT	(−) AMOUNT OF CHECK	√ T	(−) CHECK FEE (IF ANY)	(+) AMOUNT OF DEPOSIT	BALANCE 705	83
		TO/FOR Citizen's Electric					21	73
823	4/19	April electric bill	21 73				684	10
		TO/FOR Bell Phone					35	83
824	4/19	April phone bill	35 83				648	27
		TO/FOR Pleasentview Apartments					215	00
825	4/30	May rent	215 00				433	27
		TO/FOR deposit					295	73
	5/5					295 73	729	00
		TO/FOR Charge – Amay Company					113	57
826	5/7	April credit card bill	113 57				615	43
		TO/FOR						

Transparency Master 20-2

Family Business Information

Date _____

Name _____   Social security number_____

Social security number_____

Bank and savings accounts:

Checking: Bank _____   Account Number _____

Savings: Institution_____   Account Number _____

Institution _____   Account Number _____

Safe deposit box: Bank _____   Box number _____

Name, address, and phone number of:

   Banker _____

   Attorney _____

   Doctor _____

   _____

   Dentist_____

Insurance agents:

   Life _____

   Health _____

   Property _____

   Automobile _____

Credit cards:

Name	Card #	Number to call to report loss

Where the following are kept:

Life insurance policies _____   Safe deposit box key _____

Health insurance policies _____   Household inventory _____

Property insurance policies _____   Income tax returns_____

Deeds to property _____   Wills _____

Mortgages _____   Automobile title(s) _____

Birth certificates_____   Auto registration _____

Marriage certificate _____

Financial Management

Name _____

Date _____ **Period** _____ **Score** _____

Chapter 20 Test

Matching: Match the following terms and identifying phrases.

_____ 1. A spending plan that is used to control the use of money.

_____ 2. Records that show how you spend your money.

_____ 3. Records, such as personal documents, health records, education records, and employment records.

_____ 4. A rented metal box in a fireproof vault, usually at a bank.

_____ 5. Records that can prove ownership, indicate monetary value of possessions, and help determine insurance needs.

_____ 6. All the money received from salaries or wages, money gifts, tips, allowances, interest earned, dividends, income from securities, or income from rental property.

_____ 7. Expenses that vary in amount and frequency of occurrence.

_____ 8. A list of personal property including household furniture, furnishings, and equipment and the date of purchase and purchase price or appraised value of each item.

_____ 9. A list of all your important papers and where they are stored.

_____ 10. Expenses that occur regularly and stay the same or nearly the same.

_____ 11. The total amount you earn for a pay period before any deductions are subtracted from your paycheck.

_____ 12. The total amount you earn for a pay period minus the deductions.

_____ 13. Requires your signature and should only be used at the time and place a check is being cashed or deposited.

_____ 14. Common ones often say "For deposit only" and your signature or "Pay to the order of," the name of the party to receive the check, and your signature.

A. financial records

B. fixed expenses

C. flexible expenses

D. household inventory

E. income

F. personal documents

G. property records

H. record keeping inventory

I. safe deposit box

J. budget

K. restrictive endorsement

L. net pay

M. blank endorsement

N. gross pay

(Continued)

Name _____

True/False: Circle *T* if the statement is true or *F* if the statement is false.

T F 15. All personal and family records and papers should be organized and filed in some way.

T F 16. Bank records include charge account receipts and savings bonds.

T F 17. Any paper that will be needed immediately should be kept in a safe deposit box.

T F 18. A budget guides the use of a person's money.

T F 19. Budgets are only necessary for people who have lower than average incomes.

T F 20. Some sources of income include wages, money gifts, tips, allowances, and interest on savings accounts.

T F 21. Car expenses and clothing expenses are both considered flexible expenses.

T F 22. The average family spends the greatest percentage of its income on food and taxes.

T F 23. Saving part of your income might be one of your spending goals.

T F 24. For your budget to succeed, you must stick to rigid rules and avoid making adjustments in your spending categories.

Multiple Choice: Choose the best answer and write the corresponding letter in the blank.

_____ 25. Which of the following statements about important papers and record keeping is NOT true?
   A. Some personal documents may be needed to prove marital status.
   B. Canceled checks provide a complete record of spending.
   C. The household inventory is an important document in proving ownership.
   D. Charge account receipts can be used in settling credit disputes.

_____ 26. Which of the following is true about record keeping?
   A. Although some papers can be stored at home, others should be in a safer place, such as a safe deposit box.
   B. The style of record keeping you choose is not important as long as that style suits your record keeping purposes.
   C. All members of the family who are old enough to understand should know how the record-keeping system works and how information can be found.
   D. All of the above are true.

_____ 27. Which of the following is true about developing a budget?
   A. Before you can develop a budget, you need information regarding income and expenses.
   B. Income from a salary should include only take-home pay.
   C. Not all fixed expenses are monthly expenses.
   D. All of the above are true.

_____ 28. When completing a budget, remember that _____.
   A. the one type of form that is to be used is called the "budget form"
   B. budgets are more effective figured on a yearly basis than if figured on a monthly basis
   C. being flexible is an important part of managing a budget
   D. for some categories, you will not be able to estimate spending

(Continued)

Name _____

_____ 29. Which of the following is NOT true about evaluating a budget?
   A. A successful budget requires constant evaluation.
   B. If the spending figures and estimates are not close, you will have to adjust the budget.
   C. If spending is greater than income, there is no way to work out a usable budget.
   D. Reducing flexible expenses can be difficult for some families.

Essay Questions: Provide the answers you feel best show your understanding of the subject matter.

30. Explain what property records are and why they are important to save.

31. Explain three advantages of developing a budget.

32. Describe the necessary steps in developing a budget.

33. Describe alternatives a family has if they find through a budget that their spending exceeds their income.

Using Credit Wisely

Objectives

When students have completed this chapter, they will be able to
- recognize the advantages and disadvantages of credit use.
- describe types of credit and types of credit cards.
- give examples of various sources of credit and explain how a person obtains credit.
- identify and explain various laws governing credit.

Bulletin Boards

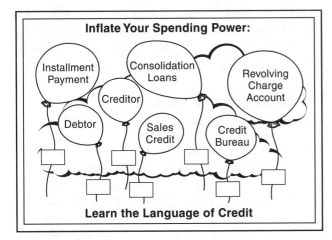

Title: *Inflate Your Spending Power: Learn the Language of Credit*

Use blue and white construction paper to make a background that looks like a sky with clouds. Place balloons made from construction paper on the board with strings hanging from them as shown. Label the balloons with vocabulary terms from Chapter 21. Attach pieces of paper with definitions for the terms on the strings of the balloons.

Title: *Weigh the Advantages and Disadvantages of Credit*

Draw a large balance with two baskets hanging from it. Label one basket *Advantages* and the other *Disadvantages*. Have students write down advantages or disadvantages and place them on the board above the appropriate basket.

Teaching Materials

Text, pages 359-375
To Review
To Challenge Your Thinking
To Do with the Class
To Do with Your Community
Student Activity Guide
  A. *Credit Advantages and Disadvantages*
  B. *Types of Credit*
  C. *Obtaining Credit*
  D. *Consumer Credit Laws*
Teacher's Resources
Types of Consumer Credit, transparency master 21-1
Chapter 21 Test
Credit, color transparency CT-21

Introductory Activities

1. Have students complete the following statements:
   - Credit is…
   - People who borrow money are…
   - People should use credit…
   Discuss the ideas and attitudes reflected in the various responses.
2. Have students discuss alternatives to using credit for different purposes, such as education, home furnishings, medical bills, and vacation.
3. *Credit,* color transparency CT-21, TR. Use this transparency as an introduction to credit. Discuss how the unwise use of credit can have significant, possibly extreme consequences. Discuss how adults and especially adolescents get "trapped" and also ways to avoid the credit "trap."

Instructional Concepts and Student Learning Experiences

Credit Use

4. *Credit Advantages and Disadvantages,* Activity A, SAG. Have students complete the chart by writing about situations that illustrate each of the advantages and disadvantages of credit listed.
5. Have students discuss the meaning of the statement, "Credit is a good servant but a bad master."
6. Have students find articles describing some of the problems or advantages of using credit. Students should share their findings in class.
7. *Types of Consumer Credit,* transparency master 21-1, TR. Review the various types of credit with the class. As you discuss each type, have students give definitions for each item.
8. As a class project, have students develop a collection of brochures and application forms for various types of credit.
9. *Types of Credit,* Activity B, SAG. Have students answer the questions about various types of credit.
10. Have students develop a chart comparing limited purpose credit cards to multipurpose credit cards.
11. Have students find information on credit card protection services and write a report based on their findings.
12. Have students develop a form that can be used to keep information on credit cards in case they are lost or stolen. Students should give the form to a person with several credit cards and ask the person to evaluate the form's usefulness.
13. Have students research to find out more about the processes involved in borrowing money from one of the credit sources listed in the text. Students should share their findings in an oral report.
14. Panel discussion. Invite representatives of local banks, savings and loans, consumer finance companies, credit unions, and life insurance companies to discuss the criteria for receiving a loan from them and loan terms.
15. *Obtaining Credit,* Activity C, SAG. Have students determine whether each factor used to evaluate credit applicants relates to character, capacity, or capital. Students should then explain how the factor might affect an applicant's credit rating.
16. Have students analyze a credit application from a bank or savings and loan. Based on the information requested, students should discuss actions they can take in the future to assure that they are good credit risks.
17. Guest speaker. Invite a representative of a credit card company or credit card department of a store to discuss credit application processing with the class.

Managing Credit Use Throughout Life

18. Have students survey persons in school age, young adult, middle adult, and later adult years. Find out how often and what types of credit they use. Report the findings to the class.
19. Search the Internet for trends in credit use for the various stages of life. Research the debt trends as well.
20. Have students ask persons in the various stages of life what advice they would give to younger persons about the use of credit. Share answers with the class.

Laws and Regulations Governing Credit

21. *Consumer Credit Laws,* Activity D, SAG. Have students complete the given charts on consumer credit laws by explaining the features of the laws and benefits of the laws to consumers.
22. Have students research one of the credit laws discussed in the text to find out why the law was introduced and how it affected consumers. Students should give an oral or written report on their findings.
23. Have students interview a person who does research for a credit bureau to find out the process involved in running a credit check. Students should write an article based on their interview.
24. Have students write a practice letter to a hypothetical creditor about a billing error.
25. Guest speaker. Invite a credit counselor to discuss the reasons why consumer credit laws were adopted and their effects on consumers and creditors.

Answer Key

Text

To Review

1. When you have an installment loan, you borrow a set amount of money and repay it plus finance charges in a series of scheduled payments. When you have a single-payment loan, you borrow an amount of money and repay that amount plus finance charges in one payment.
2. With regular charge accounts, the customer will be billed within 30 days after the purchase. The total amount billed is due. If it is not paid by the due date, the customer will be charged interest. If only a partial amount is paid, interest will be charged on the amount not paid. Revolving charge accounts differ in that the total amount does not have to be paid each month. A minimum amount that is to be paid is stated on the bill. However, a finance charge is figured on the amount unpaid.
3. commercial banks, consumer finance companies, credit unions, life insurance companies
4. true
5. Capacity, character, capital. Capacity is your ability to repay the debt from regular income. Questions on the credit application help the lender evaluate capacity. Character is whether or not you are likely to repay the debt. It is difficult to evaluate, but a person's credit history is helpful. Questions related to this appear on the credit application. Capital involves your financial resources. It includes your property and your savings. Questions on the application will indicate whether or not you will be able to repay the debt.
6. They can encounter big debts at an early age.
7. The potential for serious illness is greater, and middle-age people who are laid off as a result of business cutbacks, often have trouble finding another job.
8. responsibilities
9. Truth in Lending Law, Equal Credit Opportunity Act, Fair Credit Reporting Act, Fair Credit Billing Act
10. Notify the creditor in writing within 60 days at the address indicated on the bill. The letter should include the name, address, and account number of the consumer as well as the reason the bill is wrong. The creditor is expected to acknowledge the consumer's letter within 30 days unless the account is corrected.

Student Activity Guide

Types of Credit, Activity B

1. Cash credit is used to borrow money, and sales credit is used to purchase goods and services.
2. Cash credit might be used to purchase goods and services from sellers who do not give credit.
3. Regular installment payments would be made, and they would include the finance charges.
4. from the people who sell goods and services
5. amount of purchase, amount of finance charge, total amount to be repaid
6. It acts as a guarantee that the customer will make the installment payments.
7. regular charge account
8. revolving charge account
9. The seller has the legal right to reclaim the product.
10. Phone the company immediately and explain what has happened. They will need to know your name, your address, and the number of people who have copies of the card. They will also need to know the account number and expiration date of the card.

Teacher's Resources

Chapter 21 Test

1. I
2. K
3. B
4. E
5. H
6. A
7. D
8. I
9. J
10. C
11. G
12. F
13. F
14. T

15. F
16. F
17. T
18. T
19. F
20. F
21. T
22. F
23. D
24. B
25. A
26. C
27. A
28. C
29. B
30. (Student response. Describe two advantages and two disadvantages.)
31. (Student response.)
32. Immediately contact your credit card company by phone. As soon as the credit card company is notified, you are no longer responsible for any charges. Give the company your name, address, and the account number of your card. Make a note of the time you call, and ask the person you speak with to do the same. Ask for a written confirmation of your call. Student response for explanation.
33. (Student response.)

Types of Consumer Credit

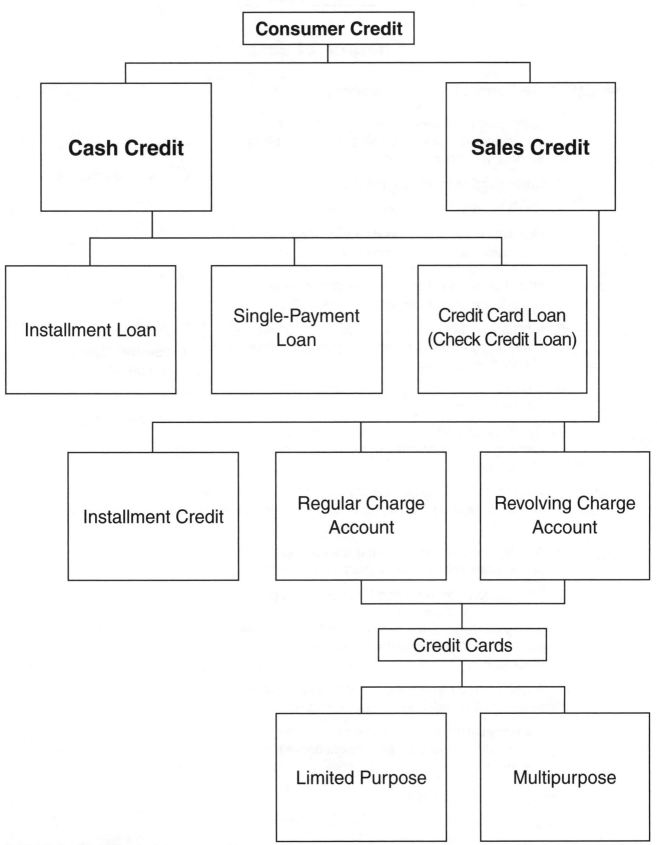

Using Credit Wisely

Name _____

Date _____ **Period** _____ **Score** _____

Chapter 21 Test

Matching: Match the following terms and identifying phrases.

_____ 1. Sales credit that allows customers to purchase goods and services on credit and pay the bill in 30 days with no interest charge.

_____ 2. Credit used to purchase goods and services.

_____ 3. Credit used to borrow money.

_____ 4. Firm which assembles credit information and other information about consumers and sells it to creditors, landlords, insurers, employers, and other businesses that are interested in a consumer's ability and willingness to repay loans.

_____ 5. A set amount of money is borrowed, and the borrower repays it plus finance charges in a series of scheduled payments.

_____ 6. A person's ability to repay debt from his or her regular income.

_____ 7. Supplying of money, goods, or services in exchange for the promise of future payment by the consumer.

_____ 8. An amount of money is borrowed, and that amount is repaid plus finance charges in one payment.

_____ 9. A charge account in which the total amount of the bill does not have to be paid each month.

_____ 10. When a borrower arranges for one loan to pay off the total amount of a variety of debts. After paying off these debts, the consumer makes one payment each month to the finance company or other lender.

_____ 11. A type of credit where the buyer makes regular payments that include the finance charges.

_____ 12. A financial institution that is run as a cooperative-owned and operated for the benefit of their members.

A. capacity

B. cash credit

C. consolidation loan

D. credit

E. credit bureau

F. credit union

G. installment credit

H. installment loan

I. regular charge account

J. revolving charge account

K. sales credit

L. single payment loan

(Continued)

Name _____

True/False: Circle *T* if the statement is true or *F* if the statement is false.

T   F   13. Creditors are the people who use credit.

T   F   14. Most limited purpose credit cards involve no membership fee or annual charge to the user.

T   F   15. Consumer finance companies have more rigid rules for qualifying for loans than commercial banks do.

T   F   16. Capital refers to the consumer's ability to repay the debt from his or her regular income.

T   F   17. Savings and loan associations were established mainly to finance home building.

T   F   18. According to the Truth in Lending Law, creditors must state the finance charge as an annual percentage rate.

T   F   19. It is legal for creditors to ask a credit applicant for age, race, or marital status when deciding whether or not to grant credit.

T   F   20. The credit bureau decides whether or not a consumer is a good or bad credit risk.

T   F   21. If a consumer is denied credit, he or she has the right to know why credit was denied.

T   F   22. If a consumer notices a billing error on a credit account, he or she should call the creditor on the phone to explain the error.

Multiple Choice: Choose the best answer and write the corresponding letter in the blank.

_____ 23. Which of the following statements about multipurpose credit cards is true?
  A. There is usually no finance charge if the total bill is paid within 30 days of the billing date.
  B. Most companies charge an annual membership fee.
  C. They can be used at a variety of businesses, department stores, and restaurants.
  D. All of the above are true.

_____ 24. The source of credit that is likely to charge the highest interest rate are_____.
  A. commercial banks
  B. consumer finance companies
  C. credit unions
  D. savings and loan associations

_____ 25. Which of the following questions on an application investigates the potential borrower's capacity?
  A. How much do you earn?
  B. Do you own or rent?
  C. How much life insurance do you have?
  D. What is the balance in your savings account?

_____ 26. Which of the following questions on an application investigates the potential borrower's capital?
  A. What is your occupation?
  B. Where have you obtained credit in the past and how much?
  C. What physical assets do you have that could be sold to repay the debt?
  D. Have you fully repaid your debts on time?

(Continued)

Name _____

_____ 27. The law that is especially important for people who have been victims of credit
discrimination is the _____.
A. Equal Credit Opportunity Act
B. Fair Credit Billing Act
C. Fair Credit Reporting Act
D. Truth in Lending Law

_____ 28. The law that is designed to ensure that credit agencies use fair and equitable
procedures in distributing credit information is the _____.
A. Equal Credit Opportunity Act
B. Fair Credit Billing Act
C. Fair Credit Reporting Act
D. Truth in Lending Law

_____ 29. The law that protects consumers against credit card abuses, computerized billing
system abuses, and other unfair billing practices is _____.
A. Equal Credit Opportunity Act
B. Fair Credit Billing Act
C. Fair Credit Reporting Act
D. Truth in Lending Law

Essay Questions: Provide the answers you feel best show your understanding of the subject matter.

30. Describe two advantages and two disadvantages of using credit.

31. Explain what limited purpose credit cards are and what multipurpose credit cards are.

32. Describe the procedures to follow if you lose a credit card and explain why these procedures are so
important.

33. Explain the meaning of the three Cs of credit.

Planning for Financial Security

Objectives

When students have completed this chapter, they will be able to
- relate savings and investment alternatives to building financial security.
- list types of life insurance, health insurance, property insurance, and automobile insurance and describe various features of each.
- describe sources of retirement income.
- relate estate planning steps toward financial security.

Bulletin Boards

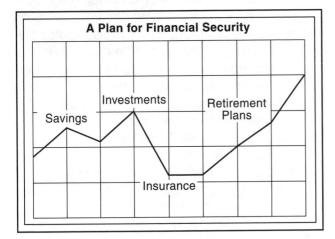

A Plan for Financial Security

Savings   Investments   Retirement Plans   Insurance

Title: *A Plan for Financial Security*

Draw a grid on the board and place a jagged line across it to represent a stock analysis chart as shown. Place the terms *Savings, Investments, Insurance,* and *Retirement Plans* on the board as shown.

Title: *Money Power for the Golden Years*

Place a large picture of senior citizens in the center of the board. Arrange pamphlets pertaining to retirement plans, savings programs, and other programs designed to assure financial security in later life around the center picture.

Teaching Materials

Text, pages 376-401
To Review
To Challenge Your Thinking
To Do with the Class
To Do with Your Community

Student Activity Guide
A. *Savings and Investment Choices*
B. *Life Insurance Match*
C. *Automobile Insurance*
D. *Understanding Insurance*
E. *Retirement Plans*

Teacher's Resources
Reading Investment Reports, reproducible master 22-1
Comparing Car Insurance Costs, reproducible master 22-2
Chapter 22 Test
Financial Security, color transparency CT-22

Introductory Activities

1. Have students brainstorm a list of financial hazards often experienced in families. Students should discuss ways that families can prepare for such hazards.
2. Have students interview an elderly person to find out what the person wishes he or she would have done differently to prepare for financial security in later years. Students should share their findings in class.
3. *Financial Security,* color transparency CT-22, TR. Use this transparency to introduce the basics of financial security and how wise application of investing, insuring, budgeting, saving, and spending can influence financial security.

Instructional Concepts and Student Learning Experiences

Savings and Investment Alternatives

4. Have students make a chart comparing the advantages and disadvantages of various kinds of savings and investments.
5. Have students debate the following statement: "Low income people barely have enough to survive on and cannot save money for emergencies."
6. Have students discuss the relationship between the level of risk and the rate of return on an investment. Students should discuss situations in which taking the risk may be worthwhile and situations in which risks are too great to be worth the possible profit.
7. *Savings and Investment Choices,* Activity A, SAG. Have students answer the questions about savings and investments.
8. Guest speaker. Invite a bank representative to discuss various savings plans. The speaker should focus on differences in interest and dividends as well as restrictions on various accounts.
9. Have students write a research report on various types of bonds, their costs, times of maturity, and yields.
10. *Reading Investment Reports,* reproducible master 22-1, TR. Have students use the master to interpret investment reports from current newspapers.
11. Guest speaker. Invite an investment counselor to discuss types of investments, types of risks involved, and the effects of inflation and recession on investments.
12. Have students make hypothetical investments in stocks and/or bonds. You may set an amount for them to invest. Students should keep track of their investments for three weeks and then report on their findings.

Insurance

13. Have students discuss how life insurance needs may change at each of the stages in the family life cycle.
14. Have students interview a life insurance agent to find out how different factors affect insurance premium rates. These factors include age, physical condition, face value of policy, and type of policy. Students should write an article based on the interview.
15. Have students research to find the differences between group life insurance and individual life insurance. Students should discuss their findings in class.
16. *Life Insurance Match,* Activity B, SAG. Have students match the terms related to life insurance to their appropriate descriptions.
17. Guest speaker. Invite a life insurance agent to discuss the advantages and disadvantages of various types of life insurance policies.
18. As a class, have students find out costs for various treatments and services at hospitals. Students should also find out costs of various types of health insurance. Students should determine the worth of insurance in relationship to the costs of medical care.
19. Divide the class into three groups. Have the first group research various policies to help make adequate health insurance available to all people using private insurance programs. The second group should research the possibilities of adopting government sponsored insurance programs for all United States citizens. The third group should research to find current questions related to health insurance that could be answered by the other two groups. Have a class discussion based on the input of the three groups.
20. Panel discussion. Invite representatives of standard health insurance companies, HMOs, and PPOs to discuss costs, coverage, benefits to, and drawbacks of various forms of health insurance.
21. Have students work as a class to develop a brochure explaining why property insurance is needed by both home owners and renters.
22. Guest speaker. Invite an insurance agent to demonstrate how to determine the amount of property insurance needed by a family or an individual. The agent also should explain some of the different features available in property insurance.
23. Have students write a short research report on the terms of the financial responsibility law in their state.
24. *Comparing Car Insurance Costs,* reproducible master 22-2, TR. Have students compare the costs of various types of coverage at three different insurance companies.

25. *Automobile Insurance,* Activity C, SAG. Have students answer the questions about automobile insurance rates and coverage.
26. *Understanding Insurance,* Activity D, SAG. Have students indicate how listed insurance terms differ.

Retirement Plans and Estate Planning

27. *Retirement Plans,* Activity E, SAG. Have students use the form provided to interview people of different ages about their retirement plans. Students should discuss the differences in responses among different age groups.
28. Have students make posters outlining a person's rights and responsibilities related to social security.
29. Have students find and read current articles on the state of the social security system. Students should share and discuss the articles in class.
30. Have students develop a form that can be used to survey local businesses. The survey should be used to obtain information about company pension programs including employee-employer contributions, amount of benefits, eligibility requirements, and other features. Students should send the surveys to employers and evaluate the results when they are returned.
31. Have students write a research report on IRAs or Keogh plans.

Answer Key

Text

To Review
1. E, A, F, D, C, B
2. Common stock entitles the stockholder to share in the profits of the firm if there are any. Common stockholders hope their stock will increase in value, and then they can sell for more money than they paid. Common stockholders also have the right to vote for company directors and on other matters. With preferred stock, the size of the annual dividend is fixed by the corporation and never changes. Dividends for preferred stock are paid before any of the other stockholders receive dividends.
3. A. term insurance
   B. permanent life insurance
   C. term insurance
   D. permanent life insurance
   E. permanent life insurance
4. basic medical coverage, major medical coverage
5. A. false
   B. true
   C. false
6. C
7. to keep people who cannot pay for property damages or injuries off the streets
8. when your car injures or kills pedestrians, people in other cars, or passengers in your car
9. A will is used to designate heirs, identify property they are to receive, and indicate who will act as administrator of the estate.
10. false

Student Activity Guide

Savings and Investment Choices, Activity A
1. A. Pros: Readily available; money may be withdrawn at any time without penalty. Cons: They pay a relatively low rate of interest; generally do not include check-writing privileges.
   B. Pros: Money earns a higher rate of interest. Cons: Money must be left in the account for a certain period of time; penalty for early withdrawal; fixed rate of interest.
   C. Pros: Earns a higher rate of interest; checks can be written. Cons: Often require a minimum deposit; may charge fees if balance falls; earnings can vary.
2. They will replace the money.
3. refers to how easily you can convert an investment into cash when you need it
4. If held for five years, bonds pay a guaranteed minimum. Interest is exempt from state and local taxes, and no federal tax is due until the bonds mature or are cashed in. Bonds are liquid and very safe.
5. knowledge of your investment objectives, types of investments available, and where to go for advice
6. A. Saving is accumulating money for a specific purpose or to use in an emergency and should be placed in a program that involves no risk of loss. Investing involves risk. You may get returns higher than your investment, but there is the possibility of loss.

B. An equity investment is made when you buy stock in a company making you part owner of that company. A fixed income investment is the lending of money to a corporation or a government agency through the purchase of bonds making you a creditor.

C. With preferred stock, the size of the dividend is fixed and never changes. These dividends are paid first. With common stock, the dividends may vary and the value of the stock changes daily.

7. State and local governments issue them to finance municipal costs and improvements.

8. Dividends are the money paid to stockholders out of the company's earnings. They may take the form of a cash payment, additional shares of stock, or a combination of both.

9. companies that invest their funds in a wide variety of stocks and bonds

Life Insurance Match, Activity B

1. N
2. F
3. K
4. I
5. G
6. B
7. M
8. E
9. A
10. D
11. C
12. H
13. L
14. O
15. J

Automobile Insurance, Activity C

1. Bodily injury liability. Cost is $138.20 and $151.20, which is more than any other coverage listed.
2. Since the car is not worth very much, the person may not want to spend much money on insurance for damages to it.
3. $1,594.40
4. It is less costly than coverage with no deductible. The family could afford to spend the $100 if they were in an accident.

Understanding Insurance, Activity D

1. Term insurance provides protection for a specific period of time and permanent insurance remains in force throughout the insured person's life.
2. Group insurance is purchased by a particular group of people and individual insurance is purchased by an individual through an insurance agent.
3. Basic medical coverage includes protection against the cost of ordinary hospital care, surgery, and doctors up to certain limits. Major medical coverage begins where basic coverage ends.
4. HMOs pay a flat fee to health care providers to provide a specific range of health care services to members. PPOs provide reduced fees on a fee-for-service arrangement to members.
5. Medicare helps pay medical costs for people over age 65 and Medicaid helps pay medical costs for low-income or unemployed people.
6. Replacement cost covers the full cost of repair or replacement and actual cash value is based on replacement cost less depreciation.

Teacher's Resources

Chapter 22 Test

1. A
2. F
3. H
4. D
5. K
6. L
7. I
8. G
9. E
10. C
11. B
12. J
13. T
14. F
15. F
16. F
17. T
18. T
19. F
20. F
21. T
22. F
23. T

24. F
25. B
26. C
27. B
28. D
29. B
30. Passbook accounts earn the lowest interest and allow the money to be withdrawn at any time. Time accounts are those in which the money must be kept in for a fixed period of time. Money market accounts pay a higher rate of interest depending upon U.S. Treasury Bill rates and often require a minimum deposit.
31. Basic medical includes protection against the cost of ordinary hospital care, surgery, and doctors up to certain limits. Major medical coverage begins where the basic coverage ends.
32. HMOs pay a flat fee to health care providers to provide health care services to members for no additional fee. PPOs provide reduced fees on a fee-for-service arrangement to members.
33. (List and explain four. Student response.)
34. If you don't have a will, the state decides who receives any property. This causes additional expense, and the state may not distribute the property as you would have wanted.

Reproducible Master 22-1

Reading Investment Reports

The stock dollar is divided into fractions of 8. Each eighth of a dollar has a value of 12 1/2 cents. This value would be $10.12 1/2 per share.

The abbreviated name of the stock company—Emerson Electronics.

The highest and lowest values for a share of the stock over the last 52-week period.

Footnotes are used to note special concerns— n notes a newly issued stock; s notes a stock split.

The symbol for the company that would appear on the New York Exchange ticker.

These figures show the amount of money paid to shareholders. This stock pays an annual dividend of $.56 per share. The dividend yield is 2.7% of the stock's price. The price/earnings ratio (price of a share of stock divided by the company's earnings per share) is 15.

Shares of stock traded this day, to be multiplied by 100— 109,000 shares traded.

Highest, lowest, and closing values of the stock this day compared to the previous day. These values indicate the amount of money you would get if you sold your stock.

The change in the closing value of the stock this day as compared to the previous day. This stock went up $3.00 per share.

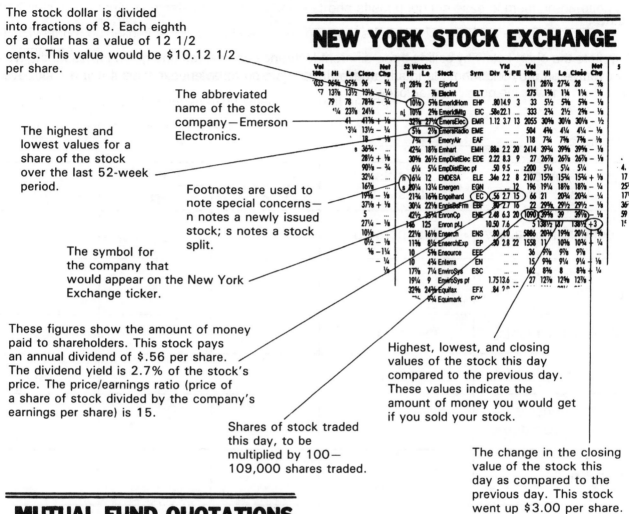

MUTUAL FUND QUOTATIONS

Investment company and type of fund. Company: Pilgrim Group.

Price at which you would buy mutual fund shares—$10.50 per share.

Price at which you would sell mutual fund shares—$16.00 per share.

This is a no-load fund, which means no commission is paid when you buy shares.

Other costs may be added to fund transactions. t—costs for buying and selling may apply. p—costs for buying may apply.

Change in the value of the fund compared to the previous day. This fund went down $.02 per share.

Reproducible Master 22-2

Comparing Car Insurance Costs

Name _____ **Date** _____ **Period** _____

Complete the chart below by calling three different insurance companies and getting rates for the types of coverage listed. (Choose a car model and year upon which to base your rates if you do not have a car.) Then answer the question that follows.

Car model: _____ Year: _____

Type of Coverage	Limits Desired	Companies		
		A	B	C
Bodily Injury Liability	(per person)			
Property Damage Liability	(per accident)			
Medical Payments	(per person)			
Uninsured Motorist	(per person)			
Comprehensive Physical Damage				
Collision	$ _____ (deductible)			
Other:				
Annual Total				

Based on your comparison, which insurance company would you choose and why? _____

_____

_____

_____

_____

_____

Planning for Financial Security

Name _____

Date _____ Period _____ Score _____

Chapter 22 Test

Matching: Match the following terms and identifying phrases.

_____ 1. The savings portion of a permanent life insurance policy; this amount of money is available while the policyholder is still living and increases with each premium payment.

_____ 2. The price of a stock; this amount changes from day to day.

_____ 3. Type of insurance where the individual's life is insured against death for a certain period of time and then the policy is terminated.

_____ 4. A certain annual percentage of the amount of money in an account which is generally paid daily, monthly, or quarterly.

_____ 5. A promise to pay the investor a certain amount of money plus interest at a specific time in the future.

_____ 6. A share of ownership in a corporation.

_____ 7. A stock in which the annual dividend is fixed by the corporation and never changes.

_____ 8. Cash value life insurance; the annual premium remains constant as long as the policy is in force.

_____ 9. The ease with which you can convert an investment into cash when it is needed.

_____ 10. Insurance that covers the repayment of a loan should the borrower die.

_____ 11. Stock that entitles the stockholder to share in the profits of the firm if there are any.

_____ 12. The amount of the investment minus the interest.

A. cash value

B. common stock

C. credit life insurance

D. interest

E. liquidity

F. market value

G. permanent life insurance

H. term insurance

I. preferred stock

J. principal

K. bond

L. stock

(Continued)

Name _____

True/False: Circle *T* if the statement is true or *F* if the statement is false.

T   F   13. Money market accounts generally pay a higher rate of interest than passbook accounts.

T   F   14. Preferred stock has more potential for increased dividends than common stock.

T   F   15. Money markets are companies that invest their funds in a wide variety of stocks and bonds.

T   F   16. The main advantage of permanent life insurance is its low cost in contrast to term life insurance.

T   F   17. Credit life insurance is usually quite expensive per dollar of insurance.

T   F   18. HMOs stress preventive medicine.

T   F   19. Medicare is the government health insurance program for needy people of all ages.

T   F   20. With homeowners insurance, the broader the coverage, the lower the premium will be.

T   F   21. All states now have financial responsibility laws related to automobile insurance.

T   F   22. United States citizens automatically receive social security benefits at age 65.

T   F   23. An annuity is an investment product sold by life insurance companies.

T   F   24. The IRA is a personal retirement plan designed for self-employed people.

Multiple Choice: Choose the best answer and write the corresponding letter in the blank.

_____ 25. An advantage of fixed income investments is that _____.
                A. they are the most effective way of producing income
                B. money is safe in these investments
                C. they are especially effective during times of inflation
                D. they are backed by the full faith and credit of the United States government

_____ 26. Government savings bonds _____.
                A. are subject to state, local, and federal taxes
                B. require a long-term investment
                C. are a very safe way to save
                D. All of the above.

_____ 27. In _____ life insurance policy, the policyholder makes payments for a certain number of years and then receives the face value of the policy.
                A. a decreasing term
                B. an endowment
                C. a limited payment
                D. a renewable term

_____ 28. Group health insurance _____.
                A. does not usually require a physical exam
                B. is less expensive than individual policies
                C. usually ends when a person leaves the group
                D. All of the above.

(Continued)

Name _____

_____ 29. Which of the following is NOT true about bodily injury liability automobile insurance?
   A. The claims can be very costly.
   B. It covers injuries to the insured or members of his or her family.
   C. This is the most important type of automobile insurance.
   D. It applies when the policyholder, a member of the immediate family, or another person with permission drives.

Essay Questions: Provide the answers you feel best show your understanding of the subject matter.

30. Describe passbook accounts, time accounts, and money market accounts.

31. Explain the difference between basic medical and major medical coverage.

32. Explain how HMOs and PPOs differ.

33. List four of the six kinds of automobile insurance coverage and explain what each covers.

34. Why is it important to have a will?

Part Seven
Managing as a Consumer

Consumer Rights and Responsibilities

Objectives

When students have completed this chapter, they will be able to

◆ describe their rights as consumers.
◆ describe various ways the consumer can become informed about products and services.
◆ give examples of federal agencies that protect the consumer.
◆ explain the relationship between consumer rights and consumer responsibilities.

Bulletin Boards

Consumer Rights and Responsibilities

Right to be informed ⟷ Responsibility to use consumer information — Right to safety and legal protection ⟷ Responsibility to use products safely

Right to choose among products and services ⟷ Responsibility to be an ethical consumer — Right to express dissatisfaction and be heard ⟷ Responsibility to protest when wronged

Title: *Consumer Rights and Responsibilities*

Develop a bulletin board to illustrate consumer rights and responsibilities and the relationship between them. Draw pictures of items that illustrate the various rights and the responsibilities that correspond to the rights. If you prefer, you may use cut out pictures from magazines or the actual objects. Place the pictures you have drawn, the pictures from the magazines, or the

actual objects on the bulletin board and draw a two-way arrow connecting the related rights and responsibilities. Have students tell how they feel about the relationship between consumer rights and responsibilities.

Title: *Informative Advertising?*

Ask students to bring in advertisements that they have seen in newspapers or magazines. Post these advertisements on the bulletin board. Before students have studied the information on advertising in the text, have them decide whether they think each advertisement offers good information and whether each is an example of good or poor advertising.

Teaching Materials

Text, pages 403-417
    To Review
    To Challenge Your Thinking
    To Do with the Class
    To Do with Your Community
Student Activity Guide
    A. *Your Rights Protected*
    B. *Persuasive Advertising*
    C. *The Responsible Consumer*
    D. *Consumer Complaints*
Teacher's Resources
    Product Warranties, reproducible
      master 23-1
    Chapter 23 Test
    Consumer Rights and Responsibilities,
      color transparency CT-23

Introductory Activities

1. Develop a display of available consumer resources. Include pamphlets, magazines, books, newspaper articles, etc. Ask each student to bring in several resources. When the display has been assembled, discuss the various types of information that has been collected and how this information can help consumers.

2. Divide the class into groups of four or five students. Ask each group to think of a situation that might occur in the United States if consumers did not have rights. Have each group perform a skit to illustrate their situation. After the performances, have students describe how they feel about living in a country where consumers do have rights.

Instructional Concepts and Student Learning Experiences

Consumer Rights

3. Discuss the meaning of the statement "Advertising is the bridge between businesses and their potential customers."

4. Discuss the bulletin board entitled *Informative Advertising?* Have students analyze each advertisement and tell whether or not they think it is informative advertising. Discuss whether students feel an advertisement can be good if it is not an informative advertisement.

5. Have students break up into small groups and discuss good and bad experiences they have had when trying to get information about products from salespeople. Then have each group choose one of the most interesting experiences and perform a skit based on that experience.

6. Ask students to do library research to learn what information is legally required on labels of food products, cosmetics, textile products, and upholstered furniture. Discuss why this is important information that consumers should know.

7. Have students select a product that has a label and shop for it comparing several brands. Ask them to look at the labels on at least four different brands. Have students write a brief report describing information on the labels that would influence their purchase decision and telling which brand they would select.

8. *Product Warranties,* reproducible master 23-1, TR. Bring samples of warranties to class and also ask students to bring samples of several warranties. Ask each student to select four warranties and fill in the chart indicating the type of product and the type of warranty. In the space provided below the chart, have students compare and contrast the information in the warranties.

9. Ask students to do library research to learn about the legal responsibilities and obligations of both the buyer and the seller and give an oral report on what they learned.

10. Obtain the free pamphlet listing the consumer publications available from the Consumer Information Center in Pueblo, Colorado. Have students select several publications that interest them and order those publications for their own use.

11. Bring as many issues of *Consumer Reports* as possible to class. Have each student take a magazine and select a product that has been tested and rated in that issue. Ask each student to write a report on what he or she learned about the product and to tell what brand he or she would select if making an actual purchase decision.

12. *Your Rights Protected,* Activity A, SAG. Students are asked to research a group that protects consumers and write a brief report about what they have learned about that group.

13. Have students list groups that work to set and enforce safety standards for products and services that protect consumers.

14. Guest speaker. Invite a government inspector of meat, other food products, or health products to speak to the class about setting and enforcing standards.

15. Ask students to express their opinions about monopolies. Have them explain why they feel monopolies are harmful to the consumer.

16. Have students discuss competition and tell whether they feel there is good competition in your community for both goods and services.

17. Panel discussion. Have a panel of outstanding salespeople from your community come to your class and speak on how they feel about their obligation to the consumer.

18. Ask students to visit several retail stores and learn about their policies for handling consumer dissatisfaction with products or services and their return policies. Have students report back what they learned to the class.

19. Ask students to role-play a situation where an irate, dissatisfied customer is complaining in person to a business and a situation where a diplomatic, but dissatisfied customer is complaining to a business. Discuss why the business would react differently to these different types of customers.

20. Guest speaker. Invite someone from the state or local consumer protection office to speak to the class on common consumer problems, helping consumers become aware of their consumer rights, and the reliability of sources of consumer information.

21. Guest speaker. Invite a lawyer to speak to your class on small claims court as a consumer resource. Ask this person to include any hints for success in small claims court.

Consumer Responsibilities

22. *Consumer Rights and Responsibilities,* color transparency CT-23, TR. Use this transparency as a basis of a discussion about consumer rights and responsibilities and how knowing them can help consumers make wise purchases.

23. Discuss the statement "Many advertising appeals and sales promotions are directed to young people because they are both present and future consumers."

24. *Persuasive Advertising,* Activity B, SAG. Students are asked to find examples of persuasive advertisements and fill in the chart with the product or service advertised, technique used, and helpful information included. Students are to bring the advertisements to class and discuss them with other class members.

25. Display equipment manuals and instruction books on use and care for various types of products and equipment in the home. Have each student look at several of the items displayed.

26. Ask students to share examples of instances they know of in which an item became unusable due to improper use or maintenance of the product.

27. Discuss how common household and personal items should be used and maintained.

28. *The Responsible Consumer,* Activity C, SAG. Students are asked to read three use-and-care-booklets and to describe important information that is included in the booklets and information they did not know before reading the booklets.

29. Ask students to write two examples of consumer attitudes and behaviors that illustrate a lack of ethics. Then have them write two examples of consumer attitudes and behaviors that illustrate ethics. Have students share their examples with others in the class.

30. Discuss how behaviors, such as shoplifting and buying products from disreputable businesses, have a negative effect on the ethical and honest consumer.

31. Ask students to interview managers of grocery stores, salespeople in clothing stores, and salespeople in furniture stores to learn the estimated costs of their losses due to the mishandling of goods by consumers and to record what they learn.

32. Discuss business practices that consumers do not like, but that are related to the irresponsible behavior of some consumers.

33. Discuss the meaning of the statement "The best defense for consumers is to make themselves heard after they have been the victim of a fraud scheme."

34. *Consumer Complaints,* Activity D, SAG. Students are asked to write a complaint letter about a consumer problem including all the information suggested in the text. If students do not have an actual complaint, they may complain about a problem that could possibly occur.

35. Have students contact a Better Business Bureau to learn about the procedures they normally follow to resolve consumer complaints.

36. Panel discussion. Invite a panel of several people who work in the consumer field to discuss consumer rights and responsibilities and common situations they experience when dealing with consumer problems in their work. Panel members might include consumer representatives from utility companies, consumer affairs professionals in business, people from the Better Business Bureau, employees from the state attorney general's office, etc.

Answer Key

Text

To Review

1. the right to be informed, the right to safety, the right to choose among products and services, the right to be heard

2. (Describe five:) advertising, salespeople, product labels, warranties and guarantees, publications, consumer organizations
3. A full warranty has no specific limitations. The product is totally guaranteed, including materials and labor, for the length of time specified. A limited warranty has some limitations, which must be clearly stated on the warranty.
4. A. false
   B. true
   C. false
5. (List four:) merchandise or service is not received as ordered, service or repairs are not satisfactory, merchandise is defective, there are credit billing problems, guarantee or warranty is unfulfilled, deposits are not refunded
6. With the bait and switch technique, an item offered at a low price is the bait. The purpose of the bait is to get the consumer in the store. Once the consumer is there, the advertiser attempts to switch the consumer to another, more expensive item. The advertiser does this by saying the store is out of the advertised item. Another approach is trying to convince the consumer the advertised item is inadequate for the consumer's needs.
7. exact product or service including model and serial numbers of applicable; price; place and date purchase was made; exact reason for dissatisfaction; anything you have done to try to solve the problem; the action you wish the company to take; your name, address, and phone number; copies of documents related to the purchase such as receipts, canceled checks, and warranties
8. to use consumer information, to use information about misleading advertising, to use information about using and caring for purchased products, to be an ethical consumer, to protest when wronged
9. BBBs are nonprofit organizations sponsored by private businesses at which consumers can complain. BBBs attempt to settle consumer complaints against local businesses.
10. $3000

Teacher's Resources

Chapter 23 Test

1. D
2. F
3. A
4. H
5. E
6. J
7. I
8. C
9. B
10. G
11. T
12. F
13. T
14. F
15. T
16. F
17. T
18. T
19. F
20. T
21. A
22. D
23. B
24. C
25. C
26. D
27. (Student response. Describe three.)
28. right to be informed, right to safety and legal protection, right to choose among products and services, right to express dissatisfaction and be heard (Student response for descriptions.)
29. (Student response.)
30. (Student response.)
31. Describe the exact product or service you are complaining about and list model numbers and serial numbers if they apply. Include what you paid and where and when you made the purchase. State the exact reason you are dissatisfied with the product or service and anything you have already done to try to solve the problem. State what action you wish the company to take to satisfy you. Be reasonable, but firm, about the action you wish to have taken. Include copies of any documents related to your purchase, such as sales slips, canceled checks, or warranties or guarantees. Be sure to include your name, address, and phone number so the company can reach you. Keep copies of all letters you send and receive.

Reproducible Master 23-1

Product Warranties

Name _____ **Date** _____ **Period** _____

Read the warranties for several products and select four warranties. Fill in the chart below with information about the warranties. Indicate the product that is covered and whether the warranty is a full warranty or a limited warranty.

Product	Type of Warranty
1.	
2.	
3.	
4.	

What information did you find that was common to all the warranties? _____

_____

_____

_____

_____

_____

_____

_____

How do the warranties you read differ? _____

_____

_____

_____

_____

_____

_____

Consumer Rights and Responsibilities

Name _____

Date _____ **Period** _____ **Score** _____

Chapter 23 Test

Matching: Match the following terms and identifying phrases.

_____ 1. Fraudulent, illegal advertising designed to cheat consumers.

_____ 2. Warranty that totally covers both materials and labor for the length of time specified.

_____ 3. An item is advertised at a low price to get the consumer in the store. Once the consumer is there, the advertiser tries to switch the consumer to another, more expensive item.

_____ 4. A product is guaranteed, but there are certain limitations.

_____ 5. Advertising that aims to satisfy psychological needs.

_____ 6. Advertising that presents a recommendation for a product or service from either a celebrity or a "typical" consumer.

_____ 7. Consumers have no choice of where to buy goods or services; they can be purchased from only one seller.

_____ 8. Similar goods and services are offered by more than one seller.

_____ 9. Advertising in which the company compares its brand with another competing brand.

_____ 10. Advertising that appeals to values of people, such as patriotism, caring for others, and the importance of family.

A. bait and switch

B. comparative advertising

C. competition

D. deceptive practices

E. emotional advertising

F. full warranty

G. institutional advertising

H. limited warranty

I. monopoly

J. testimonial advertising

True/False: Circle *T* if the statement is true or *F* if the statement is false.

T   F   11. The Fair Packaging and Labeling Act helps consumers more easily compare food products at the supermarket.

T   F   12. The Office of Consumer Affairs distributes a publication called *Consumer Reports*.

T   F   13. The Consumer Product Safety Commission protects consumers from dangerous products and encourages safe use in and around the home.

T   F   14. The Food and Drug Administration is responsible for grading meat.

(Continued)

Name _____

T   F   15. Laws that prohibit monopolies are designed to encourage competition.

T   F   16. Comparative advertising presents a recommendation for a product or service from either a celebrity or a "typical" consumer.

T   F   17. The consumer should suspect the bait and switch technique if the salesperson gives a reason why the advertised product is not available or will not work out well for the consumer.

T   F   18. Many dissatisfied consumers may be responsible for poor performance of an appliance through ignoring maintenance needs suggested by the manufacturer in the use and care booklet.

T   F   19. The purpose of consumer action panels (CAPS) is to provide valuable information to consumers who are considering buying certain products.

T   F   20. Honest consumers ultimately pay the price for shoplifting and other dishonest practices.

Multiple Choice: Choose the best answer and write the corresponding letter in the blank.

_____ 21. Informative advertising _____.
   A. makes the process of consumer decision making quicker and easier
   B. is most often developed using institutional advertising techniques
   C. tries to persuade you to buy goods or services using arguments that may or may not be valid
   D. is not a responsibility of advertisers

_____ 22. Which is NOT true about information on warranties or guarantees?
   A. This information tells the consumer in advance what to expect concerning servicing repairs and adjustments.
   B. For products selling for more than $10.00, the warranty must state if it is a full warranty or a limited warranty.
   C. The Magnuson-Moss Warranty Act simplifies the language of warranties so consumers can more easily understand them.
   D. The warranty for a product selling for less than $5.00 must include the names and addresses of the warrantors.

_____ 23. Which of the following is true about the right to choose among products and services?
   A. Laws that discourage competition are enforced to assure this right.
   B. The Federal Trade Commission is responsible for enforcing laws that assure this right.
   C. Monopolies provide consumers with a large selection of products and services.
   D. All of the above are true.

_____ 24. Which of the following is true about persuasive advertising?
   A. The bait and switch technique is an example.
   B. It is illegal.
   C. Comparative advertising is an example.
   D. It always offers a great deal of constructive information about products and services.

(Continued)

Name _____

_____ 25. Which of the following is NOT true about persuasive advertising?
   A. An advertisement that asks "Does your family deserve the best?" is aiming at psychological needs.
   B. Institutional advertising appeals to the values of many Americans.
   C. Testimonial advertising always presents the recommendation of a celebrity.
   D. All of the above are NOT true.

_____ 26. Which of the following is true of deceptive advertising?
   A. A commonly used strategy is offering a free item or service if the consumer purchases a product.
   B. If irregulars or seconds are offered, the merchant must describe this in the advertising and on the product.
   C. An advertiser must inform the consumer in the advertisement if quantities are limited.
   D. All of the above are true.

Essay Questions: Provide the answers you feel best show your understanding of the subject matter.

27. Describe three sources of consumer information.

28. List and describe the four consumer rights stated by President Kennedy.

29. Describe the meaning of the following statement: Without consumer responsibilities, consumer rights are worthless.

30. Explain the meaning of being an ethical consumer.

31. Describe information to include in a letter expressing dissatisfaction about a product or service.

Consumer Decision Making

Objectives

When students have completed this chapter, they will be able to
- explain factors affecting consumer decision making.
- describe the goals and characteristics of the United States economy.
- apply the decision-making process to their own consumer decisions.

Bulletin Boards

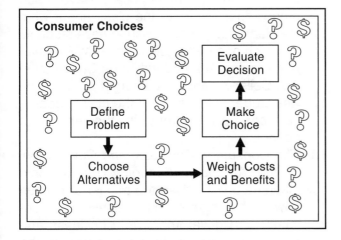

Title: *Consumer Choices*

Develop a bulletin board that illustrates the steps in the consumer decision-making process. Make a border of question marks and dollar signs. Beneath the title, place colorful rectangles of construction paper onto which the steps of the decision-making process have been written. Connect the steps with lines and arrows to show the proper order of the steps in the consumer decision-making process.

Title: *The Flow of the American Economy*

Create a bulletin board that is similar to Figure 24-5 in the text. Post one drawing to represent consumers and one drawing to represent businesses.

Include information from the text about the relationship between the consumer and business in the American economy.

Teaching Materials

Text, pages 418-432
 To Review
 To Challenge Your Thinking
 To Do with the Class
 To Do with Your Community

Student Activity Guide
 A. *Economic Research*
 B. *Our Economic System*
 C. *Consumer Decision Making in Action*
 D. *Evaluating the Decision*

Teacher's Resources
 The Consumer, Business, and Government in the American Economy, reproducible master 24-1
 Chapter 24 Test
 The American Economy, color transparency CT-24

Introductory Activities

1. Have students work in small groups to brainstorm a list of advantages to living under a capitalistic form of government. Ask each group to share items from each list with the rest of the class and make a master list of advantages on the chalkboard.
2. Ask students to describe the process they typically go through before making a purchase decision when buying both an expensive item and when buying an inexpensive item.
3. Ask students to think back on good and poor purchase decisions they have made in the past and to consider what factors led them to make that poor purchase decision. Ask for volunteers to share their experiences with others in the class.

Instructional Concepts and Student Learning Experiences

Factors Affecting Decision Making

4. *The American Economy,* color transparency CT-24, TR. Use this transparency as a basis of discussion about the circular flow of goods, services, and money in the American economy.

5. *Economic Research,* Activity A, SAG. Students are asked to find an article that relates to the topic of economics and write a report on the article by filling in the form provided. Students are asked to share what they have learned with others in class.

6. Invite two people active in local government who have opposing views on the control government should have in the American economy to come to your class. Ask them to debate the role of government in the American economy in relation to having very direct control or serving as "watchdog" with only occasional necessary actions.

7. Discuss the meaning of the statement "The wise consumer's goal is to think straight about what he or she wants according to his or her values and to translate those thoughts into consistent actions."

8. Ask students to interview four older adults to learn about some of the special purchases they made when they were teenagers and what factors affected their decision making at that time. Have students compare the factors that affected decision making years ago with the factors that affect decision making for teenagers today. Then ask students to give oral reports on what they have learned.

9. Ask students to go to the library and research socialism, communism, and capitalism. Have them take note of both similarities and differences. Ask students to write a report on what they learned.

10. Discuss why the United States economy is referred to as a mixed economy rather than a true free enterprise economy.

11. Have students choose either a goal or a characteristic of the American economy and research it extensively. Ask students to give an oral report to the class summarizing what they learned.

12. Ask each student to select one of the following economic goals: economic freedom, economic efficiency, economic growth, economic stability, economic security. Then have students develop a description of an action or an experience that illustrates either moving away from that goal or moving toward that goal. The action or experience described could be on either a government level or an individual level.

13. Discuss reasons why both inflation and deflation are undesirable conditions and explain methods the government can use to influence these conditions.

14. Ask students to research and write brief descriptions of three government programs that have been designed to help create economic security. Discuss why controversy exists over what types of programs the government should provide.

15. Ask students to describe why they feel the right to private property is important.

16. Ask students to work in small groups and ask each group to research a law or regulation that was enacted to encourage competition and discourage monopolies. Have each group report orally to the class about what they learned. You may wish to have students research one of the following laws: Sherman Act, Clayton Act, Federal Trade Commission Act, Celler-Kefauver Antimerger Act.

17. Ask students to describe the flow of goods, services, and money in the American economy.

18. *The Consumer, Business, and Government in the American Economy,* reproducible master 24-1, TR. Use the master to explain how the consumer and business, the consumer and government, and business and government relate to each other in the American economy. Check students' understanding of the concepts by having them write a brief summary of the relationship between the various sectors.

19. *Our Economic System,* Activity B, SAG. Students are asked to give examples from daily living to illustrate each characteristic of our economic system and to explain the advantages of each characteristic to people living in the United States.

20. Have each student ask an adult he or she is friendly with to let that student look through a series of check stubs or a record of spending the person has kept. Ask students to think about what might be some of the values of the person who kept the check stubs or the records. Ask students to discuss their experiences in class.

21. Randomly divide the class into groups of five to eight students. Within each group, ask students to share some of their general spending habits and compare their own habits with the habits of other students. Have students record their thoughts as they go through this process. Then have each student work individually to compare his or her spending habits with the spending habits of other family members. Ask students to consider how differences in spending might reflect differences in values. Ask for volunteers to share their thoughts with the class.

22. Ask each student to make a list of consumer goals that would be considered short-term and a list of consumer goals that would be considered long-term. Ask students to share their lists and discuss differences between long-term and short-term consumer goals.

23. Have each student make a list of 10 items he or she has purchased recently and to indicate what spending goal, if any, each item relates to. Ask volunteers to discuss their lists.

24. Discuss the meaning of the following statement: Knowing how to obtain specific consumer information is more important than learning specific facts about products that may quickly become obsolete.

25. Ask students to list examples of ways to save money by producing their own goods and services.

26. Ask students to give reasons why it would be helpful for each family member to be aware of both the goals of each family member and the goals of the family as a unit.

27. Give examples of common areas of conflicting values in families as related to consumer decisions, and ask for volunteers to give examples of conflicts related to consumer decisions that have occurred within their own families.

The Decision-Making Process in Consumer Choices

28. *Consumer Decision Making in Action,* Activity C, SAG. Students are asked to use the consumer decision-making process to make one of their own consumer decisions.

29. Ask students to give examples of situations where a lack of information or inaccurate information led a consumer to make a decision that he or she later regretted.

30. If possible, locate a copy of one or more mail order catalogs that are 20 or more years old. Bring the old catalogs to class along with several more recent catalogs. With students working in small groups, have them compare and contrast the products available then and now and the information available on those products then and now. Discuss how differences in the world today affect the ease of making consumer decisions.

31. Ask students to write down several situations that illustrate the need to think broadly when defining a consumer problem.

32. Ask for volunteers to give examples of consumer problems. Working as a class, have students practice changing several of those problems into goals. Then have each student write down two problems of his or her own and develop them into goals.

33. Ask for several volunteers to share the goals they developed in the previous activity. Then ask students to suggest possible alternatives for reaching the goals and discuss reasons why an alternative may be suitable for one person but not for another person.

34. Discuss the meaning of the statement "How knowledgeable a consumer is will certainly affect the quality of the alternatives considered and selected."

35. Ask students to choose alternatives for solving a consumer problem and develop a chart to help in weighing the facts to decide the best alternative. Ask students to share with the class factors that would influence their choice of the best alternative.

36. Ask each student to develop a written example of a real or fictitious situation that indicates how information gained from evaluation can be helpful in future decision making.

37. *Evaluating the Decision,* Activity D, SAG. Students are asked to complete forms to analyze poor consumer decisions that they or someone they know has made. They are also asked to state how the knowledge gained from the poor decision could be used to make better consumer decisions in the future.

Answer Key

Text

To Review

1. Economics is a study of the process people and societies use to make choices about making and spending their money. Capitalism is the economic system in the United States. (Student response for description.)

2. A. false
   B. true
   C. true

3. Competition forces business firms to keep searching for more efficient practices so they can offer better products and services at lower prices.

4. Goals give you direction. They are something toward which you can work.

5. beginning stage—many decisions at this stage affect family income; expanding stage—heavy demands are put upon budget; developing stage—costs related to children, such as educational costs, may still be quite high; launching stage—financial stability is gained; aging stage—careful planning is necessary for many

6. They think about their problem in terms of a specific product rather than more broadly.

7. When information is in black and white, it is easier to weigh facts and choose the best alternative.

8. Values, resources

9. time, research

10. More information is better; learning about products' functions and features can help choose between alternatives.

Teacher's Resources

Chapter 24 Test

1. G
2. L
3. K
4. H
5. B
6. D
7. J
8. I
9. F
10. C
11. A
12. E
13. F
14. T
15. T
16. F
17. F
18. T
19. F
20. T
21. F
22. T
23. A
24. C
25. D
26. D
27. C
28. B
29. (Student response for diagram and explanation.)
30. (Student response.)
31. Changing the problem into a goal clarifies the problem and gives you direction in choosing alternatives. Goals often force you to deal with values and set priorities.

Reproducible Master 24-1

The Consumer, Business, and Government in the American Economy

In our economic system, consumers, business, and government work together toward stable economic growth. Each of these sectors has certain dependencies on and expectations of the other sectors.

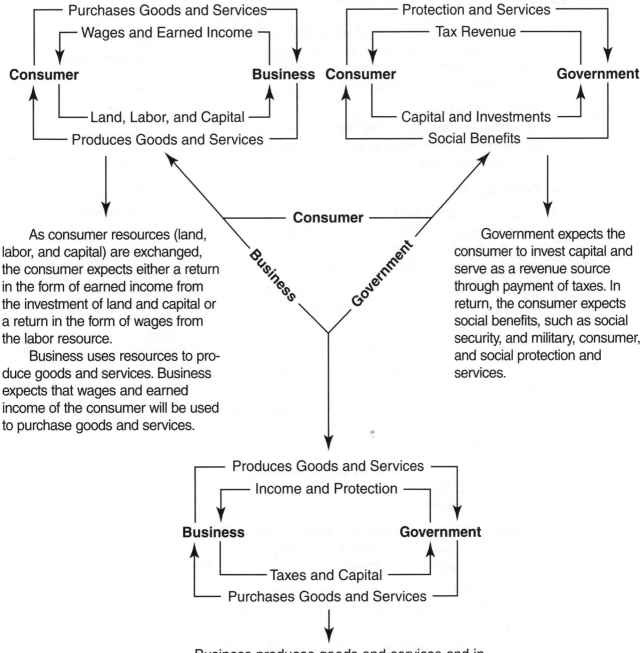

As consumer resources (land, labor, and capital) are exchanged, the consumer expects either a return in the form of earned income from the investment of land and capital or a return in the form of wages from the labor resource.

Business uses resources to produce goods and services. Business expects that wages and earned income of the consumer will be used to purchase goods and services.

Government expects the consumer to invest capital and serve as a revenue source through payment of taxes. In return, the consumer expects social benefits, such as social security, and military, consumer, and social protection and services.

Business produces goods and services and in return, expects the government to purchase the goods and services. Business pays taxes and makes capital investments just as the consumer does. In return, business expects trade and import restrictions and protection for patents from the government.

Consumer Decision Making

Name _____

Date _____ **Period** _____ **Score** _____

Chapter 24 Test

Matching: Match the following terms and identifying phrases.

_____ 1. Occurs when the prices of goods and services rise without a corresponding increase in the production of goods and services; the demand for goods and services is greater than the supply.

_____ 2. Economic system in which there is considerable government planning to promote the well-being of the citizens; the government owns and operates most industries.

_____ 3. Working to earn an income.

_____ 4. Economy in which consumers have freedom of choice; choices involve what will be produced, how much will be produced, and the price that will be paid for goods and services.

_____ 5. System of government where the government owns the land and almost all industries and plans all production.

_____ 6. The study of the process people and societies use to make choices about making and spending their money.

_____ 7. Involve the way the Federal Reserve Board regulates money and credit to achieve a stable and growing economy.

_____ 8. An economy in which individuals make most decisions, but the economy is in part regulated by the government.

_____ 9. Policies that involve the way the federal government adjusts taxes and government spending to influence economic conditions.

_____ 10. Condition that exists when prices are falling; supply of goods and services is greater than the demand.

_____ 11. Form of government that allows private ownership of land and produced goods.

_____ 12. State that exists when there is a high level of employment without inflation or deflation.

A. capitalism

B. communism

C. deflation

D. economics

E. economic stability

F. fiscal policies

G. inflation

H. market economy

I. mixed economy

J. monetary policies

K. profit motivation

L. socialism

(Continued)

Name _____

True/False: Circle *T* if the statement is true or *F* if the statement is false.

T F 13. The choices you make as a consumer do not affect society as a whole.

T F 14. In the United States, individuals make most economic decisions, but the economy is, in part, regulated by the government.

T F 15. People in business are free to decide when and where to advertise.

T F 16. Competition is desirable for all products and services.

T F 17. Producers are the powerful force that influences what goods and services are produced.

T F 18. Every consumer choice made is like a vote in the marketplace.

T F 19. High inflation has helped families reach their economic goals.

T F 20. Having children involves a long-term economic commitment.

T F 21. Because of the legal changes that have taken place, divorce is no longer costly.

T F 22. In general, the more education you have, the higher your salary and the greater your job security is.

Multiple Choice: Choose the best answer and write the corresponding letter in the blank.

_____ 23. The economic goal that refers to making the best use of limited resources is economic _____.
A. efficiency
B. growth
C. security
D. stability

_____ 24. Economic stability _____.
A. refers to an increase in standard of living
B. can exist at a time of inflation
C. is influenced by adjustments of taxes and government spending
D. All of the above.

_____ 25. Which of the following is true about goals and consumer decision making?
A. Goals are more abstract than values.
B. Although goals are difficult to develop, prioritizing them is easier.
C. Values are based on a person's goals.
D. None of the above are true.

_____ 26. Which of the following is true about consumer resources?
A. Money is the resource most often used for obtaining consumer resources.
B. Skills can be valuable consumer resources.
C. In a rapidly changing world, knowing how to obtain specific consumer information becomes more important than learning specific facts about products.
D. All of the above are true.

(Continued)

Name _____

_____ 27. Which of the following is NOT true about consumer decision making?
   A. Most consumer problems are the result of poorly made decisions based on insufficient or inaccurate information.
   B. Rational decisions result from certain logical steps.
   C. Making choices is easy in today's world because there are so many choices.
   D. All of the above are NOT true.

_____ 28. When defining the problem in consumer decision making, it is best NOT to _____.
   A. think broadly about the consumer problem
   B. think of your needs in terms of a specific product
   C. state the problem in terms of a goal
   D. deal with values and set priorities

Essay Questions: Provide the answers you feel best show your understanding of the subject matter.

29. Draw a diagram illustrating the circular flow of goods and services in the American economy. Label your diagram.

30. Explain how spending patterns differ depending on the stage in the family life cycle. Include the young married couple, young family, family in its middle years, couple when children leave home, and retired couple.

31. Explain how stating your problem in terms of a goal can help you make a decision or solve a problem.

Meal Management— Planning and Shopping

Objectives

When students have completed this chapter, they will be able to
- ◆ recognize resources valuable to efficient meal management.
- ◆ describe guidelines in meal planning.
- ◆ demonstrate skills in time management leading to efficient planning and shopping.
- ◆ recognize advantages and disadvantages of shopping at different types of food stores.
- ◆ relate the choice of brands to intended use.
- ◆ explain ways to avoid wasting food.

Bulletin Boards

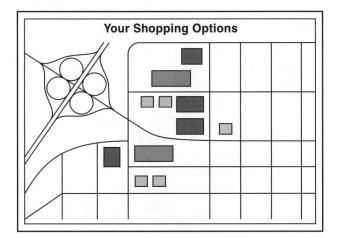

Title: *Your Shopping Options*

Cover the bulletin board with a map of your community. Cut out various store shapes from colored construction paper. Attach these to the map to highlight store locations in your community. Feature the variety of shopping options available today, such as supermarkets, neighborhood grocery stores, warehouse stores, specialty stores, food cooperatives, and convenience stores.

Title: *Food Budgeting Resources*

Display a variety of resources that might be helpful in planning meals to meet the food budget. These resources might include grocery ads; shopping lists; national brand, house brand, and generic labels; and unit price tags. You may wish to involve students in gathering these resources.

Teaching Materials

Text, pages 435-450
   To Review
   To Challenge Your Thinking
   To Do with the Class
   To Do with Your Community
Student Activity Guide
   A. *Advertised Specials*
   B. *Efficient Meal Planning*
   C. *Efficient Grocery Shopping*
   D. *Unit Pricing*
   E. *Deciding Where to Shop*
   F. *Using Leftovers to Avoid Waste*
Teacher's Resources
   Meal Patterns in Planning, reproducible master, 25-1
   Comparing Brands, reproducible master 25-2
   Chapter 25 Test
   Take the Guesswork Out of Meal Management, color transparency CT-25

Introductory Activities

1. Have students brainstorm a list of factors that might affect the amount that people spend on food. Write student responses on the chalkboard. As they study the chapter, have students note how many of their ideas are mentioned.

2. Have students contact the Consumer Information Center in Pueblo, Colorado, to obtain available materials on meal planning and food budgeting or access the Internet for similar information.

3. *Take the Guesswork Out of Meal Management,* color transparency CT-25, TR. Use this transparency as a basis of discussion about how to make meal management easier. Discuss strategies from the chapter that students could practice and become skilled at for better management of family meals.

Instructional Concepts and Student Learning Experiences

Guidelines in Meal Planning

4. Have students conduct research to find out who is eligible for food stamps and under what conditions.

5. Guest speaker. Invite a financial counselor to speak to your class about how to develop a family food budget.

6. Have students role-play a situation showing what might happen if someone on a limited income were to shop for food without any preplanning.

7. Ask each student to write a paragraph explaining how meal planning can help avoid food waste.

8. Guest speaker. Invite a supermarket manager to explain to your class how food prices are set. Ask the speaker to discuss what brands are carried in his or her store and give tips on how consumers can get the best buys.

9. Have students make a list of library resources or Internet sites they can use to help them plan meals.

10. Ask each student to try one new recipe or food to expand his or her food interests. Have students give brief oral reports describing what new foods they tried, why they tried those particular foods, and why they did or didn't like them.

11. Have students study current food ads for two different stores in your area. Ask students to decide which store they would choose to shop at and state the reason for their choice.

12. *Advertised Specials,* Activity A, SAG. Have students use newspaper ads for a large supermarket to plan two meals. Have students write menus for the meals and make shopping lists of the items they would need to buy to prepare them. Then have students circle the specials they would buy from the ads.

13. Give each student a coupon for a food product. Ask students to explain why they would or wouldn't use their coupons.

14. Give students a "typical" weekly shopping list with the price of each item on the list. Have students divide the list into categories, such as dairy products, canned goods, produce, staple foods, meats, etc. Have students total the cost of each category and then compare the cost of protein foods with the cost of other food categories.

15. Have students choose one type of meat, poultry, or fish that would be suitable for a main dish. Ask them to describe how their choice could be used in three different ways as a main dish for the heavier meal of the day. Then have them describe how it could be used in three different ways for a lighter meal of the day.

16. Have students discuss store practices that encourage impulse buying.

17. Ask students to give suggestions for preparing a complete and organized shopping list.

Time Management in Meal Planning

18. *Efficient Meal Planning,* Activity B, SAG. Have students plan a meal that can be prepared in 45 minutes. The meal should involve the use of at least one time-saving piece of equipment, at least one convenience food, and some advance preparation.

19. Guest speaker. Ask an efficiency expert to give your students general tips for managing their time more efficiently. Ask the speaker to relate these suggestions to time management in the kitchen.

20. Ask each student to interview two meal managers to find out what they feel their greatest problems are related to time management. Have students share and discuss their findings in class.

21. Discuss with students the advantages and disadvantages of planning meals on a weekly basis, a biweekly basis, and a monthly basis.

22. Ask each student to develop a plan for what he or she would consider to be an ideal kitchen planning center. Have students describe how their centers are arranged and list the items that would be stored there. Then have students sketch a floor plan of this area.
23. *Meal Patterns in Planning,* reproducible master, 25-1, TR. Have students develop a day's menus using light, moderate, and heavy meal patterns.
24. Have students brainstorm a list of timesaving equipment available for use in the kitchen.
25. Have each student select a timesaving piece of equipment, such as a microwave oven or food processor. Have students research the different models of their chosen appliances that are available. Then have them give brief oral reports about price range, features, safety factors, use, and care.
26. Have students visit the housewares section of a department or hardware store. Have them make a list of all the utensils that they feel would be especially valuable for saving time in food preparation.
27. Have each student choose a piece of timesaving kitchen equipment and demonstrate its use to the class.
28. Divide the class into two groups. Have one group make a list of all the types of finished convenience food products that are available in most supermarkets. Have the other group make a list of all the types of semi-prepared convenience food products that are available.
29. Have students develop a bulletin board or display showing pictures or packages of some of the many convenience foods that are available.
30. Ask students to analyze the menus they developed in Learning Experience 23 to determine what foods could be prepared in advance to save meal preparation time later.
31. Have students discuss the advantages of a well-planned shopping list.
32. Give students a set of recipes that could be used to prepare a meal. Have each student develop a complete shopping list of items that would be needed to prepare the recipes. Then have students compare their lists and discuss any differences they find.
33. *Efficient Grocery Shopping,* Activity C, SAG. Have students draw a floor plan of the grocery store at which their families usually shop. Have them label the sections where various types of foods are found.
34. Guest speaker. Invite an extension home living agent to give your students suggestions for foods that can be prepared in advance and stored in the refrigerator or freezer to save meal preparation time later. Also ask the speaker to discuss how to store these foods safely.
35. Have students interview managers of local grocery stores to find out when their stores are most and least busy. Ask students to share their findings in class and discuss how this information could help them save time when shopping.

Shopping Skills

36. *Deciding Where to Shop,* Activity E, SAG. Have students list the advantages and disadvantages of shopping at various types of stores. Then they are to compare prices of three items at three of these store types. Discuss their findings.
37. Create a display of food packages and labels showing a variety of brands available at supermarkets in your area. Ask students to identify which items are name brands, which are house brands, and which are generic products.
38. Have students compare the quality of the name brand, house brand, and generic versions of a product such as canned peaches or tomatoes. Ask students to suggest the best uses for each version of the product.
39. Have students visit a grocery store and make a list of all the different brands they can find available of the items in the shopping list used in Learning Experience 14. Have students share their findings in class.
40. *Comparing Brands,* reproducible master 25-2, TR. Have students visit two different grocery stores to price name brand, house brand, and generic versions of the products listed. Then ask students to use their findings to decide which brands they would use and at which store they would shop.
41. Have students discuss the value of unit pricing as a consumer aid.

42. Create four or five price labels for a particular food item and have students decide which would be the best buy.
43. *Unit Pricing,* Activity D, SAG. Have students use the information on unit price tags for the name brand, house brand, and generic versions of two different products to complete the charts. Then have them use the charts to determine which version of each product would be the best buy for their intended use.

Avoiding Waste

44. Have each student give a brief oral report on how to properly store a food to avoid waste. Each class member should report on a different food item.
45. Have students make a display of a variety of containers designed for storing foods.
46. Have students write a reaction paper to the statement "The garbage disposal is often the best fed member of the family." Ask volunteers to share their papers in class.
47. Discuss with students how attitudes about eating habits and behavior are related to food waste.
48. Have students develop a survey about food waste in the home. Ask each student to use the survey to interview two people who have the primary responsibility for managing meals in their homes. Have students write an article for a local newspaper summarizing their findings and analyzing the implications.
49. Have students brainstorm a list of creative ways to use leftovers.
50. *Using Leftovers to Avoid Waste,* Activity F, SAG. Have students decide how to use four main dish leftovers for dinners and lunches.

Answer Key

Text

To Review

1. (List four:) Look for new foods at the store and try them. Collect new recipe ideas from resources such as cookbooks. Look for new ways of fixing familiar foods. Get new ideas from friends about snacks and favorite meals. Garden at home to can, freeze, and preserve foods.
2. your budget, needs, storage space, and the storage life of the item you are considering buying

3. (List four:) macaroni, spaghetti, rice, potatoes, bread, soups (Students may justify other responses.)
4. Having a complete shopping list makes shopping simpler and helps you avoid impulse buying, which adds to food costs.
5. (Describe five. Student response.)
6. (List three:) blender, slow cooker, mixer, food processor, microwave oven, conventional oven, freezer (Students may justify other responses.)
7. Finished, semiprepared
8. national brands—quality products widely advertised across the country; house or store brands—processed to be distributed by a supermarket chain, an association of independent stores, or other stores with numerous outlets; economy brands—a lower-quality house brand distributed by many large supermarket chains; generics—products with plain labels and black lettering that are less costly and of a lower quality
9. The left side of the unit price tag lists the unit price. This might be the price per pound, quart, dozen, or other measurement. The right side of the tag lists the name, weight, and price of the item.
10. Food is sometimes wasted through improper storage. Food may be left on dinner plates and thrown away. Leftovers may be placed in the refrigerator, forgotten, and wasted.

Teacher's Resources

Chapter 25 Test

1. G
2. C
3. F
4. D
5. J
6. H
7. I
8. E
9. B
10. A
11. F
12. T
13. F
14. T
15. T
16. F
17. F
18. F
19. T

20. F
21. F
22. T
23. B
24. C
25. D
26. B
27. C
28. A
29. (Student response.)
30. (List three:) Expand food choices, use weekly advertisements, plan around the main dish, make a shopping list.

31. You need to choose the brand according to how you intend to use the food. The less expensive brands may not look as attractive as the name brands. Therefore, you might want a name brand if you are serving a fruit or vegetable as it comes out of the can.

32. Be sure you are looking at comparable items. A heat and serve soup should not be compared with a condensed soup to which you would add water. Some types of paper products may have variations, such as larger sizes or double thicknesses.

33. (Explain four:) Store food properly after you have purchased it. Serve food family style so each person can take as much food as he or she will eat. Store leftover foods in clear glass or plastic containers so the contents are visible. Organize refrigerator storage so leftovers are stored in a certain section. Make plans to include leftovers in meals.

Reproducible Master 25-1

Meal Patterns in Planning

Name _____ **Date** _____ **Period** _____

Use the following chart outlining light, moderate, and heavy meal patterns to develop a day's meal plans in all three categories.

Light Breakfast	Light Lunch	Light Dinner
Fruit _____ Cereal and/or bread _____ _____ Beverage _____	Soup or salad _____ Bread or sandwich _____ _____ Fruit _____ Beverage _____	Meat, poultry, or fish _____ Vegetable _____ Salad_____ Bread _____ Beverage _____
Moderate Breakfast	**Moderate Lunch**	**Moderate Dinner**
Fruit _____ Cereal and/or bread _____ _____ Beverage _____ Protein food _____ Potato, rice, or pasta_____ _____	Main dish _____ Vegetable or salad _____ _____ Fruit _____ Beverage _____	Meat, poultry, or fish _____ _____ Potato, rice, or pasta_____ Vegetable _____ Salad_____ Bread _____ Beverage _____
Heavy Breakfast	**Heavy Lunch**	**Heavy Dinner**
Fruit _____ Cereal _____ _____ Main dish or bread product _____ Protein food _____ Beverage _____	Main dish _____ Vegetable and/or salad_____ _____ Bread _____ Fruit _____ Dessert _____ Beverage _____	Soup _____ Meat, poultry, or fish _____ _____ Vegetable _____ Salad_____ Bread _____ Dessert _____ Beverage _____

Reproducible Master 25-2

Comparing Brands

Name _____ **Date** _____ **Period** _____

For each item in the chart, list the price of a name brand, house brand, and generic product found at each of two different stores. Also list which name brands and house brands you are pricing. (When possible, price the same brands at both stores.) After completing the chart, answer the questions that follow.

Item	Store A	Store B
All-purpose flour, 5 pounds Name brand House brand Generic	_____ _____ _____	_____ _____ _____
Tomato sauce, 8 ounces Name brand House brand Generic	_____ _____ _____	_____ _____ _____
Peanut butter, 18 ounces Name brand House brand Generic	_____ _____ _____	_____ _____ _____
Peach halves, 29 ounces Name brand House brand Generic	_____ _____ _____	_____ _____ _____
Vegetable oil, 24 ounces Name brand House brand Generic	_____ _____ _____	_____ _____ _____

1. Overall, which brand would you be most likely to buy? _____

   Why?_____

   _____

2. Which store would you be mostly likely to shop at?_____

   Why?_____

   _____

Meal Management—Planning and Shopping

Name _____

Date _____ **Period** _____ **Score** _____

Chapter 25 Test

Matching: Match the following terms and identifying phrases.

_____ 1. Feature a specific type of product and offer a great deal of variety in that type of product.

_____ 2. Products packaged with plain labels and bold black lettering; quality may vary from one purchase to the next.

_____ 3. Serve local, loyal customers who care more about convenience than price.

_____ 4. The top brand is usually comparable in taste and texture to name brands but lower in price.

_____ 5. Reduce prices by cutting their overhead costs; require customers to pack their own purchases.

_____ 6. Another name for house brands.

_____ 7. Offer the greatest overall selection of items.

_____ 8. Generally the most expensive products on the market.

_____ 9. Individuals trade work for savings in food prices.

_____ 10. A form of house brand that has a slightly lower quality than name brands.

A. economy brands

B. food cooperatives

C. generics

D. house brands

E. name brands

F. small independent stores

G. specialty stores

H. store brands

I. supermarkets

J. warehouse stores

True/False: Circle *T* if the statement is true or *F* if the statement is false.

T F 11. The amount of money spent on food usually indicates the quality of meals.

T F 12. The main dish is often an expensive part of the meal.

T F 13. The Internet can be used to find nutritional information, but not recipes.

T F 14. Soups are one way to extend meat in a main dish.

T F 15. Having a complete shopping list helps prevent impulse buying.

T F 16. At specialty stores, customers are expected to pack their own purchases.

T F 17. House brands are generally the most expensive products on the market.

(Continued)

Name _____

T   F   18. An advantage of generic foods is their consistent quality.

T   F   19. Unit pricing tells what a product costs per standard unit, such as a pound or a quart.

T   F   20. Vegetables and fruits should be washed before they are stored.

T   F   21. Eggs are best stored in an open tray in the refrigerator.

T   F   22. Casseroles, stews, soups, and other one-dish meals that combine meat with vegetables are usually timesaving recipes.

Multiple Choice: Choose the best answer and write the corresponding letter in the blank.

_____ 23. When preparing a shopping list, what would be the least helpful?
     A. Referring to a chart indicating can sizes and quantity.
     B. Arranging items on the list in alphabetical order.
     C. Referring to an equivalent chart.
     D. Attaching your coupons to the list.

_____ 24. Which of the following is NOT true about meat?
     A. Cutting your own meat from a large roast can help you save money.
     B. Buying poultry whole helps save money.
     C. Roasts with the bone removed are usually lower priced than those with the bones.
     D. All of the above.

_____ 25. Food costs can be limited by _____.
     A. using advertised specials for the main dish
     B. using a main dish that combines meat with an extender
     C. adding to leftovers to create a main dish for the lighter meal of the day
     D. All of the above.

_____ 26. Which of the following is NOT true about the unit pricing tag?
     A. It tells what a product costs per unit.
     B. It can be used to compare all food products.
     C. It will give the name, weight, and price per item.
     D. All of the above.

_____ 27. The most expensive brands generally are _____ brands.
     A. economy
     B. generic
     C. name
     D. house

_____ 28. Which of the following is NOT true about food waste?
     A. There is very little food waste in the United States.
     B. Leftover foods are often placed in the refrigerator and forgotten.
     C. A permissive attitude about eating habits can be a cause of food waste.
     D. All of the above.

(Continued)

Name _____

Essay Questions: Provide the answers you feel best show your understanding of the subject matter.

29. Explain why the way meals are planned has a strong effect upon the ease of meal preparation.

30. Give three guidelines to follow that can help you meet a food budget and yet satisfy family members.

31. Explain why the least expensive brand may not always be the best product for your needs.

32. Describe a caution to keep in mind when using unit pricing.

33. List four ways to avoid food waste.

Meal Preparation

Objectives

When students have completed this chapter, they will be able to
- ◆ recognize resources valuable to efficient meal management.
- ◆ relate time management to the organization of the work area.
- ◆ develop time plans for meal preparation and describe work simplification procedures to prepare meals efficiently.
- ◆ describe procedures in food preparation that will help retain nutrients.
- ◆ explain different ways food can be heated.
- ◆ recognize the effect of cooking equipment on food preparation.
- ◆ demonstrate food preparation procedures that can help them avoid common problems.

Bulletin Boards

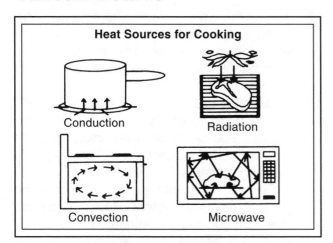

Title: *Heat Sources for Cooking*

Use pictures or drawings of a range top, broiler, convection oven, and microwave oven to illustrate conduction, radiation, convection, and microwaves, respectively, as heat sources for cooking. Place red arrows on the pictures or drawings to indicate the heat flow in each of the different cooking methods.

Title: *Nutrients Saved/Nutrients Lost*

Place pictures or drawings in two columns to show cooking methods that help preserve nutrients and cooking methods that cause nutrient loss. For instance, vegetables being washed under a faucet could be shown opposite vegetables being soaked in water to illustrate nutrient loss in water. Food boiling vigorously could be shown opposite food simmering gently to illustrate nutrient loss to heat. Food wrapped in plastic wrap could be shown opposite food sitting in open air to illustrate nutrient loss to oxidation.

Teaching Materials

Text, pages 451-477
  To Review
  To Challenge Your Thinking
  To Do with the Class
  To Do with Your Community
Student Activity Guide
  A. *Storage in the Kitchen*
  B. *A Time Plan for Meal Preparation*
  C. *Preparation Techniques*
  D. *Avoiding Problems in Preparation*
  E. *Retaining Nutrients in Food*
  F. *Understanding Heat*
Teacher's Resources
  Materials for Cookware, transparency
    master 26-1
  Chapter 26 Test
  Efficient Meal Preparation, color
    transparency CT-26

Introductory Activities

1. *Efficient Meal Preparation,* color transparency CT-26, TR. Use this transparency as an introduction to the basics of meal preparation.
2. Think of two dinner menus—one that would not appeal to students and one that would. Assemble pictures of the foods in each menu. Ask students to look at the two groups

of pictures and write a list of factors that make one meal appeal to them more than the other.

3. Survey students to find out how many of them are involved in preparing meals for their families. Ask those who have meal management experience what they find most challenging about meal preparation.

Instructional Concepts and Student Learning Experiences

Efficient Meal Preparation

4. Have students discuss how each of the following factors could affect the management of time in meal preparation: family size, number of persons helping with meal preparation, knowledge and skill of meal manager, equipment, organization of kitchen equipment, and space.

5. Field trip. Take your class to a business that sells kitchen cabinets and/or designs kitchen space. Have your students note the shapes of the model kitchens and the placement of the work centers. Ask students to analyze the advantages and disadvantages of each model.

6. Have students conduct an experiment to determine the most efficient arrangement of work centers for preparing a meal.

7. Guest speaker. Invite an interior designer, architect, or space planner to talk to your class about how to increase kitchen storage capacity.

8. *Storage in the Kitchen,* Activity A, SAG. Have students draw a diagram of a kitchen showing the three work centers. Then have them indicate where listed pieces of equipment would most logically be stored in the kitchen.

9. Have students debate the statement "Having too much equipment in the kitchen can make meal management as difficult as having too little."

10. Panel discussion. Invite a panel of experienced cooks to discuss methods they use to simplify meal preparation.

11. Review with students the steps of the problem-solving process. Then have students use these steps to solve the following problem: Before leaving for work, Sam forgot to take the roast out of the freezer that he intended to serve for dinner this evening.

12. Discuss with students how a person's cooking experience will affect his or her time plan for meal preparation.

13. Have each student develop a time plan for preparing the same dinner menu. Then have students compare their time plans and discuss any differences.

14. *A Time Plan for Meal Preparation,* Activity B, SAG. Have each student write a dinner menu and develop a time plan for preparing it.

15. Have each student choose a task that he or she does regularly in the kitchen. On paper, have students break these activities down into steps. Then have them analyze the activities to see if they can be simplified in any way.

16. Have each student choose a piece of kitchen equipment that he or she has not often used. Ask students to make a point of using these pieces of equipment as often as possible during the next two weeks. After that time, have students write an evaluation of how their skills in using these pieces of equipment have improved. The evaluation should also explain how these pieces of equipment have helped students simplify food preparation tasks.

Nutrition and Meal Preparation

17. Review the water-soluble vitamins with students. Have students make a chart of foods high in these vitamins. Discuss how these foods should be cooked to avoid nutrient loss in water.

18. *Retaining Nutrients in Food,* Activity E, SAG. Have students use the text and one other credible source of nutrition information to develop a list of procedures that are helpful in retaining nutrients. Discuss the lists in class.

19. Divide the class into groups. Assign each group a different nutrient. Have the groups research cooking techniques that can be used to preserve their assigned nutrient. Have students compile their findings into a brochure on cooking tips for nutritious eating. Distribute the brochure throughout the school.

20. Have students find recipes in which they could use the cooking liquid from vegetables in order to avoid throwing away the nutrients that have leached into the water. Have students discuss the negative effects of overcooking foods.

21. Have students inspect a variety of food storage containers. Ask them to analyze the tightness of the seals on the containers and evaluate their effectiveness for keeping oxygen out of foods.

The Significance of Heat in Cooking

22. *Understanding Heat,* Activity F, SAG. Have students complete sentences related to the significance of heat in cooking.
23. Guest speaker. Invite a physics teacher to speak to your class about the different methods of heat transfer.
24. Have students visit the cookware section of a department or hardware store. Have them note the variety of materials and finishes available. Discuss their findings in class.
25. *Materials for Cookware,* transparency master 26-1, TR. Use the master to discuss with students the advantages and disadvantages of various cookware materials.
26. Guest speaker. Invite a cookware representative to demonstrate and explain the use of a pressure cooker.
27. Have students conduct an experiment to compare the cooking time and quality of a food prepared in a regular saucepan with that of the same food prepared in a pressure saucepan. Discuss the reason for the time difference.

Food Preparation Techniques

28. *Preparation Techniques,* Activity C, SAG. Have students analyze given situations and suggest cooking procedures that would eliminate possible problems.
29. *Avoiding Problems in Preparation,* Activity D, SAG. Have students explain how to prevent a variety of common problems in food preparation.
30. Have students develop a display showing the variety of milk and milk products that are available in stores today.
31. Prepare a milk product, such as pudding or cream soup, as a cooking demonstration for students. As you demonstrate, emphasize cooking techniques that prevent film, sticking and scorching, and curdling.
32. Have students research the difference between natural and processed cheeses and ripened and unripened cheeses. Plan to have a cheese tasting so students can sample

these different types of cheese as they share their findings in class.
33. Have students microwave two one-inch cubes of Cheddar cheese, one on high power and the other on medium power. Both cubes should be microwaved for the same amount of time—about 45 seconds to 1 minute, or until melted. Have students compare the appearance and texture of the two samples. Ask them to explain why the samples differ and draw conclusions about microwaving cheese.
34. Have students make French dressing and mayonnaise. Have them compare the characteristics of the two products and discuss the emulsifying effect of the egg in the mayonnaise.
35. Have students use pictures to create a poster or bulletin board showing various ways eggs can be used in meals.
36. Discuss with students the relationship between meat tenderness and the location of meat cuts in an animal.
37. Guest speaker. Invite a butcher to speak to your class about the use of moist heat and dry heat cooking methods for preparing various cuts of meat.
38. Have students prepare various kinds of fish using different techniques, such as frying, poaching, broiling, and baking.
39. Divide the class into lab groups. Have each group stir 1/2 cup boiling water into 1 tablespoon flour. Then have each group stir a second 1/2 cup boiling water into 1 tablespoon flour combined with one of the following: 1 tablespoon melted shortening, 1 tablespoon cold water, or 2 tablespoons sugar. Ask each group to compare the texture and appearance of their two starch pastes and report their observations to the rest of the class.
40. Have students prepare two batches of biscuits. Have them prepare the first batch following a standard recipe. Have them prepare the second batch from the same recipe but omitting the baking powder. Have students compare the two products as the basis for a discussion on the function of leavening agents.
41. Have students examine the labels from a variety of cooking oils and fats to determine the origin of the products and give suggested uses.

42. Place cut bananas, apples, and pears on two plates. Dip the fruit on one plate in lemon or orange juice. After 30 minutes, allow students to compare the fruit on the two plates. Discuss with them the cause and prevention of browning of cut fruit.

43. Cook samples of green, red, and white vegetables to demonstrate how adverse color changes can take place during cooking. Cook a second sample of the same vegetables demonstrating techniques to avoid these color changes.

Serving the Meal

44. Have students demonstrate how to set a table correctly.

45. Role-play various mealtime situations and have students practice rules of etiquette.

Answer Key

Text

To Review

1. preparation center, cooking and serving center, cleanup center (Student response for equipment in each center.)

2. (List three:) Decide in which of the work centers that piece of equipment is used most. Decide how often it is used. The more often it is used, the more accessible it should be. Consider the weight of an item. Heavy items should be stored in a place that is convenient to reach.

3. Decide the time the meal is to be served. Decide the time to begin each specific food by figuring the amount of time needed to prepare the product. Determine from the serving time when preparation should begin. Finally, integrate the schedules for preparing these different foods into a logical sequence of activities.

4. (Name three. Student response.)

5. D, C, B, A

6. A film or scum can form when milk is heated. The milk can stick to the bottom and sides of the pan and scorch. The milk may curdle, creating small, soft lumps.

7. A. false B. true C. false D. false E. false

8. D, C, A, B

9. Baking powder or baking soda—Carbon dioxide is formed when these products come in contact with liquid giving volume to the product. Yeast—When mixed with a warm liquid and sugar, carbon dioxide is formed. The gas expands the gluten structure, and causes the bread to rise. Egg whites—When beaten, egg whites can hold a large quantity of air, forming a foam. A thin film of egg white protein surrounds each cell giving rigidity to the foam structure. Steam—In heating, steam forms and expands the structure as in popovers or cream puffs.

10. Vegetable oils are pressed or extracted from a variety of seeds, such as corn, cottonseed, peanut, safflower, and soybean. The oils are then purified by a variety of methods and are sold in liquid form to be used in salad dressings, frying, and baking. Vegetable shortenings are made from vegetable oils and are hydrogenated to make them solid. In addition to changing the consistency, this process changes the color, flavor, and odor and improves the keeping quality.

Student Activity Guide

Preparation Techniques, Activity C

1. To prevent the film, use a covered container or stir the milk while it heats. Beating the milk while it heats will prevent the skin from forming. To prevent lumps, don't use milk that is about to sour. Cook at low temperatures.

2. Take eggs out of refrigerator and let them warm up to room temperature. Be sure no fat is present. Be sure no yolk gets in the white. Use a glass, metal, or ceramic bowl. Don't add sugar until egg white has reached almost full volume. Use a gentle folding motion to combine with other ingredients.

3. (Student response. Examples might include foods such as broiled steak, fish, or hamburgers; baked chicken; and roast ham, turkey, or beef.)

Understanding Heat, Activity F

1. material
2. radiation
3. conduction
4. convection
5. center
6. microwave
7. short cooking time
8. Metal
9. Aluminum, copper, magnesium
10. Glass, steel

11. absorber
12. polished
13. weight
14. moisture content

Teacher's Resources

Chapter 26 Test
1. F
2. J
3. A
4. G
5. D
6. C
7. B
8. E
9. H
10. I
11. T
12. T
13. T
14. T
15. T
16. F
17. F
18. T
19. F
20. T
21. T
22. F
23. D
24. A
25. C
26. D
27. A
28. C
29. B
30. D
31. C

32. Analyze the activity and break it down into detailed steps. Decide if you are using any unnecessary steps and if the steps are arranged in logical order. Check to see if all supplies and equipment needed are available. Storage of some equipment may need to be reorganized.
33. Determine in which of the work centers the equipment is most often used and decide how often it is used. The more you use a piece of equipment, the more accessible it should be. Heavy items should be easy to reach.
34. (Student response. List and describe three.)
35. (A) Mix the flour with the melted fat first. Then slowly add the liquid. Stir the two together to distribute the heat and allow the starch granules to swell evenly over moderate heat. (B) Mix the starch product with a small amount of cold water or liquid before adding it gradually to the hot liquid. (C) Mix the starch or flour with other ingredients, such as sugar and seasonings to separate the starch.
36. (Student response. List five.)

Transparency Master 26-1

Materials for Cookware

Material	Advantages	Disadvantages
Aluminum	Conducts heat rapidly and evenly. Durable.	Darkens and pits due to minerals in food and water.
Cast iron	Holds heat well. Distributes heat evenly.	Heavy. Will rust if not dried before storing.
Copper	Conducts heat well.	Reacts with food when heated to form poisonous compounds. Must be lined with another material for cooking.
Stoneware	Retains heat so food stays at serving temperature. Can be used in conventional or microwave oven. Can be used for cooking and serving.	Breaks and chips easily.
Enamel (glass baked on metal)	Available in attractive patterns. Maintains heat distribution of base metal.	Chips easily. May be heavy if base metal is iron.
Glass	Allows food to be seen while cooking. Available in attractive designs.	Chips and breaks easily. Conducts heat unevenly. Cannot hold up under extreme temperature changes.
Stainless steel	Will not rust, corrode, or stain. Keeps brightness under normal care. Durable.	Conducts heat slowly and unevenly. Develops hot spots. May darken if overheated.
Stainless steel with copper or aluminum bottom of both metals	Heats quickly and evenly. Durable. Attractive.	Copper bottoms discolor and need to be cleaned.

Meal Preparation

Name _____

Date _____ **Period** _____ **Score** _____

Chapter 26 Test

Matching: Match the following terms and identifying phrases.

_____ 1. Causes a food product to increase in volume.

_____ 2. Heat created by electromagnetic waves or rays that go directly to the object being heated.

_____ 3. The substance that makes green vegetables green.

_____ 4. Flecks of fat in meat.

_____ 5. A mixture that forms when liquids that do not ordinarily mix are combined.

_____ 6. Using circulating currents of hot air to cook food.

_____ 7. The transference of heat from the heat source to a container to the substance being heated.

_____ 8. The swelling and subsequent thickening of starch granules as they are heated in water.

_____ 9. High-frequency radio waves that generate heat in the food itself.

_____ 10. Exposure to oxygen.

A. chlorophyll

B. conduction

C. convection

D. emulsion

E. gelatinization

F. leavening agent

G. marbling

H. microwave

I. oxidation

J. radiation

True/False: Circle *T* if the statement is true or *F* if the statement is false.

T F 11. Work simplification is a resource that can help you conserve time and energy.

T F 12. Each kitchen has three work centers: the preparation center, the cooking and serving center, and the cleanup center.

T F 13. Equipment that is used often should be easily accessible.

T F 14. The greatest loss of nutrients during food preparation occurs when foods are soaked or cooked in water.

T F 15. Vitamin C is easily destroyed when exposed to oxygen.

T F 16. Radiation is a fairly slow method of transferring heat.

T F 17. Stainless steel and glass are excellent conductors of heat.

T F 18. Milk is more likely to boil over when there is a film or scum on top.

T F 19. Eggs act as emulsifying agents in soufflés, popovers, and angel food cakes.

(Continued)

Name _____

T   F   20. The best way to cook meat depends on the meat's tenderness and the size of the cut.

T   F   21. Because butter and margarine burn or smoke at the lowest temperature of any fat, they are not suitable for frying.

T   F   22. When fruits are cooked with sugar, they tend to lose their shape.

Multiple Choice: Choose the best answer and write the corresponding letter in the blank.

_____ 23. Work simplification _____.
   A. involves analyzing an activity to see if it is done in the most efficient way
   B. conserves both time and energy
   C. may involve using tools and equipment to simplify the task
   D. All of the above.

_____ 24. Which of the following items would be best stored in the preparation center of the kitchen?
   A. electric mixer
   B. cookbooks
   C. coupons
   D. dishwashing detergent

_____ 25. Which of the following items would be best stored in the cooking and serving center of the kitchen?
   A. blender
   B. scouring pads
   C. frying pan
   D. vegetable peeler

_____ 26. Which of the following items would be best stored in the cleanup center of the kitchen?
   A. dinner plates
   B. baking pans
   C. pot holders
   D. dish towels

_____ 27. The best way to prevent nutrient loss in fruits and vegetables is to _____.
   A. cook them in a minimum of water
   B. soak them before cooking
   C. chop them as finely as possible
   D. wash them after cutting

_____ 28. When cooking with milk, the best way to keep it from curdling is to _____.
   A. use high heat
   B. add acid, such as tomato juice, directly to the milk
   C. use fresh milk
   D. use milk that has been refrigerated for at least two weeks

(Continued)

Name _____

_____ 29. Which of the following is NOT true about an emulsion?
    A. An emulsion is a mixture that forms when liquids that ordinarily do not mix are combined.
    B. Mayonnaise is an emulsifying agent.
    C. Emulsions can be temporary or permanent.
    D. An egg yolk can be used to create a permanent emulsion.

_____ 30. A method of cooking meat that would be most suitable for less tender cuts is _____.
    A. frying
    B. broiling and grilling
    C. roasting
    D. braising

_____ 31. Which of the following is true about leavening agents?
    A. As yeast mixes with a warm liquid and sugar, oxygen is formed, causing the bread to rise.
    B. Gluten is a leavening agent in flour.
    C. Eggs and steam are leavening agents for sponge cakes.
    D. Baking soda and egg whites are the leavening agents in angel food cake.

Essay Questions: Provide the answers you feel best show your understanding of the subject matter.

32. Describe steps in using work simplification as a resource.

33. What should a person consider when deciding where to store kitchen equipment?

34. List and describe three methods of cooking meat.

35. Describe three ways to cook with starch to avoid lumping.

36. List at least five rules of mealtime etiquette.

Planning and Shopping for Clothes

Objectives

When students have completed this chapter, they will be able to

- explain how clothing is related to basic human needs.
- describe the significance of fashion in clothing selection.
- develop a wardrobe plan.
- explain how the elements of design relate to clothing.
- apply the decision-making process to clothing selection.
- describe various shopping guidelines.
- explain the factors that influence the performance of a garment.

Bulletin Boards

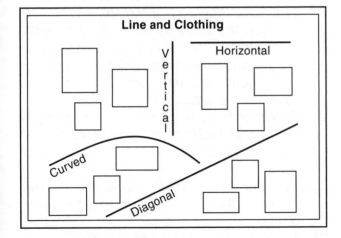

Line and Clothing

Title: *Line and Clothing*

Use and label the four types of line to divide the board into four sections as shown. Within each section, place pictures of clothing illustrating each type of line.

Title: *The Effect of Color*

Using illustrations from magazines and catalogs, develop two series of fashion pictures leading from dark colors to light colors and from dull colors to bright colors. Have students discuss the different effects created by the different colors.

Teaching Materials

Text, pages 479-502
To Review
To Challenge Your Thinking
To Do with the Class
To Do with Your Community

Student Activity Guide
A. *The Significance of Clothing*
B. *A Clothing Inventory*
C. *Elements of Design*
D. *Knowledge and Skill in Clothing Selection*

Teacher's Resources
Color and You, reproducible master 27-1
Cost of Clothing Per Wearing, reproducible master 27-2
Chapter 27 Test
The Color Wheel, color transparency CT-27

Introductory Activities

1. Give a demonstration on accessories using students from the class. Demonstrate how accessories can add interest and individuality, hide less desirable features, play up attractive features, and provide a way to wear the same outfit but give it a different look.

272 Goals for Living

2. Gather pictures of fashions that have been popular at different points in history and in different countries and display them for the class. Have students discuss how the different fashions met various needs for people at that time or in that place.

Instructional Concepts and Student Learning Experiences

The Significance of Clothing

3. Have students choose a famous person and determine how that person's lifestyle and priorities affect his or her clothing choices. Have students share their findings with the class.
4. Panel discussion. Invite students from other countries to discuss how traditional clothing in their native land differs from clothing in this country.
5. *The Significance of Clothing,* Activity A, SAG. For each of the factors listed, students should write a specific situation in which clothing selection would be influenced by that factor.
6. Have students discuss how clothing can affect self-concept.
7. Have students discuss why they think teens tend to wear different clothing styles than adults. Students should discuss what the differing styles say about teens' and adults' self-images.
8. Assign each student a different period of time in history. Have students research to find information and illustrations on styles of that time period. Have students present their findings in chronological order. Students should discuss trends that they observe.
9. Have students discuss current clothing styles, noting which styles are classics and which are fads.

A Wardrobe Plan

10. Have students discuss the advantages and disadvantages of having a wardrobe plan.
11. Guest speaker. Invite a clothing consultant from a local store to give a demonstration on wardrobe planning tips.
12. Have students work as a class to develop a list of criteria for a well-planned wardrobe.
13. *A Clothing Inventory*, Activity B, SAG. Have students complete a clothing inventory chart and answer questions about it.

14. Have students discuss why it might be functional in some parts of the country to have two clothing inventories.
15. Have students develop a commercial designed to "sell" the idea of developing a wardrobe plan.
16. Have each student make a list of his or her roles. Students should list clothing and accessories needed for each role.
17. Have students work in groups to compare their clothing needs. Students should discuss why clothing needs may differ or be similar among group members.
18. Have a group of students develop a demonstration to show how posture can affect the way clothing looks on a person.
19. Have students make posters highlighting how aspects of personal analysis can help a person choose flattering clothing.

The Elements of Design

20. *Elements of Design,* Activity C, SAG. Have students use the instructions provided to select an outfit that uses line, color, and texture in a way that would be attractive on them.
21. Have students develop a demonstration to show how line, color, and texture can be used to emphasize positive features and disguise negative features.
22. Have students find pictures of clothing that create illusions of length or width using line. Students should share their pictures in class.
23. *The Color Wheel,* color transparency CT-27, TR. Use the color wheel to illustrate basic color information. Illustrate how primary, secondary, and intermediate colors are found on the wheel. Discuss how various color schemes are produced.
24. Collect pictures of clothing with a variety of collars and necklines. Have students discuss which face shapes would look best with each type.
25. Have students use blue, yellow, and red paint to create their own color wheels by mixing colors.
26. *Color and You,* reproducible master 27-1, TR. Have students determine how various colors make them feel and how they could use various colors to express their personality in their wardrobes.

27. Arrange a display of fabric swatches in a variety of textures. Have students discuss each texture in terms of garments and body types for which it would be appropriate.
28. Have students brainstorm a list of adjectives to describe various textures. Have students discuss how textures can be used to express various aspects of personality based on the list of adjectives developed.

Knowledge and Skill in Clothing Selection

29. Have students write an evaluation of a recent clothing purchase.
30. Panel discussion. Invite representatives from the clothing industry to suggest guidelines for buying clothing. Representatives might include store managers, buyers, wardrobe consultants, seamstresses or tailors, and clothing care specialists such as dry cleaners.
31. Have students develop a list of resources available in the community to help people learn clothing construction techniques.
32. *Cost of Clothing Per Wearing,* reproducible master 27-2, TR. Have students use the chart to determine the cost of various types of clothing per wearing.
33. Have students bring to class a variety of clothing advertisements. Have students evaluate them in terms of helpfulness to the consumer.
34. Have students bring a garment to class that has not performed well in some way. Students should share the problem and explain what has been learned from this experience.
35. Have students develop a display of fabric swatches. Each swatch should be labeled with fiber content, fabric weave, and fabric characteristics.
36. *Knowledge and Skill in Clothing Selection,* Activity D, SAG. Place a variety of fabric samples in a box. There should be at least four samples for every student in the class. Have students select and evaluate four samples using the form provided.
37. Have each student choose a fabric finish and research the qualities of the finish. Students should share their findings in class.
38. Have students write a research report on the benefits of and drawbacks to fabric finishes.

39. Have students collect six hangtags and compare the information on each.
40. Have students write a research report on the history of legislation related to clothing labeling.
41. Have students develop a list of local clothing stores that do alterations on clothing if garments do not fit properly. Students should also list any costs involved in alterations.
42. Have students examine similar garments in various price ranges and evaluate their construction. Students should draw conclusions on the relationship between price and construction and share their findings in class.
43. Guest speaker. Invite a seamstress or tailor to demonstrate methods of judging proper fit of clothing.

Answer Key

Text

To Review

1. A. Style refers to the specific characteristics or distinctive form or shape of clothing while fashion refers to the style, which is popular at a certain period of time.
   B. Fads are styles accepted by a large number of people for only a short period of time while classics are styles that are worn year after year by a large segment of the public.
2. First take a clothing inventory to be sure of what clothes you have. Then consider your various needs for clothing and check to see what needs are not covered by your present wardrobe. You will probably have to set priorities for your needs since most people cannot immediately buy all they need. Information from a personal analysis and your knowledge of the elements of design are both resources, which should help you in planning to select garments.
3. Line, color, texture. Line in a garment has a large effect on whether or not a garment looks good on your figure. Line can be used to emphasize your strengths and make you more attractive. Color can enhance your appearance and create the effect you want. Colors that coordinate with your skin, hair, and eyes will do the most for you. The texture of the garment you choose can make you appear smaller or larger.

4. hue, value intensity
5. B, D, C, F, A, E
6. plain weave, twill weave, satin weave
   A. satin weave
   B. twill weave
   C. twill weave
   D. plain weave
   E. satin weave
   F. twill weave
   G. satin weave
7. (Give two examples.) dyeing, printing, permanent press, water proofing
8. Provides instructions for proper garment care.
9. fit
10. (Student response. Name eight.)

Teacher's Resources

Chapter 27 Test
1. D
2. B
3. E
4. G
5. C
6. H
7. K
8. I
9. J
10. L
11. F
12. A
13. T
14. T
15. F
16. T
17. T
18. F
19. T
20. F
21. F
22. F
23. A
24. B
25. A
26. B
27. C
28. C
29. D
30. (Student response.)
31. When fashions are first introduced, they are followed by a few daring people. As a style rises in acceptance, it is copied and adopted by those who want to look "smart" and "fashionable." The cycle continues, and the fashion gains widespread acceptance and mass conformity. After reaching its peak, the fashion declines and then finally disappears. Unless a style is accepted as a classic, it eventually completes the fashion cycle, and consumers experiment with newer styles.
32. Take a clothing inventory to be sure of what clothes you have. Then consider your various needs for clothing and check to see what needs are not covered by your present wardrobe. You will probably have to set priorities for your needs. Use information from a personal analysis and knowledge of the elements and principles of design to help you select garments.
33. (Student response. List four.)

Reproducible Master 27-1

Color and You

Name _____ **Date** _____ **Period** _____

Different colors produce different feelings in people. You can use colors to express different aspect personality in your clothing. Describe how each of the colors below makes you feel. Then answer the questions that follow.

Red: _____

Yellow: _____

Green: _____

Navy blue:_____

Royal blue: _____

Purple: _____

Brown: _____

Maroon: _____

Forest green: _____

Pink: _____

Light blue:_____

Lavender: _____

Black: _____

White: _____

Gray:_____

Orange:_____

Shocking pink: _____

Chartreuse:_____

1. Which of the colors listed above would fit your personality most of the time?_____

_____

2. Which colors would fit your personality if you were in a fun, playful mood? _____

_____

3. Which colors would fit your personality if you were in a serious mood? _____

_____

4. Which colors might you use to catch someone's attention?_____

_____

5. Which colors are least expressive of your personality most times?_____

_____

6. How can you apply the information from this activity to your wardrobe planning? _____

_____

Reproducible Master 27-2

Cost of Clothing Per Wearing

Name _____ **Date** _____ **Period** _____

Use the form below to determine the cost per wearing of various types of clothing. An example is given for you. Then answer the questions that follow.

Garment	Initial cost	How often worn	First year cost per wearing	Estimated wear life	Final cost per wearing
Crew neck sweater	$35	Once per week for 8 months of the year	(35 ÷ 32) $1.09	5 years	(35 ÷ 160) $.22

1. Which article of clothing has the lowest initial cost? _____

2. How does this article of clothing rank in terms of first year cost per wearing and final cost per wearing? _____

_____

3. Which article of clothing has the lowest first year cost per wearing? _____

_____

4. Which article of clothing has the lowest final cost per wearing? _____

_____

5. How do these items rank in terms of initial cost? _____

_____

6. What conclusions can you make about the costs and value of garments based on this activity? __

_____

_____

Planning and Shopping for Clothes

Name _____

Date _____ **Period** _____ **Score** _____

Chapter 27 Test

Matching: Match the following terms and identifying phrases.

_____ 1. The characteristic that gives a color a name and makes it unique.

_____ 2. Chain or independent stores that sell a large variety of goods and services.

_____ 3. The brightness or dullness of a color.

_____ 4. The colors that cannot be created by mixing other colors.

_____ 5. Chain or independent stores that attempt to undersell other merchants on certain lines and types of merchandise.

_____ 6. Colors that are produced when equal amounts of any two primary colors are mixed.

_____ 7. Chain or independent stores that sell a variety of consumer goods in a low price range.

_____ 8. The darker color that is created when black is added to a normal value.

_____ 9. Chain or independent stores that specialize in a limited type of merchandise.

_____ 10. The colors related to red, yellow, or orange.

_____ 11. Stores that are stocked with extra merchandise from a manufacturer's normal production.

_____ 12. The colors related to blue and green that give a subdued, quiet feeling.

A. cool colors

B. department stores

C. discount stores

D. hue

E. intensity

F. manufacturer's outlet stores

G. primary colors

H. secondary colors

I. shade

J. specialty stores

K. variety stores

L. warm colors

True/False: Circle *T* if the statement is true or *F* if the statement is false.

T F 13. Style relates to specific characteristics or the form or shape of clothing.

T F 14. Classics have a long period of acceptance and are worn year after year by a large segment of the public.

T F 15. When doing a clothing inventory, you should throw away clothing that needs repair or alteration.

T F 16. Quality is usually related to price.

T F 17. Blending yarns is a way to combine the best features of different fibers.

(Continued)

Name _____

T F   18. There are three basic weaves: the plain weave, the basket weave, and the satin weave.

T F   19. The twill weave can be identified by its characteristic diagonal line.

T F   20. Printing is a functional finish on a fabric.

T F   21. Durable finishes last only until the first time the garment is washed or dry cleaned.

T F   22. Narrow seams in a garment generally indicate high quality construction.

Multiple Choice: Choose the best answer and write the corresponding letter in the blank.

_____ 23. The term that refers to the style that is popular at a certain time is _____.
A. fashion
B. fad
C. classic
D. high fashion

_____ 24. All of the following are elements of design except _____.
A. line
B. organization
C. texture
D. color

_____ 25. Lines that are formed when a garment is sewn are called _____.
A. structural lines
B. decorative lines
C. prominent lines
D. lines of emphasis

_____ 26. The lightness or darkness of a hue is known as its _____.
A. validity
B. value
C. balance
D. contrast

_____ 27. Colors that are made by mixing a primary color with the secondary color next to it are
called _____ colors.
A. internal
B. integral
C. intermediate
D. None of the above.

_____ 28. The texture of a fabric _____.
A. can do little to disguise figure irregularities
B. can be described by words, such as light, bright, and dark
C. describes the way a fabric feels and the way the surface appears
D. None of the above.

_____ 29. Herringbone is a variation of the _____ weave.
A. plain
B. basket
C. satin
D. twill

(Continued)

Name _____

Essay Questions: Provide the answers you feel best show your understanding of the subject matter.

30. Explain how psychological needs influence clothing selection.

31. Describe the steps of the fashion cycle.

32. Describe the steps in developing a wardrobe plan.

33. List four items that indicate quality in the construction of clothing.

Caring for Clothing

Objectives

When students have completed this chapter, they will be able to

- provide proper routine and periodic care and repair of their own clothing.
- suggest guidelines for clothing storage.
- demonstrate use of care labels as a resource in laundry techniques.
- explain procedures to follow in stain removal.
- describe products that contribute to better care and cleaning of clothes.
- relate specific laundry procedures to the resulting appearance of clothing.

Bulletin Boards

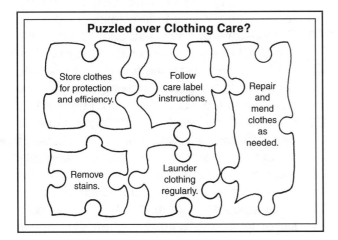

Puzzled over Clothing Care?

Store clothes for protection and efficiency.

Follow care label instructions.

Repair and mend clothes as needed.

Remove stains.

Launder clothing regularly.

Title: *Puzzled over Clothing Care?*

Place large puzzle pieces cut from poster board or construction paper on the board as shown. Place the following labels on the pieces: *Store Clothes for Protection and Efficiency, Follow Care Label Instructions, Remove Stains, Launder Clothing Regularly,* and *Repair and Mend Clothes as Needed.* Place pictures to illustrate these points on the appropriate puzzle pieces.

Title: *What's the Purpose?*

Place labels from various laundry products on one side of the board. On the other side, write purposes for each of the products in a random order. For instance, the purpose for starch might be "to add body to the garment." Provide string and push pins so that students can connect the appropriate labels and purposes.

Teaching Materials

Text, pages 503-515
  To Review
  To Challenge Your Thinking
  To Do with the Class
  To Do with Your Community
Student Activity Guide
  A. *Your Clothing Care Habits*
  B. *Clothing Storage*
  C. *Care Labels*
  D. *A Comparison of Laundry Products*
Teacher's Resources
  Reading Care Labels, reproducible master 28-1
  Stain Removal Guide, reproducible master 28-2
  Chapter 28 Test
  Clothing Care Labels, color transparency CT-28

Introductory Activities

1. *Your Clothing Care Habits,* Activity A, SAG. Have students use the form provided to evaluate their own clothing care habits. Students should save the activity and write suggestions for improving the way they care for clothing as they study the chapter.
2. Plan a "fashion show" using students or faculty from outside the class as models. The clothing modeled should be attractive, but show signs of improper care. For instance, a

dark suit might have lint on it; a dress might be wrinkled. Use the show as a springboard for a class discussion on how proper clothing care affects the appearance of clothes and the image of the person wearing them.

Instructional Concepts and Student Learning Experiences

Techniques of Clothing Care

3. Have students demonstrate to the class a simple technique for clothing repair. Students should provide a handout illustrating the technique. Place the handouts together to form a booklet on clothing repairs.
4. Have students develop lists of clothing care tasks that should be done daily, weekly, and seasonally.
5. Have students develop a list of tips for protecting clothes from such hazards as moisture, dust, moths, and sunlight.
6. Have students make drawings or models of plans for increasing storage space in a closet. Students should share their plans with the class.
7. Have students examine a product designed to improve closet storage. Students should report to the class on the type and function of product, cost, and quality.
8. *Clothing Storage*, Activity B, SAG. Have students mount or draw pictures of various storage products.

Laundry and Cleaning Techniques

9. Have students discuss tips for minimizing the work involved in doing laundry. Students should try one of the tips and report on the results.
10. *Care Labels,* Activity C, SAG. Have students complete the chart using information from six care labels.
11. Have students develop a checklist of guidelines for using care labels properly.
12. *Clothing Care Labels,* color transparency CT-28, TR. Use this transparency to illustrate examples of some of the international clothing care symbols that appear on clothing. Discuss how care labels help save money and time, as well as protect the consumer.

13. *Reading Care Labels,* reproducible master 28-1, TR. Distribute care labels or copies of care label instructions to students. Have students use the chart to interpret the meaning of the instructions on the care labels.
14. Have students visit a supermarket and record information on various stain removal products. Students should record information on how the products are used, types of stains removed, and cost.
15. *Stain Removal Guide,* reproducible master 28-2, TR. Provide students with stained fabrics. Have students try the methods listed to remove the stains.
16. Have students test the effectiveness of four stain removal products as a class experiment. Have the class evaluate the results.
17. *A Comparison of Laundry Products,* Activity D, SAG. Have students evaluate various laundry products using the form provided.
18. Have students interview consumers to find out what products they use for laundry care and why. Students should share their findings in class.
19. Have students research to find out how the elements in water affect the chemical structure of laundry products. Students should report their findings to the class.
20. Demonstrate or have a student demonstrate the effect of excessive agitation on wool fabric during hand washing and during machine washing. Illustrations showing the physical changes to the wool fiber should be used.
21. Have students visit an appliance store to evaluate two washing machines. Students should compare price, features, warranty, etc. Have students determine which washing machine they would select and explain why.
22. Have students work as a class to develop a list of factors to consider when selecting a dry cleaner.
23. Guest speaker. Invite the manager or owner from a dry cleaning business to speak on the dry cleaning process and clothing storage techniques.

Answer Key

Text

To Review

1. (Name five. Student response.)
2. A. May get mildew or smell musty.
   B. Moths lay eggs, hatch, and while in the larvae stage, eat the wool.
   C. Silverfish are attracted to starch and may eat holes in the wool.
3. false
4. If a garment is washed or ironed with a stain, it may be difficult, if not impossible, to get out. If not removed promptly, you may forget what caused the stain and may not know what to use to remove it.
5. greasy, nongreasy
6. Soaps combine with minerals in hard water to form a deposit or scum that gathers dirt from the water and sticks to the clothes and the inside of the washing machine. Detergents contain chemicals that soften and tie up the water minerals to permit cleaning.
7. if stained; heavily soiled
8. It can cause damage and discoloration to fabric.
9. White clothes are separated from those that have color to prevent them from becoming dull, grayish, or taking on colors from other clothes. Synthetics, particularly those with a permanent press finish, should be washed in warm water with a cool rinse. They are separated from white cottons, which are best washed in hot water. Delicate items are separated because they might be stretched out of shape or made rough by the agitation. They should be either washed by hand or washed on the delicate cycle. Heavily soiled clothing should be separated from clothing that is slightly soiled to prevent the other clothing from becoming dingy.
10. removes oil stains; less shrinkage; less agitation abrasion; safe on most colors, prints, and finishes

Teacher's Resources

Chapter 28 Test

1. F
2. D
3. C
4. B
5. A
6. H
7. E
8. G
9. F
10. F
11. F
12. T
13. T
14. T
15. T
16. T
17. F
18. F
19. A
20. D
21. C
22. D
23. Store each item as close as possible to the place where it will be used. Store frequently used items where they can be easily reached. Store items together if they are used together. Store similar items together. (Student response for an example of each storage principle.)
24. Stains should be worked on while the substance is wet or still on the surface of the fabric. Washing or ironing a stained garment often makes removing the stain more difficult, if not impossible. Hot water can cause certain stains to become permanent. You may also forget what caused the stain if you do not remove it promptly.
25. Detergents and soaps. Detergents work better in hard water. They contain chemicals that soften and tie up the water minerals to permit cleaning. When soaps are used in hard water, minerals combine with the soap and form a deposit or scum. This deposit gathers dirt from the water and sticks to the clothes.
26. Bleaches are used to clean, whiten or brighten fabrics, and remove soils and stains. Chlorine bleaches are the strongest bleaches, and they disinfect and deodorize. They should never be used on wool, silk, or crease-resistant or permanent press clothes. Frequent use of chlorine bleach will weaken fabrics. Oxygen bleaches are much safer for general bleaching purposes and stain removal. They can be used on most washable fabrics and colors. Oxygen bleaches do not act as a disinfectant.

Reproducible Master 28-1

Reading Care Labels

For Machine Washing	
When Label Reads:	**It Means:**
Washable Machine washable Machine wash	Wash, bleach, dry, and press by any customary method including commercial laundering.
Home launder only	Same as above but do not use commercial laundering.
No bleach	Do not use bleach.
No starch	Do not use starch.
Cold wash Cold setting Cold rinse	Use cold water from tap or cold washing machine setting.
Warm wash Warm setting Warm rinse	Use warm water 90°F to 110°F
Hot wash Hot setting	Use hot water (hot washing machine setting) 130°F or hotter.
No spin	Remove wash load before final machine spin cycle.
Delicate cycle Gentle cycle	Use appropriate machine setting; otherwise wash by hand.
Permanent-press cycle	Use appropriate machine setting; otherwise use medium wash, cold rinse, and short spin cycle.
Wash separately	Wash alone or with like colors.
For Hand Washing	
When Label Reads:	**It Means:**
Hand washable Hand wash	Launder only by hand in lukewarm (hand comfortable) water. May be bleached. May be dry cleaned.
Hand wash only	Same as above, but do not dry clean.
Hand wash separately	Hand wash alone or with like colors.
No bleach	Do not use bleach.
Damp wipe	Clean surface with damp cloth or sponge.

(Continued)

For Drying

When Label Reads:	It Means:
Tumble dry Machine dry	Dry in tumble dryer at specified setting—high, medium, low, or no heat.
Tumble dry Remove promptly	Same as above, but in absence of cool-down cycle remove at once when tumbling stops.
Drip dry Hang dry Line dry	Hang wet and allow to dry with hand shaping only.
No squeeze No wring No twist	Hand dry, drip dry, or dry flat only.
Dry flat	Lay garment on flat surface.
Block to dry	Maintain original size and shape while drying.

For Ironing or Pressing

When Label Reads:	It Means:
Cool iron	Set iron at lowest setting.
Warm iron	Set iron at medium setting.
Hot iron	Set iron at hot setting.
No iron No press	Do not iron or press with heat.
Steam iron Steam press	Iron or press with steam.
Iron damp	Dampen garment before ironing.

Miscellaneous

When Label Reads:	It Means:
Dry clean Dry clean only	Garment should be dry cleaned only
Professionally clean only Commercially clean only	Do not use self-service or home dry cleaning.
No dry clean	Use recommended care instructions. No dry cleaning materials to be used.

Reproducible Master 28-2

Stain Removal Guide

Adhesive tape: Remove as much gummy material as you can with a dull knife. Rub the remaining residue with a white rag dipped in a dry-cleaning solvent.

Blood: Soak in cold water. Rub heavy-duty detergent into the spot, then launder in cold water. Can also soak in product containing enzymes.

Candle wax: Solidify the wax by rubbing it with an ice cube, then carefully scrape off as much as possible with a dull knife. Then place the stain between several layers of white paper towel or white tissue and press with a warm iron. Repeat as necessary. If any stain remains, apply dry-cleaning fluid.

Chewing gum: Make the gum hard by putting ice on it. Remove as much as you can with a dull knife. Put dry-cleaning fluid on the remaining spots. Then launder in hot, soapy water.

Coffee and tea: Soak with laundry product containing enzymes or rub with liquid laundry detergent and water. Launder using chlorine bleach, if safe for fabric.

Cosmetics: Apply undiluted, heavy-duty liquid detergent to stain. Work with your fingers to form suds. Rinse well. Repeat if necessary. If the garment is not washable, use a spot remover. Rub the edges of the stain lightly with a cloth to prevent a circle from forming.

Deodorants: Rub liquid detergent on stain. Wash in the hottest water that is safe for the fabric.

Eggs: Scrape off the dried egg and soak the stain in cold water. Pretreat with a prewash stain remover.

Fruit juices and soft drinks: Pretreat by soaking in warm water using a detergent containing enzymes. If stain remains, use bleach, if safe for fabric. If the garment cannot be bleached, apply white vinegar.

Grass: Pretreat by soaking in warm water using a detergent containing enzymes. If stain persists, launder using a safe bleach.

Grease and oil: Dampen area and rub heavy-duty detergent into stain. Launder in hot water using bleach if safe for fabric and plenty of detergent. If stain persists, sponge with a cleaning fluid.

Ink (ballpoint): Sponge stain with rubbing alcohol or spray with hair spray until wet looking. Can also use a prewash stain remover. Rub detergent into stained area and launder.

Mayonnaise and salad dressing: Rub detergent into dampened stain. Rinse and let dry. If greasy stain remains, sponge with cleaning fluid.

Mildew: Rub detergent into dampened stain. Launder in hot water using chlorine bleach (if safe for fabric), or oxygen bleach.

Milk and ice cream: Soak in cold water. Pretreat with a prewash stain remover and rinse. If stain persists, sponge it with a cleaning fluid.

Mustard: Pretreat using a liquid detergent with enzymes, or a spray-type stain remover. Launder in hottest water suitable for fabric.

Perspiration: Rub detergent into dampened stain, or pretreat with stain remover. If the stain has discolored the fabric, the discoloration can sometimes be removed by sponging fresh stains with ammonia and old stains with white vinegar.

Caring for Clothing

Name _____

Date _____ Period _____ Score _____

Chapter 28 Test

Matching: Match the following terms and identifying phrases.

_____ 1. A safer product that can be used on most wash-able fabrics to clean, whiten, or brighten.

_____ 2. Substances that make fabrics soft and reduce static electricity and wrinkling.

_____ 3. Products that destroy germs.

_____ 4. Substances used for cleaning that are made with petroleum, natural fats, and oils; they contain chemicals that soften and tie up the water to permit cleaning.

_____ 5. A strong product that is used to clean, whiten, or brighten fabrics, to remove soils and stains, and to deodorize and disinfect.

_____ 6. Substances used for cleaning made by combining lye with fats and oils; when used in hard water, they form a deposit or scum.

_____ 7. Used to hold the minerals in solution in the wash water before the soap is added.

_____ 8. Remove minerals in the wash water by forming a solid that settles out.

A. chlorine bleach

B. detergents

C. disinfectants

D. fabric softeners

E. nonprecipitating water softeners

F. oxygen bleach

G. precipitating water softeners

H. soaps

True/False: Circle *T* if the statement is true or *F* if the statement is false.

T   F   9. Most knit sweaters should be stored on hangers so they do not wrinkle.

T   F   10. Placing mothballs with your wool clothes will protect them from moisture.

T   F   11. Care labels are not legally required on most garments.

T   F   12. If a care label is marked "machine wash and dry," you can launder and dry the garment by any method at any temperature.

T   F   13. You can assume bleaching a garment is safe if the label doesn't warn against it.

T   F   14. If the label says "dry clean only," the garment should not be washed.

T   F   15. Fabric softeners should not be added to the wash cycle.

(Continued)

Name _____

T   F   16. If chlorine is not mentioned in the description of a bleach, it is probably an oxygen bleach.

T   F   17. If you use a presoak product, a soap or detergent is not necessary.

T   F   18. Permanent press and wash-and-wear garments should not be put in the clothes dryer.

Multiple Choice: Choose the best answer and write the corresponding letter in the blank.

_____ 19. Periodic care of clothing does NOT include _____.
A. watching for needed repairs
B. seasonal storage
C. cleaning closets
D. organizing drawers

_____ 20. Which of the following is NOT true about stain removal?
A. Stains should be removed as soon as possible.
B. Hot water causes some stains to become permanent.
C. Most stains will come out with either dry cleaning fluid or detergent.
D. Solvents are best for stain removal because they do not produce a ring when used.

_____ 21. An advantage of nonprecipitating water softeners over precipitating water softeners is they _____.
A. also serve as a fabric softener
B. are generally stronger than precipitating water softeners
C. are less likely to change dye colors
D. can be used without a detergent or soap

_____ 22. Which of the following statements about laundry procedures is true?
A. Medium hot water is recommended for fabrics that tend to bleed or shrink easily.
B. Heavily soiled items will get the cleanest washed in cold water.
C. Faster agitation keeps synthetic fabrics from wrinkling.
D. Sorting laundry avoids the problems of color transfer, shrinkage, graying, and lint collection.

Essay Questions: Provide the answers you feel best show your understanding of the subject matter.

23. List the four storage principles and give an example of each principle.

24. Why is it important to remove stains as soon as possible?

25. Name the two basic types of laundry cleaning products. Then tell which product works better in hard water and explain why.

26. Explain why bleaches are used and tell the difference between the two types of bleaches.

Part Ten
Managing Housing

Planning and Selecting Housing

Objectives

When students have completed this chapter, they will be able to

◆ describe ways housing can help satisfy human needs.

◆ explain factors that affect satisfaction with housing.

◆ identify the advantages and disadvantages of various housing alternatives.

◆ describe the legal aspects of renting an apartment or home.

◆ explain how a home purchase may be financed and the legal aspects of purchasing housing.

Bulletin Boards

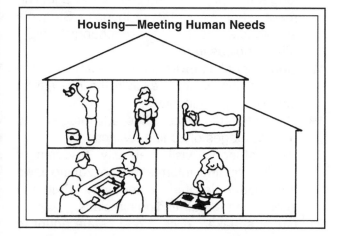

Housing—Meeting Human Needs

Title: *Housing—Meeting Human Needs*

Draw the outline of a house on the board and divide the house into sections to represent rooms. Place pictures in each section to represent family members having needs met. Needs might include self-expression (decorating), rest (sleeping), privacy (reading alone), love and acceptance (playing a game together), and nourishment (cooking). Have students discuss the needs represented by the pictures.

Title: *Renter's Checklist*

Use Chart 29-24 in the text as the basis for a renter's checklist to write on the board. With each written point, include illustrations, articles, or written descriptions pertaining to the point.

Teaching Materials

Text, pages 517-551
  To Review
  To Challenge Your Thinking
  To Do with the Class
  To Do with Your Community

Student Activity Guide
  A. *Homes Meeting Human Needs*
  B. *Factors Affecting Housing Satisfaction*
  C. *Rental Considerations*
  D. *Housing Alternatives*
  E. *Financing a Home Purchase*

Teacher's Resources
  Housing Meets Needs, reproducible master 29-1
  Figuring Monthly Housing Loan Payments, reproducible master 29-2
  Chapter 29 Test
  Home Financing Options, color transparency CT-29

Introductory Activities

1. *Housing Meets Needs,* reproducible master 29-1, TR. Have students read the descriptions of people and determine some of their needs. Students should then describe a house that would be designed to meet those needs. Have students share their descriptions in class.

2. Have students discuss how housing needs may change throughout the various stages of the family life cycle.

Instructional Concepts and Student Learning Experiences

The Home—Meeting Human Needs

3. Have each student write a definition of what home means to him or her. Then have students work in small groups to form a definition of home that can be used whether the home is an apartment, house, or condominium. Have groups share their definitions with the class.

4. *Homes Meeting Human Needs,* Activity A, SAG. Have students complete the chart by listing ways that the home can help satisfy human needs.

5. Have students research to find information on housing of the 1800s. Students should share their findings with the class and discuss how such housing may have met needs differently than current housing does.

6. Ask an architect to speak to the class about the concept of universal design.

7. Have students discuss ways that housing can help satisfy a person's need to stay healthy and fit.

8. Have students survey students outside the class to find out what home means to them. As a class, students should try to find references to various psychological needs in the definitions.

9. Have students discuss ways that the home can fulfill the need for self-expression.

10. Divide the class into small groups. Assign each group a list of values and have the groups develop descriptions, drawings, or models of homes that would reflect the assigned values.

11. Have students write a fictional story about a family going through the stages in the life cycle and resulting changes in their housing related to space.

12. Have students develop plans for using one room in a home for different functions.

13. Guest speaker. Invite an architect or interior designer to demonstrate how housing units can be designed in different ways to meet various space needs.

14. Have students find illustrations of well-planned, orderly storage and share them with the class.

15. Have students develop a list of items within a typical home that need to be stored. Students should determine how often each item is needed. Then students should develop a plan for storing items so items needed more often can be easily reached. Students should make drawings or models of their storage plans.

Factors Affecting Satisfaction with Housing

16. *Factors Affecting Housing Satisfaction,* Activity B, SAG. Have students interview a family about their satisfaction with their housing and use the information gained to answer the given questions.

17. Guest speaker. Invite a representative of the city council or planning board to discuss any long range plans for the community affecting roads, shopping areas, or industry. Students should discuss how these changes might affect choices in housing.

18. Guest speaker. Invite a representative of the local zoning office to explain the process in establishing zoning laws.

19. Have students discuss the advantages and disadvantages of zoning restrictions.

20. Have students visit their city government building to find information on zoning laws and codes in their community. Students should share their findings in class.

21. Guest speaker. Invite a real estate agent to discuss the importance of the neighborhood in making housing selections.

22. On small sheets of paper, have each student write one positive and one negative influence in his or her neighborhood. Mix the strips together and have students discuss randomly chosen influences and their effects on housing satisfaction.

Housing Alternatives

23. Have students interview people in various types of housing. Students should ask why they chose their housing. Students should share their findings in class and compare the various reasons given.
24. *Rental Considerations,* Activity C, SAG. Have students discuss leases with three different people who have rented housing. Students should use information gained to complete the given chart on rental considerations.
25. Have students diagram different decisions related to the decision to buy housing. Students should discuss their diagrams in class.
26. Have students interview people who have recently bought or sold homes through real estate agents to find out the role of the real estate agent in buying or selling a home. Students should write a short report on their findings.
27. Have students debate the advantages and disadvantages of buying a manufactured home.
28. Have students collect pictures and descriptions of a variety of single-family homes. Students should list advantages and disadvantages of buying each home.
29. Have students visit a condominium or cooperative community to find information on the rights and responsibilities of people in the community. Students should share their findings in class.
30. *Housing Alternatives,* Activity D, SAG. Students are asked to name advantages and disadvantages of the types of housing listed.
31. Panel discussion. Invite a real estate agent, banker, city official, and other concerned people to discuss the community responsibilities involved in home ownership.
32. Guest speaker. Invite a representative of the home building industry to discuss construction features in housing related to safety, durability, and cost of upkeep.

33. *Home Financing Options,* color transparency CT-29, TR. Use this transparency to illustrate the various financing options available to consumers. Explain each type of financing and under what conditions a consumer would consider applying for each type to purchase housing.
34. *Figuring Monthly Housing Loan Payments,* transparency master 29-2, TR. Have students work together to determine monthly payments on mortgages of various amounts and at various interest rates.
35. *Financing a Home Purchase,* Activity E, SAG. Have the students compare the variety of options for financing a home.
36. Guest speaker. Invite a lawyer to class to discuss the legal aspects of buying and selling a home.

Answer Key

Text

To Review
1. (Student response.)
2. true
3. social or group activities, private or personal activities, work activities (Student response for three specific space needs in each category.)
4. (Student response.)
5. true
6. (Student response. Explain three.)
7. B
8. D
9. The binder covers a detailed description of the property, total purchase price, amount of the down payment, and date for closing the sale and delivering the deed to the new owner.
10. Formal transfer of property.

Teacher's Resources

Figuring Monthly Housing Loan Payments, reproducible master
See illustration below. *Note: Mortgage rates and purchased prices may vary according to location and current economic conditions. This activity is designed to show how monthly housing loan payments are calculated. In some instances, property tax and insurance are included in the monthly payment.

Purchase Price*	% Down Payment	Amount of Down Payment	Amount of Loan	Interest Rate*	Years	Monthly Payment
36,000	20%	7,200	28,800	9%	25	241.63
40,000	10%	4,000	36,000	8 ½%	30	276.84
40,000	15%	6,000	34,000	8%	30	249.56
45,000	20%	9,000	36,000	9%	20	324.00
52,000	10%	5,200	46,800	9 ½%	20	436.18
60,000	5%	3,000	57,000	11%	25	558.60
75,000	10%	7,500	67,500	8%	40	469.13
100,000	10%	10,000	90,000	12%	30	926.10

Chapter 29 Test

1. G
2. A
3. D
4. F
5. K
6. I
7. H
8. E
9. C
10. J
11. B
12. L
13. T
14. F
15. T
16. F
17. F
18. F
19. T
20. T
21. F
22. F
23. T
24. F
25. A
26. B
27. D
28. C
29. A
30. B

31. The "live" storage area would contain items you might use every day and would be easily accessible. "Dead" storage would contain items used rarely, if ever. These items could be stored in an attic or a less accessible area of a hall closet.
32. (Student response. Name four.)
33. (Student response. Name three advantages and three disadvantages.)
34. (Student response. Name two advantages and two disadvantages.)
35. In a condominium, there is individual ownership of the units with joint interest in the common property. Condominium owners are financially responsible for both their own units and the common areas. In a cooperative, you are part of a group that owns the building or complex. Each person owns stock in the complex. There is only one mortgage and tax bill that is paid by the corporation. Monthly payments from cooperative members are used to meet these expenses. Cooperative members often have more restrictions than condominium owners.

Reproducible Master 29-1

Housing Meets Needs

Name _____ **Date** _____ **Period** _____

Housing satisfies many needs for families and individuals. If people are aware of these needs, they can choose housing designed to help satisfy their needs in the best ways possible. Below are three descriptions of individuals or families. Read the descriptions and determine any housing needs they may have. Then describe a home that would help satisfy those needs. Discuss your descriptions in class.

1. Yolanda is a single, 23-year-old sales representative for an insurance company. Yolanda enjoys living on her own, but she does not spend much time at home during the week. When she does have free weekend time, Yolanda likes to spend as much time as possible relaxing, reading, or exercising. Although she likes her home to be orderly, she does not have much time for cleaning. Yolanda is saving money for college, so she wants to keep her housing costs as low as possible for now.

   Housing needs:_____

   _____

   _____

   The following housing would satisfy those needs: _____

   _____

   _____

   _____

2. The Benson's have just had a baby girl. They have been living in a two-bedroom apartment with their three-year-old son, Mike, but now they need more space. The Bensons feel strongly about having plenty of space for the children to play, indoors and out. Mrs. Benson has been wanting to quit her job at a local restaurant to start a catering business. Mr. Benson is an accountant who often needs to do work at home.

   Housing needs:_____

   _____

   _____

   The following housing would satisfy those needs: _____

   _____

   _____

   _____

3. Tyrone Jackson is retiring in four months. He and his wife Roberta are still living in the home where they raised their four children. The Jacksons still enjoy gardening, but they no longer want to spend the time and energy needed to care for their large yard. Besides, they would like to spend more time traveling with friends.

   Housing needs:_____

   _____

   _____

   The following housing would satisfy those needs: _____

   _____

   _____

   _____

Reproducible Master 29-2

Figuring Monthly Housing Loan Payments

Name _____ Date _____ Period _____

Mortgage Rates*

(Monthly principal and interest payments per $1,000 principal)

Years	8%	8½%	9%	9½%	10%	11%	12%
15	9.56	9.85	10.14	10.44	10.75	11.37	12.00
20	8.36	8.68	9.00	9.32	9.65	10.32	11.01
25	7.72	8.05	8.39	8.74	9.09	9.80	10.53
30	7.34	7.69	8.05	8.41	8.78	9.52	10.29
35	7.10	7.47	7.84	8.22	8.60	9.37	10.16
40	6.95	7.33	7.71	8.10	8.49	9.28	10.09

Complete the chart below by using the table above and the following formulas:

Purchase Price x (% Down Payment ÷ 100) = Amount of Down Payment
Purchase Price - Amount of Down Payment = Amount of Loan
Chart Figure Based on Interest Rate and Years x (Amount of Loan ÷ 1,000) = Monthly Payment

Purchase Price*	% Down Payment	Amount of Down Payment	Amount of Loan	Interest Rate*	Years	Monthly Payment
36,000	20%	7,200	28,800	9%	25	241.63
40,000	10%			8 ½%	30	
40,000	15%			8%	30	
45,000	20%			9%	20	
52,000	10%			9 ½%	20	
60,000	5%			11%	25	
75,000	10%			8%	40	
100,000	10%			12%	30	

*Note: Mortgage rates and purchased prices may vary according to location and current economic conditions. This activity is designed to show how monthly housing loan payments are calculated. In some instances, property tax and insurance are included in the monthly payment.

Planning and Selecting Housing

Name _____

Date _____ **Period** _____ **Score** _____

Chapter 29 Test

Matching: Match the following terms and identifying phrases.

_____ 1. Most common type of loan used in home financing.

_____ 2. An apartment you buy.

_____ 3. A loan insured by the Federal Housing Administration and provided by an approved lending institution.

_____ 4. An agreement between a renter and a landlord.

_____ 5. The circulation from one room to another and from place to place within a room; the way people move around in a home.

_____ 6. A refundable payment often equal to one or two months rent that is used to cover damages in an apartment or substitute for rent should a renter fail to pay rent or leave before the end of a lease.

_____ 7. A legal document that acts as security for the lender until the debt is repaid.

_____ 8. Seizing property and selling it to pay off the debt when a borrower fails to make the agreed monthly payments.

_____ 9. The report that involves the review of legal documents and public records of a property.

_____ 10. A one-family home detached from any other building, a townhouse, or a manufactured home.

_____ 11. When a group of people buy a building or complex and each owns stock in the corporation that owns the complex.

_____ 12. A loan guaranteed by the Veterans Administration which is granted to a qualified veteran of the U.S. Armed Forces and is obtained through a regular lending agency.

A. condominium

B. cooperative

C. abstract of title

D. FHA-insured loan

E. foreclosure

F. lease

G. conventional loan

H. mortgage

I. security deposit

J. single-family dwelling

K. traffic pattern

L. VA-guaranteed loan

(Continued)

Name _____

True/False: Circle *T* if the statement is true or *F* if the statement is false.

T   F   13. A person's home environment exerts a powerful influence on him or her.

T   F   14. Very low humidity is more harmful to home furnishings than to people.

T   F   15. Storage needs in a room will depend upon what activities take place in that room.

T   F   16. Most families have very similar storage needs.

T   F   17. Zoning regulations are always helpful to taxpayers.

T   F   18. A densely populated area offers more opportunities for privacy.

T   F   19. The number of people living in rental apartments is increasing rapidly.

T   F   20. If a lease contains objectionable clauses, you may want to refuse the lease or try to negotiate with the owner.

T   F   21. All security deposits are completely refunded after the renter moves out of the apartment.

T   F   22. FHA loans are provided by the Federal Housing Administration and insured by an independent lending institution.

T   F   23. The length of a conventional loan is usually between 15 and 30 years.

T   F   24. If you are buying a house without the services of a real estate agent, you will not need a lawyer at the closing.

Multiple Choice: Choose the best answer and write the corresponding letter in the blank.

_____ 25. A traffic pattern _____.
   A. should move through a room without interfering with conversation
   B. cannot be improved in an existing home without making structural changes
   C. is most convenient if it allows you to go from the entryway through the living room to the kitchen
   D. is most convenient if traffic lanes are narrow

_____ 26. Open storage units _____.
   A. may cause you to forget about what items you have stored
   B. are a good choice for a young child's bedroom
   C. offer protection for china dishes
   D. are a good place to store valuable items

_____ 27. Which of the following should influence where an item is stored?
   A. The size of the item.
   B. The purpose of the item.
   C. How often the item is used.
   D. All of the above.

_____ 28. A good lease may include all but which of the following items?
   A. Length of time the property is being rented.
   B. Renter and landlord names.
   C. Negotiable time for rental payment.
   D. A sublet cause.

(Continued)

Name _____

_____ 29. An advantage of renting is that _____.
  A. beyond the regular monthly payment, there are no further charges for upkeep and repairs
  B. renters receive a tax break
  C. you can make inside or outside changes to suit your personal decorating preferences
  D. rent tends to be very reasonable during housing shortages

_____ 30. Which of the following is true about buying a single-family dwelling?
  A. When you own a home, you do not need property insurance.
  B. Home ownership is normally a safe investment.
  C. Owning a home is a disadvantage when figuring income tax.
  D. All of the above are true.

Essay Questions: Provide the answers you feel best show your understanding of the subject matter.

31. What types of items should be stored in a "live" storage space, and what types of items should be stored in a "dead" storage space?

32. Describe four ways the community and neighborhood in which you live may influence your satisfaction with your housing.

33. Give three advantages and three disadvantages of renting housing.

34. Give two advantages and two disadvantages of owning a home.

35. Explain the differences between a condominium and a cooperative.

Furnishing and Caring for the Home

Objectives

When students have completed this chapter, they will be able to
- relate the use of the elements and principles of design to an attractive home.
- explain characteristics that may influence selection of various home furnishings.
- list tips on how to maintain a clean home.
- describe ways maintenance helps avoid housing problems and repair.

Bulletin Boards

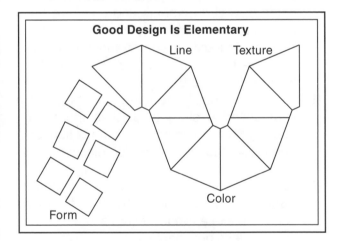

Good Design Is Elementary

Line Texture

Color

Form

Title: *Good Design Is Elementary*

Arrange examples of various forms, lines, colors, and textures as shown. For form, use catalog or magazine pictures of furniture. For line, use wallpaper samples of different patterns. For color, use large paint samples. For texture, use fabric samples. Label the elements appropriately.

Title: *Know Your Home Care Resources*

Draw the outline of a house on the board. Inside, place copies of brochures, pamphlets, and book covers related to home care and maintenance.

Teaching Materials

Text, pages 552-581
 To Review
 To Challenge Your Thinking
 To Do with the Class
 To Do with Your Community
Student Activity Guide
 A. *Design in Home Furnishings*
 B. *Color Schemes*
 C. *Selecting Home Furnishings*
 D. *Preventive Maintenance*
Teacher's Resources
 Using Rhythm in Design, reproducible master 30-1
 Routine Home Care, reproducible master 30-2
 Chapter 30 Test
 Elements and Principles of Design, color transparency CT-30

Introductory Activities

1. Have students discuss how values might influence a person's taste in home furnishings and design.
2. Have students survey several adults to find out what tasks are involved in routine maintenance of a house or an apartment. Students should compile a master list of maintenance tasks based on the results of the survey.

Instructional Concepts and Student Learning Experiences

Design in Home Furnishings

3. *Elements and Principles of Design,* color transparency CT-30, TR. Use this master as a basis of discussion about the elements and principles of design. Have students look at the illustration and comment about how the

elements and principles are used in designing an attractive home. Ask students to provide other examples of home furnishings that illustrate good use of the elements and principles of design.

4. Have students find a pair of pictures of rooms that show contrasting use of lines. For instance, one room may use more vertical lines and the other may use more horizontal lines. Students should mount the pictures side by side on a piece of paper. Under the pictures, have them write descriptions of the feelings created by the use of line in the rooms.

5. Guest speaker. Invite an interior designer or decorator to demonstrate how the elements and principles of design can be used to create a pleasing home environment.

6. Have students discuss the meaning of the statement "Form follows function." Students should discuss the results of creating home furnishings that have interesting but nonfunctional forms.

7. *Color Schemes,* Activity B, SAG. Have students select and mount pictures to illustrate monochromatic, accented neutral, analogous, and complementary color schemes. Students should define each color scheme and list the colors used in each room.

8. Have students create drawings or models to illustrate how the same room design can create different feelings just by changing the room's color scheme.

9. Have students discuss ways to use color to emphasize or de-emphasize certain features of a room.

10. Have students research to find information on studies related to color and emotions. Students should share their findings in class and discuss how they can be applied to the decoration of rooms.

11. Create a display of pictures illustrating different types of textures. In each picture, one main type of texture should dominate. Students should view the pictures and discuss the feelings created by the different textures.

12. Have students develop and share demonstrations of how texture affects the color of objects.

13. Supply the class with several home accessories. Have students try different arrangements to illustrate formal and informal balance with the accessories.

14. Have students discuss situations in which choosing furniture of the wrong proportions can make a room seem cramped, overpowering, or empty.

15. *Using Rhythm in Design,* reproducible master 30-1, TR. Have students work in groups to select and mount pictures that illustrate each type of rhythm. Students should then write definitions of each type of rhythm in their own words.

16. Have students discuss their reactions to the following statement: "Emphasis is more effective in a room with a simple design."

17. *Design in Home Furnishings,* Activity A, SAG. Have students select and mount a picture of a room that they find attractive. Then have them analyze the use of design in the room.

The Selection of Home Furnishings

18. Have students visit a local paint and wallpaper shop. Students should choose two similar types of wall treatments and compare them in terms of appearance, quality, and price. Students should determine which of the two products they would choose and why. Share findings in class.

19. Guest speaker. Invite a representative of a floor covering store to discuss the advantages and disadvantages of various floor coverings. The guest should also discuss points to consider when buying a floor covering.

20. Have students make a drawing or model to illustrate how a window treatment can be used to make a window seem smaller, larger, more or less noticeable, etc.

21. Have students brainstorm a list of needs that furniture can satisfy. Students should focus on needs other than the obvious intended purpose of a piece of furniture such as providing a place to sit.

22. Guest speaker. Invite a representative of a drapery store or department to display and describe various types of window treatments. The guest should also discuss points to consider when buying window treatments.

23. Have students work in groups to develop and conduct an experiment that tests the durability of a furniture feature. Features to test might include upholstery fabrics, wood joints, or wood finishes. Have students list points to consider when selecting furniture. The lists should include signs of quality construction in furniture.

24. Field trip. Make arrangements for the class to visit a furniture store. Have a representative of the store describe the various styles of furniture in the store. The representative should also point out features to look for when selecting furniture.
25. Have students browse through lighting catalogs to discover the variety and price range of light fixtures. Have each student choose three fixtures that they like and describe how they would use them in a home.
26. Have students create a lighting plan for a room. Students should explain their choices.
27. *Selecting Home Furnishings,* Activity C, SAG. Have students choose one of the furnishings listed and write a research report on factors to consider when selecting the furnishing.

Maintaining a Clean Home

28. Have students demonstrate various cleaning techniques.
29. Have students prepare a list of cleaning tips that can be used in maintaining a clean home.

Preventive Maintenance

30. Have students discuss the following statement: "Care and maintenance of home furnishings and equipment is a resource as valuable as money."
31. *Preventive Maintenance,* Activity D, SAG. Have students complete the chart by listing six routine home tasks that are steps in preventive maintenance. Students should describe the damage that might occur if these tasks are not done.
32. Have students analyze a use-and-care manual for an appliance and report to the class on the types of information included in the manual.
33. Have students work as a class to develop a chart of proper cleaning products and techniques for various household surfaces. Students should discuss how using proper cleaning methods helps increase the life of a product.
34. *Routine Home Care,* reproducible master 30-2, TR. Have students discuss each group of tasks in terms of their effects on the items being cared for. In groups, have students decide how often each cleaning task should

be performed, such as weekly, monthly, semiannually, or annually.
35. Have students list cleaning tasks that are performed rather regularly in the home and develop a schedule for accomplishing those tasks in the most efficient ways.
36. Have students research to find preventive maintenance techniques for one appliance. Students should give an oral report/demonstration to the class on their findings.
37. Have students develop a list of resources including agencies, books, and pamphlets that would be helpful resources for home maintenance. Distribute all or part of the list to the community through a school district mailing or newsletter.
38. Have students make posters focusing on signs of impending maintenance problems in the home.

Answer Key

Text

To Review
1. balance, proportion, rhythm, emphasis
2. (List two for each type:)
   A. wide, restful, steady, masculine
   B. high, strong, formal
   C. active, stimulating
   D. graceful, feminine
3. monochromatic, complementary
4. With formal balance, identical objects are placed in a mirror image on either side of the center. Informal balance does not have an obvious center. It is more casual.

5. (Describe two:) Rugs can be shifted to change traffic wear. They can be sent to the cleaners to be cleaned.

6. traditional: C, F
   country: D
   contemporary: B, E
   eclectic: A

7. pressed, veneered

8. Incandescent lights have a tungsten filament that is heated by electricity to the temperature at which it glows. These lights are not very efficient in terms of energy consumption because more energy is converted into heat than light. However, the incandescent light gives off a pleasant warm golden glow.

   Fluorescent lights produce light by releasing electricity through a mercury vapor sealed within a tube rather than by heat. Fluorescent lights seem to distort colors, but they are the cheapest to use. The life of a fluorescent light is shortened each time you turn it on.

9. false

10. (List three. Student response.)

Teacher's Resources

Chapter 30 Test

1. L
2. D
3. C
4. A
5. G
6. B
7. E
8. K
9. H
10. J
11. I
12. F
13. F
14. T
15. F
16. F
17. T
18. T
19. F
20. T
21. T
22. T
23. F
24. F
25. T
26. T
27. D
28. A
29. B
30. C
31. D
32. A
33. C
34. B
35. A
36. B

37. (Define three:) Monochromatic color scheme: uses various values and intensities of one color. Accented neutral scheme: uses a neutral, such as brown, gray, or white, as the main color in a variety of values and intensities, and the neutral is supplemented with an accent color. Analogous color scheme: uses colors that are next to each other on the color wheel. Complementary color scheme: uses two colors that are opposite each other on the color wheel. (Student response for an example of each color scheme.)

38. Warm colors give a feeling of warmth and activity and are often used in family rooms and kitchens. Warm colors advance and make a room or a wall seem smaller than it is. Warm colors can make a cool room with a northern or eastern exposure seem warmer. Reds, yellows, oranges, and browns have this warming effect. Cool colors are considered restful and relaxing and may be more appropriate for a living room or a bedroom. Because cool colors recede, they can make a room look larger. Pale, dull colors give an illusion of space. In warm rooms with a southern or western exposure, colors such as blue, green, and lavender can create a cooler, more soothing atmosphere.

39. Preventive maintenance is routine maintenance care. Preventive maintenance allows you to recognize when repairs need to be made. It can save you time and money, and it can also help you create a safer living environment.

40. (Student response. List three preventive maintenance steps outside the home and three inside the home.)

Reproducible Master 30-1

Using Rhythm in Design

Names _____ **Date** _____ **Period** _____

Use pictures from magazines to illustrate each of the types of rhythm listed below. Then use your own words to describe each type of rhythm.

Repetition: _____

_____

_____

_____

Gradation: _____

_____

_____

_____

Transition: _____

_____

_____

(Continued)

Name _____

Opposition: _____
_____
_____
_____

Radiation: _____
_____
_____
_____

Reproducible Master 30-2

Routine Home Care

Appliances:

Remove contents— clean
  refrigerator

Defrost/clean freezer

Dust/vacuum refrigerator
  coils

Clean stove top

Clean oven

Clean microwave

Vacuum dryer filter
  and vent

Clean ventilating fans

Vacuum furnace filters

Walls:

Dust ceilings

Dust walls

Wash walls

Dust furnace vents

Remove grates—vacuum
  vents

Wipe switches and outlets

Dust doors and woodwork

Wash doors and woodwork

Windows:

Dust blinds

Wash blinds

Vacuum drapes/curtains

Wash windows and tracks

Wash screens

Floors:

Dust floors

Sweep floors

Wash floors

Wax/treat floors

Dust baseboards

Wash baseboards

Vacuum carpet

Vacuum beneath furniture

Clean carpet

Ceilings:

Wash ceilings

Lights and Accessories:

Dust light fixtures

Wash light diffusion bowls

Vacuum lampshades

Dust picture frames

Clean pictures

Dust accessories

Wash accessories

Wash kitchen canisters

Dust mirrors

Clean mirror glass

Fixtures:

Scour sink

Polish fixtures

Disinfect toilet

Wipe up bathtub/shower

Scour shower/bathtub

Furniture:

Dust furniture

Polish/oil/wax furniture

Vacuum upholstered
  furniture

Clean upholstered furniture

Vacuum mattresses

Turn mattresses

Wash slipcovers

Cupboards, Drawers, Closets, Cabinets, Shelves:

Remove contents and
  wash

Dust and wash shelves

Replace shelf liner

Wash drawers and drawer
  dividers

Sort through and organize

Miscellaneous:

Wash trash baskets

Dust books

Launder blankets

Launder mattress pads

Launder throw rugs

Launder shower curtains

Furnishing and Caring for the Home

Name _____

Date _____ **Period** _____ **Score** _____

Chapter 30 Test

Matching: Match the following terms and identifying phrases.

_____ 1. The movement of the eye across a design.

_____ 2. Lighting that is directed on a particular area and is used for activities such as reading, washing dishes, or playing the piano.

_____ 3. Unupholstered furniture made of wood, such as cabinets, chests, desks, and dressers.

_____ 4. Decorative lighting.

_____ 5. Exists when identical objects are arranged in a mirror image on either side of the center.

_____ 6. A sense of equilibrium.

_____ 7. The focal point of a room—the center of interest.

_____ 8. The relationship of one part to another part or one part to the whole.

_____ 9. Lighting that maintains a low level of light throughout a room to assure safety and ease in moving about.

_____ 10. Exists when varied weights are placed at different distances from the balancing point, creating balance; there is no obvious center point.

_____ 11. Lighting elements that have a tungsten filament that is heated by electricity to the temperature at which it glows.

_____ 12. Elements that produce light by releasing electricity through a mercury vapor sealed within a tube rather than by heat.

A. accent lighting

B. balance

C. case goods

D. directed lighting

E. emphasis

F. fluorescent lighting

G. formal balance

H. general lighting

I. incandescent lights

J. informal balance

K. proportion

L. rhythm

True/False: Circle *T* if the statement is true or *F* if the statement is false.

T   F   13. Good taste is acquired by simply following certain rules in decorating.

T   F   14. Horizontal lines tend to suggest feelings of rest, steadiness, and masculinity.

T   F   15. Because the colors of a complementary color scheme have one common color, they blend very well and have a harmonious effect.

T   F   16. Transition is a type of rhythm created when a variety of sizes of objects are used.

(Continued)

Name _____

T   F   17. The point of emphasis in a living room might be a fireplace.

T   F   18. If walls are of textured plaster, paint is the best finish.

T   F   19. Double-hung windows are hinged and open like a door in the center or at the sides.

T   F   20. The picture window is usually a large window that is permanently closed.

T   F   21. Austrian shades are very formal and feature graceful scallops of fabric between the vertical cords.

T   F   22. Portable lamps are most often used for direct lighting.

T   F   23. Plants, paintings, photographs, and collections are considered functional accessories.

T   F   24. Although preventive maintenance is important to the home owner, it is not important to the renter.

T   F   25. The best way to find a good service repair person is to talk with other people.

T   F   26. A large portion of the money you spend on repairs goes for labor.

Multiple Choice: Choose the best answer and write the corresponding letter in the blank.

_____ 27. An example of an accented neutral color scheme is _____.
   A. blue with red accents
   B. black with white accents
   C. blue with pink accents
   D. brown with peach accents

_____ 28. An example of a complementary color scheme is _____.
   A. blue and orange
   B. blue and red
   C. orange and green
   D. green and yellow

_____ 29. Rough textures tend to _____.
   A. advance
   B. absorb light
   C. make a color appear more intense
   D. reflect light

_____ 30. Rhythm through _____ occurs when lines or patterns extend outward from a central axis.
   A. gradation
   B. opposition
   C. radiation
   D. repetition

_____ 31. The features of a room that create a background for other furnishings are _____.
   A. walls
   B. ceilings
   C. floorings or floor coverings
   D. All of the above.

(Continued)

Name _____

_____ 32. Which of the following statements about flooring is NOT true?
   A. Wood is considered a resilient flooring.
   B. Vinyl flooring vs. tile floorings are popular because of their ease of installation.
   C. Carpeting tends to make a room look more spacious.
   D. Rugs can be used both on hard surface floorings and on top of carpeting.

_____ 33. The decorating look that uses a combination of furniture styles is _____.
   A. contemporary
   B. country
   C. eclectic
   D. traditional

_____ 34. When a piece of furniture is labeled veneered wood, it means the piece is made _____.
   A. of solid wood
   B. by gluing several layers of wood on top of each other with the grain at right angles
   C. of wood scraps, chips, and shavings
   D. of plastic with a woodlike grain

_____ 35. Preventive maintenance does NOT _____.
   A. require many technical skills
   B. require some knowledge about equipment and systems in the home
   C. save time and money
   D. involve checking or cleaning items that are presently working

_____ 36. Which of the following is true about having service people make repairs?
   A. You will pay labor only for the time the service person spends in your home.
   B. You should have the model number and serial number of the equipment to be repaired when you call for repair work.
   C. Most charges for repairs are for equipment parts.
   D. All of the above.

Essay Questions: Provide the answers you feel best show your understanding of the subject matter.

37. Define three of the four color schemes discussed in the text and give an example of each color scheme.

38. Describe the effects you can create by using warm colors in a room and the effects you can create by using cool colors in a room.

39. Explain what is meant by preventive maintenance. Why is this task so important?

40. List three preventive maintenance steps outside the home and three preventive maintenance steps inside the home.

Career Planning

Objectives

When students have completed this chapter, they will be able to

◆ explain the importance of career planning.

◆ recognize how attitudes about careers develop.

◆ explain how interests, abilities, and personality may relate to career choices.

◆ describe a variety of sources of career information.

◆ explain how management relates to careers.

Bulletin Boards

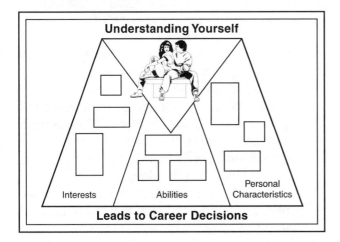

Title: *Understanding Yourself Leads to Career Decisions*

Cut a triangle of construction paper and draw pictures of a male and female teenager on it, or cut the pictures from magazines and attach them to the triangle. Place the triangle on the bulletin board as shown. Using three different colors of construction paper, cut sections to be labeled *interests*, *abilities*, and *personal characteristics*

and place them on the bulletin board beneath the triangle as shown. Have students bring in pictures of themselves involved in various activities that illustrate their interests, abilities, and personal characteristics. Ask each student to place his or her pictures on the appropriate sections of the bulletin board. Examples of interest pictures include young people involved in activities, hobbies, and recreation. Examples of abilities pictures include someone using mental abilities by reading, typing, or working on a computer and someone using physical skills doing anything from playing a violin to pounding a nail. Examples of personality pictures include people in groups, people working alone, and pictures indicating values.

Title: *Changing Occupational Trends*

Develop a bulletin board that illustrates changing trends in occupations by posting magazine pictures or photographs. Some ideas for pictures to post include people working at home, careers in health care and working with the older adults, corporate child care centers, and men and women in nontraditional work roles, such as female executives, female truck drivers, male nurses, and male flight attendants.

Teaching Materials

Text, pages 583-603
   To Review
   To Challenge Your Thinking
   To Do with the Class
   To Do with Your Community
Student Activity Guide
   A. *Attitudes Toward Careers*
   B. *Knowing Yourself*

C. *Specific Knowledge About Careers*
D. *Jobs Involving Management*

Teacher's Resources

Making Use of Management Skills,
   reproducible master 31-1
Start Your Own Business—The
   Opportunities Are Limitless, reproducible
   master 31-2
Chapter 31 Test
Career Planning, color transparency CT-31

Introductory Activities

1. Ask each student to write his or her own definition of the words "job" and "career." Discuss definitions read by volunteers. Emphasize the fact that entering a career requires planning, but getting a job does not. Then explain that through study of this chapter, students will learn how to develop career plans of their own.
2. Have students make a list of their interests, abilities, and personal characteristics. Encourage them to add to their lists as they study the chapter and identify additional characteristics that should be added.

Instructional Concepts and Student Learning Experiences

Career Planning

3. *Career Planning,* color transparency CT-31, TR. Use this transparency to emphasize how a person's future success in a career depends on the "fit" of characteristics that come from past training or experiences. Ask students to share examples of each component listed on the puzzle pieces. Students might match possible careers that would complement various combinations of individual components.
4. *Attitudes Toward Careers,* Activity A, SAG. Ask students to recall experiences that have given them either positive or negative attitudes toward various types of careers. Then have them explain how these attitudes might influence their career planning. Ask volunteers to share their responses with the class.
5. Have students discuss how a family's lifestyle is affected by the careers of its members.

6. Have students discuss how the jobs they choose can contribute to their long-range career plans.
7. Panel discussion. Invite a panel of shift workers to discuss the pros and cons of not working during typical business hours.
8. Have each student interview someone who has been in a career for at least 10 years. Have students ask the interviewees to list all the jobs they have had and identify the ones they feel have most helped them reach their career goals. Have students report their findings in class.

A Self-Study in Relation to Career Plans

9. Have students take an interest inventory.
10. Have students brainstorm lists of careers in which each of the following abilities would be important: verbal, reading, math, reasoning, and finger dexterity.
11. Have each student write a one-page essay about one of his or her achievements and what it indicates about the student's abilities.
12. Panel discussion. Invite several people who fill the roles of both homemaker and wage earner to discuss the challenges and benefits of the dual role lifestyle.
13. Panel discussion. Invite a panel of shift workers to discuss the pros and cons of not working during typical business hours.
14. Have students role-play situations in which a personality conflict inhibits a worker's job success. Create some situations in which a worker's personality traits are found offensive by his or her fellow employees. Create other situations in which the philosophy of the work environment conflicts with the worker's values. Discuss the role-plays in class.
15. Have students brainstorm a list of the different reasons people value their jobs. Discuss the list.
16. Guest speaker. Invite a career counselor to speak to your class about the causes of career burnout, how it might be prevented, and how to cope with it. If possible, have the counselor bring along several individuals who have experienced this problem to participate in a panel discussion.
17. *Knowing Yourself,* Activity B, SAG. Have students conduct a self-study in relation to career plans.

Learning About Career Options

18. Have students visit the career information section of the school or public library and make a list of all the available resources.
19. Have each student select one of the career information resources found in the school or public library and outline the types of information it provides. Have students share their findings in class.
20. Have students write to the U.S. Department of Labor, trade associations, professional organizations, and labor unions to obtain information about careers that interest them. Gather all the information received by students in a career information resource file in your classroom.
21. Have each student select a career area of interest. Have students use specific questions to interview three people working in that area to learn details about their work. Then ask students to write a paper comparing the information from the three sources and summarizing what they have learned.
22. Guest speaker. Invite someone from your state apprenticeship and training bureau to speak to your class about apprenticeship training for various trades.
23. Have students look in the classified ads of a local newspaper to find listings of part-time jobs. Ask students to identify careers to which these positions relate.
24. Have students read articles from recent periodicals about popular work schedule options. Have them summarize what they have read in brief oral reports.
25. *Specific Knowledge About Careers,* Activity C, SAG. Have each student complete the worksheets based on his or her research of two careers of interest.

Management-Related Careers

26. Divide the class into small groups and assign each group a career. Have each group list 10 decisions someone working in that career might have to make. Then have each group use the steps of the decision-making process to make one of the decisions on their list.
27. *Making Use of Management Skills,* reproducible master 31-1, TR. Have students suggest how managers could use their skills to solve problems in given situations.

28. *Jobs Involving Management,* Activity D, SAG. From the chart on management in the text, have each student select two management careers of interest from each educational level. Then have students write a paragraph for each job they selected explaining how management is a part of it.
29. *Start Your Own Business—The Opportunities Are Limitless,* reproducible master 31-2, TR. Have students review given information about business opportunities. Then have each student make a chart including job descriptions and trait requirements for five businesses that he or she might like to start.
30. Have each student read an article from a current periodical about recent changes in existing occupations and/or occupational predictions for the future. Have students report their findings in class.

Answer Key

Text

To Review

1. A career is a succession of productive experiences throughout life that make your life more satisfying and help move you toward a career goal. A job is just one work experience that may involve not planning. A job may be good or bad depending on whether it helps move you toward your career goals.
2. Classifying your interests helps you see how they relate to various occupations and encourages you to learn more about those areas of work. Classifying your interests will encourage you to develop skills related to those interests.
3. abilities
4. (List four:) *Occupational Outlook Handbook, Occupational Outlook Quarterly,* school and public libraries, pamphlets from the United States Department of Labor, talking with people who work in an area that interests you, part-time or summer jobs, the Internet
5. planning, implementing, controlling, evaluating
6. Managers are responsible for other people. Being able to communicate ideas to those people, listen attentively, interpret what they say, and respond to them makes it more likely that managers' plans will be carried through.

7. The manager who is familiar with the work being done is more likely to be accepted by the workers. The manager and the workers are working together toward goals everyone understands.

8. A. false
   B. true

9. (List six:) technology, the aging population, dual-career families, more leisure, travel, home maintenance, home security, computers, flex-time, mobility, entrepreneurship

10. A compressed workweek is a system in which an employee can divide the hours of a standard workweek into three or four days instead of five.

Teacher's Resources

Chapter 31 Test

1. E
2. D
3. F
4. C
5. B
6. A
7. T
8. F

9. F
10. T
11. T
12. F
13. T
14. F
15. F
16. T
17. T
18. T
19. A
20. B
21. D
22. A
23. (Student response.)
24. (Student response.)
25. (List three:) public libraries (Students may list specific publications), Department of Labor, people working in various careers, summer or part-time job experiences, the Internet (Student response for descriptions.)
26. (Explain three:) problem solving and decision-making skills, the management process, organizational skills, outlook skills, communication skills (Student response for explanations of skills.)

Reproducible Master 31-1

Making Use of Management Skills

Name _____ **Date** _____ **Period** _____

Read each of the following situations and consider how the managers involved could use their skills to solve the problems described. Write your suggestions in the space provided.

1. Jerry is the manager of a 24-hour convenience store. One night last week, no one showed up to work the late shift. The next morning, at a time when the store is usually not busy, three employees reported to work. How could Jerry use his management skills to prevent this problem from occurring again in the future?

   Organizational skills: _____

   _____

   Communication skills: _____

   _____

   Attitude skills: _____

   _____

2. Nelda is the manager of a bakery that is known for having excellent muffins. Each batch of muffins has always been prepared individually from scratch. Recently, one of Nelda's employees suggested that they could make up large containers of a baking mix. The mix would contain the flour, salt, and baking powder that are used in all the bakery's muffins. How could Nelda use her management skills to respond to this suggestion?

   Organizational skills: _____

   _____

   Communication skills: _____

   _____

   Attitude skills: _____

   _____

3. Anthony is the manager of a pizzeria that is known for offering a large variety of toppings. Last week, Anthony's vegetable supplier told him that a shipping strike was causing a shortage of tomatoes, mushrooms, green peppers, and onions. Until the strike ends, the prices of these vegetables will be very high. These are also some of the most popular toppings on the menu. How could Anthony use his management skills to handle this problem?

   Organizational skills: _____

   _____

   Communication skills: _____

   _____

   Attitude skills: _____

   _____

Reproducible Master 31-2

Start Your Own Business—
The Opportunities Are Limitless

Review the following information about business opportunities. Then use a separate sheet of paper to make your own chart including job descriptions and trait requirements for five businesses that you might like to start.

Business to Start	Job Description	Traits Required
Babysitting	Care for young children and do light housekeeping.	Outgoing personality and ability to get along well with children.
Bicycle Repair	Service working bicycles to help keep them in good working order. Rebuild and recondition broken bicycles.	Mechanical aptitude.
Children's Party Service	Plan and conduct parties for children.	Outgoing, enjoy children.
Computer Service	Maintain mailing lists, print labels, forms, and other items stored on computer disks.	Analytical skills, excellent knowledge of computers and software.
Garage Sale Service	Collect, price, and resell used items for others.	Good organizational skills. Ability to keep good records.
Janitorial Service	Do general cleaning of home and office areas. Do special cleaning tasks such as washing windows and walls.	High standards of cleanliness and no allergies to dust.
Musical Entertainment	Play one or more instruments to provide music appropriate for specific events.	Outgoing personality and an expert level of skill in playing an instrument.
Lawn Care	Cut grass, pull weeds, trim hedges, plant flowers.	Skill in using lawn care equipment and knowledge of local plants.
Recycling Service	Collect recyclable items and take them to a recycling center.	Good organizational skills.
Painting Service	Paint rooms, houses, fences, and other small and large items.	Careful attention to detail. Artistic aptitude is also helpful.
Tutoring	Help children do homework and understand lessons in subjects with which they are having difficulty in school.	Patience, ability to communicate, and a high level of achievement in the subjects in which you are tutoring.
Word Processing Service	Word process letters, reports, and other written materials.	Excellent keyboarding, spelling, and grammar skills.

Career Planning

Name _____

Date _____ **Period** _____ **Score** _____

Chapter 31 Test

Matching: Match the following terms and identifying phrases.

_____ 1. Combining on-the-job work experience with traditional class work.

_____ 2. A succession of productive work experiences throughout life that make your life more satisfying.

_____ 3. What you like; your preferences for activities, events, and ideas.

_____ 4. Abilities that seem to come naturally.

_____ 5. A goal you have accomplished—something you feel you did well.

_____ 6. Skills and activities you can perform successfully.

A. abilities

B. achievement

C. aptitudes

D. career

E. cooperative education

F. interests

True/False: Circle *T* if the statement is true or *F* if the statement is false.

T F   7. Career planning involves setting goals.

T F   8. Career plans are less important to women today than they were in the past.

T F   9. Having a job and having a career are exactly the same.

T F 10. Becoming more aware of your interests can guide you toward a career you will like.

T F 11. If mathematical abilities come naturally to a person, it is said that he or she has a mathematical aptitude.

T F 12. Personality has little effect on success in a career.

T F 13. One of the best ways to learn details about a career is to talk with people who are working in that field.

T F 14. Flextime allows employees to divide the hours of a standard workweek into three or four days.

T F 15. Apprenticeship training is usually not accepted by leading labor unions.

T F 16. People in higher-level management positions tend to use specific vocational skills less than people who are in lower level positions.

T F 17. You can qualify for entry-level positions after graduating from high school.

T F 18. In the future, there will probably be more jobs in caring for older adults, health care, and hospital administration.

(Continued)

Name _____

Multiple Choice: Choose the best answer and write the corresponding letter in the blank.

_____ 19. Which of the following is NOT true regarding a successful career?
A. A successful career depends upon the amount of money earned.
B. Success in a career is a highly personal matter.
C. A successful career means different things to different people.
D. A career that is successful for you might not be successful for your best friend.

_____ 20. Classifying interests _____.
A. is always done by dividing them into three categories: those that have to do with data, those that have to do with people, and those that have to do with things
B. can guide you toward developing skills related to those interests
C. is more helpful for older adults than for teenagers
D. will help you to pursue only the interests that are related to possible careers

_____ 21. Which of the following is true about achievements in relation to self-study?
A. An achievement is something you have accomplished.
B. Skills you have and use are responsible for your achievements.
C. Considering your achievements helps you to learn more about your abilities.
D. All of the above are true.

_____ 22. Three management positions that require a college degree or more are _____.
A. teacher, architect, dietitian
B. exercise instructor, cook, carpenter
C. electrician, banker, teacher's aide
D. physician, dental hygienist, bank teller

Essay Questions: Provide the answers you feel best show your understanding of the subject matter.

23. Describe how early life experiences can affect feelings and decisions related to careers.

24. Explain the difference between a job and a career.

25. List three sources of career information and describe how each can be helpful.

26. Explain three skills that successful managers at all levels in the workplace have and use.

Finding a Job

Objectives

When students have completed this chapter, they will be able to

- recognize sources of job leads and how to use them.
- explain job-seeking skills.
- write a cover letter and develop a resume.
- describe personal traits leading to job success.
- list several responsibilities of the employer to the employee.

Bulletin Boards

Title: *Job Seeker's Tools*

Make a large-scale toolbox by drawing or cutting it from construction paper. Arrange labeled samples of cover letters, resumes, application forms, interview questions, employment tests, and portfolio materials flowing from the toolbox on the bulletin board.

Title: *Classified Ads*

Design the bulletin board to look like a newspaper page. Arrange actual classified ads in columns, following the types of headings that are used in your local paper. Select ads for entry-level positions that would appeal to your students.

Teaching Materials

Text, pages 604-623
- *To Review*
- *To Challenge Your Thinking*
- *To Do with the Class*
- *To Do with Your Community*

Student Activity Guide
- A. *Application Letter*
- B. *Resume Development*
- C. *Traits Leading to Job Success*
- D. *Personal Traits and Job Success*

Teacher's Resources
- *Application Form,* reproducible master 32-1
- *Questions Frequently Asked During Job Interviews,* reproducible master 32-2
- Chapter 32 Test
- *Climb the Stairway to Job Success,* color transparency CT-32

Introductory Activities

1. Have each student select an ad from the classified section of your local newspaper for a position that appeals to him or her. Students will complete other activities in this chapter in reference to these chosen positions.
2. Have each student interview two people who currently have jobs and who have worked for several years. Have students find out how these people found their jobs and what kinds of traits and skills have helped them be successful in their jobs. Have students share their findings in class.
3. *Climb the Stairway to Job Success,* color transparency CT-32, TR. Use this transparency to show the "steps" necessary for getting a desirable job. Discuss the importance of each and ways to successfully accomplish each item listed. Comments can be written directly on the transparency.

Instructional Concepts and Student Learning Experiences

Sources of Job Leads

4. Guest speaker. Invite a guidance counselor to speak to your class about the job placement functions of your school's guidance office.

5. Have each student poll 10 employed friends or family members to find out if they know of any current job openings at their places of employment. (These do not have to be entry-level positions.) Have students report their findings in class.

6. Have students look at the classified ads in a local newspaper. Discuss how listings are organized and what categories are used.

7. Have students use a phone book to identify private and public employment agencies in your area.

8. Have students contact a government employment service for information on civil service positions.

Job-Seeking Skills

9. Guest speaker. Invite an employer to speak to your class about what he or she looks for in a cover letter and a resume.

10. *Application Letter,* Activity A, SAG. Have each student write a letter of application for the job in the classified ad he or she selected in Learning Experience 1.

11. Discuss with students the two types of resumes in terms of how they are organized and the advantages and disadvantages of each.

12. *Resume Development,* Activity B, SAG. Have each student develop his or her own chronological resume including the information suggested in the text.

13. Have each student develop a functional resume.

14. Have each student develop a personal data sheet. Then have students work in small groups to critique each other's sheets and suggest ways to improve them.

15. Ask students to describe the characteristics of a well-prepared application form.

16. *Application Form,* reproducible master 32-1, TR. Have students fill out the sample application form. Then discuss parts of the form students found difficult to complete. Also discuss the importance of being fully prepared to supply such information when applying for a job.

17. Have each student write a list of questions he or she would ask an applicant interviewing for the job selected in Learning Experience 1.

18. Have students role-play interviewing for the jobs they selected in Learning Experience 1. Following each role-play, discuss the strengths and weaknesses displayed by both the interviewer and the interviewee with the class.

19. *Questions Frequently Asked During Job Interviews,* reproducible master 32-2, TR. Use this master as the basis for discussing interviews and typical interview questions. Allow students to practice responding to the various questions.

20. Distribute sample civil service tests or other employment tests to students. Discuss what kinds of information employers hope to discover by administering various types of tests to potential employees.

21. Have students brainstorm a list of items they might include in a portfolio. Discuss with students how a good portfolio should be organized. Show samples if possible.

Traits Leading to Job Success

22. Panel discussion. Invite a panel of employers to discuss employee traits that lead to success on the job. Also ask them to explain how they evaluate these traits during an interview.

23. Have students write a one-page paper explaining how they feel attitude is related to job success.

24. Have students role-play contrasting examples of positive and negative attitudes on the job.

25. Divide the class into small groups. Give each group a hypothetical situation in which a recently hired employee indicates through comments or performance that he or she may not be capable of doing the job. Ask the groups to discuss how they would handle the situations if they were the employers.

26. Have students discuss how the capability of one employee can affect the work of others and the business as a whole.
27. Have students write research reports on the costs of employee theft.
28. Have students discuss what is meant by the statement "One form of dishonesty on the job is stealing time."
29. *Traits Leading to Job Success,* Activity C, SAG. Have each student identify three traits related to job success that he or she would like to develop. Then have students list steps they might take to improve in each area.
30. *Personal Traits and Job Success,* Activity D, SAG. Have students explain why listed traits are likely to help people be successful at their jobs.

Employer Responsibilities

31. Ask each student to make a list of employer responsibilities and rank them in order of importance. Then have students compare their rankings and discuss any differences.
32. Have students contact the Department of Labor in your state for information about employer responsibilities related to the employment of minors.
33. Have each student interview two employers to find out what means they use to evaluate their employees. Have students report their findings in class.
34. Have students develop a survey about the various types of fringe benefits offered by employers. Have each student use the survey to interview two persons with full-time jobs. Have students compile their findings in an article for the school newspaper about average benefits students might be able to expect when they enter the working world.
35. Panel discussion. Invite a panel of representatives from various unions to discuss how their unions were formed, services the unions offer, and problems they currently face.

Answer Key

Text

To Review
1. (List and explain six. Student response.)
2. A. true
   B. false

3. qualifications, chronological, functional
4. This keeps you from being eliminated and gives you a chance to discuss salary with the employer.
5. Learn as much as you can about the company or firm that is interviewing you. Learn as much as you can about the job for which you are interviewing. Prepare questions to ask the interviewer. Plan ahead regarding your grooming. Find out where the interview will take place so you will arrive on time.
6. (Describe three. Student response.)
7. to display the applicant's work, special awards and accomplishments, and recognition publications to a potential employer
8. personal traits
9. B, F, D, E, C, A
10. (List six:) prompt payment of salary, safe working conditions, training procedures, evaluation, information related to fringe benefits, legal responsibilities

Teacher's Resources

Chapter 32 Test
1. D
2. A
3. C
4. F
5. E
6. H
7. B
8. G
9. T
10. T
11. T
12. F
13. F
14. F
15. F
16. T
17. F
18. F
19. C
20. B
21. A
22. D
23. A
24. (List and explain three:) family and friends, school placement office, newspaper advertisements, employment agencies, civil service, direct approach, Internet (Student response for explanations.)

25. the position you are interested in; how you learned the position is available; your qualifications, which might appeal to the reader; a statement indicating why your training, education, and experience would benefit the employer; accomplishments that relate to the position; remark about your attached resume; request for an interview; indication that you will call in a few days

26. (Student response.)

27. (List and describe four:) positive attitude, attitude of cooperation, attitude that accepts criticism, attitude that accepts change, capability, initiative, honesty and dependability (Student response for descriptions.)

Reproducible Master 32-1

Application Form

Name _____ **Date** _____ **Period** _____

Fill out this sample job application form as completely, neatly, and accurately as possible.

Application for Employment

Personal Information

Date _____ Social Security Number _____

Name _____

       Last   First   Middle

Present Address _____

         Street   City   State

Permanent Address _____

         Street   City   State

Phone No. _____

If related to anyone in our employ,   Referred
state name and department.   by

Employment Desired

Position	Date you can start	Salary desired
Are you employed now?	If so, may we inquire of your present employer?	
Ever applied to this company before?	Where?	When?

Education

	Name and Location of School	Years Completed	Subjects Studied
Grammar School			
High School			
College			
Trade, Business, or Correspondence School			

Subject of special study or research work _____

(Continued)

What foreign language do you speak fluently?		Read fluently?	Write fluently?

U.S. Military or Naval service	Rank	Present membership in National Guard or Reserves

Activities other than religious
(civic, athletic, fraternal, etc.)

(Exclude organizations the name or character of which indicates the race, creed, color or national origin of its members.)

Former Employers List below last three employers starting with the last one first.

Date Month/Year	Name and Address of Employer	Salary	Position	Reason for Leaving
From				
To				
From				
To				
From				
To				

References Give below the names of two people not related to you whom you have known for at least one year.

	Name	Address	Job Title	Years Acquainted
1				
2				

Physical Record

Have you any disabilities that might affect your job performance?

In case of emergency notify		
Name	Address	Phone No.

I authorize investigation of all statements contained in this application. I understand that misrepresentation or omission of facts called for is cause for dismissal.

Date	Signature

Reproducible Master 32-2

Questions Frequently Asked During Job Interviews

What are your strengths?

What are your weaknesses?

How would you describe your personality?

What kinds of people do you like?

What kinds of people do you dislike?

Are you ambitious? Please explain.

What makes you angry?

Do you like to work? Why?

How do you spend your leisure time?

What classes do you enjoy most in school?

Why are you leaving your present position?

Were you ever fired from a job?

Did you ever quit a job? Why?

What have you learned from previous work experiences?

What do you find hardest about working?

What are your long-term career objectives?

In what kinds of positions are you most interested?

In choosing a job, what are your most important considerations?

What interests you most about this position?

Why do you think you are right for this job?

What do you know about our company (our business)?

What can you contribute to this organization?

What kind of salary do you have in mind?

How much money do you want to be earning five years from now?

Do you get to work on time?

Can you delegate responsibility? Give an example.

Can you work under pressure? Are you bothered by deadlines?

Are you willing to travel?

Are you willing to relocate?

May we contact your present employer?

May we contact your references?

Do you have any questions you want to ask?

Finding a Job

Name _____

Date _____ **Period** _____ **Score** _____

Chapter 32 Test

Matching: Match the following terms and identifying phrases.

_____ 1. A letter to an interviewer indicating your interest in the position and expressing your thanks for the interview.

_____ 2. A person's potential for doing a job.

_____ 3. Doing what you are expected to do; being at work every day and being on time.

_____ 4. Completing a given task, finding something else that needs to be done, and doing it.

_____ 5. Extra features granted to an employee above and beyond regular salary.

_____ 6. A concise summary of your qualifications for a job documented by past accomplishments.

_____ 7. A letter of application to an employer that states your interest in an interview.

_____ 8. An attractive presentation of work samples in some type of a folder or other container.

A. capability

B. cover letter

C. dependability

D. follow-up letter

E. fringe benefits

F. initiative

G. job portfolio

H. resume

True/False: Circle *T* if the statement is true or *F* if the statement is false.

T F   9. Using family members and friends as sources of job leads is perfectly acceptable.

T F   10. Civil service positions require a competitive examination to qualify for appointment.

T F   11. The cover letter is a sales letter that is meant to sell yourself in order to get an interview.

T F   12. The chronological resume emphasizes marketable skills without the emphasis of time-related work history.

T F   13. Because most application blanks require the same basic information, they are an unimportant step in job seeking.

T F   14. It is impossible to prepare for a job interview since you do not have any idea of the questions that will be asked.

T F   15. A job portfolio is necessary for anyone who is applying for a job.

T F   16. A very high percentage of employees who lose their jobs do so during the first month of employment.

T F   17. Accepting criticism from an employer simply means listening politely.

T F   18. The number of allowances claimed is indicated by the employee on a W-2 form.

(Continued)